The Life and Times of
Madan Lal Dhingra

The Life and Times of
Madan Lal Dhingra

Vishav Bandhu

Ocean Books Pvt. Ltd.
ISO 9001:2015 Publishers

Published by
Ocean Books (P) Ltd.
4/19 Asaf Ali Road,
New Delhi-110 002 (INDIA)
e-mail: info@oceanbooks.in

ISBN 978-81-8430-229-5
The Life and Times of
MADAN LAL DHINGRA
by Shri Vishav Bandhu

Edition
2025

Price
₹ 400.00 (Rupees Four Hundred only)

Printed at
Shree Sai Printers, Sahibabad

****

Dedicated

to

Prof. Malwinder Jit Singh Waraich

****

Preface

Madan Lal Dhingra was the first Indian revolutionary who caused a sensation in the British administration by assassinating a high profile British Officer in London. His daring act received a wide condemnation at home and abroad. G.K. Gokhale, Surendranath Banerjee, Bipin Chandra Pal criticized it and Mahatma Gandhi called it 'an act of cowardice'. His family disowned him, declared him eccentric and his act detestable. The firm and determined Madan Lal Dhingra did not budge from his stand, braved all accusations and court ordeals with utmost courage and confidence without flinching even once or breaking down. He refused to obtain the services of a lawyer. He did not beg for clemency and kissed the *altar* of death with a smile. The West might have heard of such heroic deeds but had not seen one, till they came across Madan Lal Dhingra. Not even once did he show any remorse for his act and proudly roared in the court justifying his action, "...it was an attempt to shed English blood intentionally and of purpose as a humble protest against the inhuman transportation and hanging of Indian youth." "I may be reborn of the same mother and I may re-die for the same sacred cause, till my mission is done and She stands free..."

For my present work I am deeply indebted to Prof. Malwinder Jit Singh Waraich for providing the source material and guidance for my entire project, without which this work could not have been undertaken and completed.

My special thanks are due to Mr. Anil Mahajan, my uncle who helped me in editing and suggesting suitable changes. I am also thankful to Dr. Babusha Maingi (History Department), for helping in setting up the bibliography and index, Prof. Shilpi Seth for setting up source material and Prof. Amit Sayal for tracing some material. My thanks are due to my wife who stood by me through thick and thin and supported me in the completion of my work.

—Vishav Bandhu

Contents

1

Madan Lal Dhingra and Historic Antecedents

Madan Lal Dhingra was the first Indian revolutionary who assassinated a British Officer in London, for the freedom of his 'Motherland'. He belonged to a rich and influential family of Amritsar. His father, Dr. Sahib Ditta Mal, a qualified eye surgeon, was having a roaring practice in the city. Rai Sahib, Dr. Sahib Ditta Mal, a British loyalist to the core, was proud of his association and fidelity to the Crown and Madan Lal Dhingra, despised and detested it. The difference in outlook, opinion, and commitment created a void between the two.

The partition of Bengal in 1905 generated a wave of xenophobia resulting in rise of national consciousness among the people. It charged their emotions, and encouraged them to aspire for the freedom of the country. The burgeoning young

Madan Lal Dhingra too got swayed by the wave that had engulfed most of the educated Indian elite under its spell and he joined the group of freedom lovers while studying at Lahore, much to the obvious annoyance of his father, who immediately called him back, thus putting an end to his studies. One day, the determined Madan Lal Dhingra, left his family to free himself from its influence and to earn dignity. But this venture was short-lived. After a struggle of a few months in India, his brother persuaded him to go to England for higher studies. There, he came in contact with the like-minded comrades at India House. It was a centre of Indian revolutionaries, aspiring for and propagating the cause of India's independence and soon he started making plans to free his Motherland. He believed, "the only lesson required in India is to learn how to die and the only way to teach it is by dying alone". The soul is immortal and "if everyone of my countrymen takes at least two lives of Englishmen before his body falls, the mother's salvation is a day's work". Armed with new ideology, he assassinated Curzon Wyllie in London, thus causing a sensation and bewilderment in the Western world.

The information regarding the murder of William Hutt Curzon Wyllie, began trickling in at Lahore only on July 3, and was published on July 4, in the Sunday edition of *The Tribune.* It informed that Curzon Wyllie, the Political *Aide-de-Camp* to Lord Morley, the Secretary of State for India had been killed by a student from Punjab, one hour before midnight on July 1, 1909.[1] On that night "At Home" was being organized for the Indians by the National Indian Association at the Jehangir Hall of the Imperial Institute, London. The reception was to close at midnight, but by 11 O'clock the visitors had started leaving. Curzon Wyllie also decided to move out. It was Madan Lal Dhingra, who engaged him in conversation and they were standing a yard distance from each other in the vestibule. In between the conversation, Madan Lal Dhingra raised his hand and fired rapidly around four or five bullets on him. One bullet shattered Curzon Wyllie's right eye, and another bullet pierced his face below the left eye. Curzon Wyllie fell flat on the floor.[2] Other two shots were fired at the man who Dhingra thought was about to attack him. He was Dr. Lalcaca from Shanghai, who had come to celebrate his holidays in England.[3] The weapon however was quickly wrested from Dhingra, and he offered no further resistance.[4] A vast number of visiting cards were found in the possession of the student, rendering his identification impossible. *The Tribune* wrote that gravity of the crime in the heart of the Empire had lashed London police into activity and they were looking for evidence in every direction busy attempting to unravel the tangled affair. It was reported that police had taken the charge of the India House and that as many as 200 Indian students were under surveillance. The British Government was already in communication with the French Government for the arrest and extradition of Shyamji Krishna Varma, the owner of the India House. The idea that had caught favour with the authorities in England was that the deed was not merely an individual act committed on the personal enmity but was result of a deep-rooted conspiracy. It was also reported that the deceased had expressed his desire to meet Madan Lal Dhingra, son of Sahib Ditta Mal, his friend in India. Wyllie had also written a letter to Madan Lal Dhingra in this regard but received no positive response.

The Dhingra family went under a great shock after they received the news of their son's misdeed. Immediately, it set out to set its score in the eyes of the British Government. The act had been committed, the fate of the actor had been sealed, and now it was the time to save the prestige of the family.

Sahib Ditta Mal, lost no time in openly condemning the act of his son and publicly declared him an eccentric since childhood. *The Pioneer* published his letter in which he had expressed his deep regard and gratitude to the deceased Curzon Wyllie, and openly admitted, "Whom my cursed son killed in a fit of madness".[5] The purpose of the letter was loud and clear. Similar views were expressed by the elder brothers of Madan Lal Dhingra, Mohan Lal and Behari Lal, in a letter addressed to Dunlop Smith, "We felt the deepest agony at the mere thought of the London tragedy, for Sir Curzon Wyllie was one of our kindest friends…."[6] The family considered it as a most disgraceful, mindless misdeed of their son. Sahib Ditta Mal had sent another telegram to his youngest son Bhajan Lal in London, advising him to refer mental unsoundness of Madan Lal Dhingra and abhorrence of the act by the family.[7] The family snapped all ties with Madan Lal Dhingra and declared, "...we shall not consider Madan Lal a martyr, as the extremists would desire; we look upon him as a lunatic, who could not be influenced by the traditions and instincts of the family and his act as a detestable act".[8]

Dr. Sahib Ditta Mal repudiated Madan Lal Dhingra on behalf of his family and did not show any slightest tinge of sympathy with his son's ill-deed. Dr. Dhingra's emphatic condemnation of the crime, wrote *Pioneer*, "Must be accepted as genuine by Anglo-Indians as well as by his own countrymen, and there will even be sympathy for the respectable family thus brought to shame and disgrace".[9] The family succeeded in its purpose to prove its innocence and disgust at the deed but it left a big scar on the personality of great martyr Madan Lal Dhingra.

Shaheed-i-Azam Sardar Bhagat Singh, mindful of the neglect by the society in general, of such rebels, opines, "he was not a '*Neta*', whose biography may have been published and quickly sold. Nor was he an '*Avtar*' descending on earth about whom the *pundits* and devotees could weave anecdotes of divinehood since his birth, suggesting that he was in fact born 'different'. Nor are we cognizant of any rare feats of Dhingra's infancy or childhood on the basis of which we could have said, that 'all this foreshadowed greatness'. He was a hapless rebel. His own father had disowned him. Even the nationalist leaders like Bipin Chandra Pal who was known as radical, showered the choicest abuses on him".[10] The people in general and family in particular, perhaps feared the repercussion of the British Government and the result was, no one dared or tried to collect information or highlight Madan Lal Dhingra's early life.[11]

Today, the ancestral house of Madan Lal Dhingra, earlier known as 'Dhingra Buildings' has been squeezed to a small apartment, is situated, next to 'Regent Cinema' in *Katra Sher Singh*, Amritsar.[12] The house is presently occupied by Vikram Dhingra, the son of Mukund Lal Dhingra.[13] The family had very little knowledge about Madan Lal Dhingra. The act of Madan Lal Dhingra had disgraced the family and no one dared to talk about him before independence. In 1947, the city experienced a terrible carnage due to partition. Freedom had been won, but after paying a heavy price of life and property. The coming two decades were spent in settlement and to recuperate the loss suffered in 1947. The new leaders were busy in reaping the fruits of independence won and no one had time and energy to think about the martyrs of yester-years. It was in the seventies that the interest in the martyr was invoked by the efforts of 'Freedom Fighters Association' and few other revolutionaries, who repeatedly requested the government to bring back the remains of Madan Lal Dhingra from the prison, Pentonville, in London.[14] This invigorated the interest of the government and writers in Madan Lal Dingra and it prompted many to take up a serious research on the life of the Martyr.[15] Earlier works related to the Martyr were mostly in the form of articles and references, besides some biographical sketches.[16] The Punjab Government also arose from its slumber and affirmed to install a statue of the Martyr in the city and the then Chief Minister declared that the government had undertaken the house of Madan Lal Dhingra and will maintain it as a memorial.[17]

On December 13, 1976, the body of the Martyr was brought to India.[18] On December 20, 1976, the remains of Madan Lal Dhingra were consigned to the flames according to the Hindu rites at a special platform raised in the cattle fair grounds; where the government had acquired a five hectare plot for raising a statue and a memorial to the Martyr.[19] A plan was prepared to build a memorial at the cremation site in Amritsar. For a site of about 4 acres, the local Improvement Trust asked the State Government to deposit ₹ 14.52 lacs.[20] *The Tribune* had reported, "The Punjab Government had acquired two hectares of land at Amritsar for building a memorial to the Martyr". Parliamentary Secretary, Gurcharan Singh Nihalsinghwala, said that house belonging to Madan Lal Dhingra had also been acquired which would be preserved.[21] The present Dhingra family provided whatever little information they had regarding him such as newspaper cuttings, photographs related to the emersion of his ashes.[22]

The city of Amritsar has today two important monuments attributed to the Dhingra family, a statue of the Martyr, Madan Lal Dhingra and a building known as 'Baradari', dedicated to Dr. Sahib Ditta Mal. The monument of Madan Lal Dhingra was installed in Mall Mandi and was inaugurated on 8 September, 1992, by the then Chief Minister of Punjab, Sardar Beant Singh.

The following inscription is placed under the statue of the Martyr Madan Lal Dhingra, installed at Mall Mandi, Amritsar.

"I AM PROUD TO HAVE THE HONOUR OF LAYING DOWN MY LIFE FOR MY COUNTRY. BUT REMEMBER WE SHALL HAVE OUR TIMES IN THE DAYS TO COME."

—MADAN LAL DHINGRA

FEARLESS FREEDOM FIGHTER

MADAN LAL DHINGRA, BORN ON 18TH FEBRUARY, 1887, IN AMRITSAR: MARTYRED ON 17TH AUGUST, 1909 IN LONDON

WHO WAS HANGED FOR SHOOTING SIR CURZON WYLLIE IN LONDON (ENGLAND) ON 1ST JULY, 1909

THIS BRAVE SON OF INDIA HAPPILY KISSED THE GALLOWS AND SACRIFICED HIS LIFE AT THE *ALTAR* OF FREEDOM.

The date of birth ascribed to Madan Lal Dhingra in the above inscription is 18 February 1887, our next point of contention and discussion.

Kesar Singh in his novel, *Amar Shaheed Madan Lal Dhingra* claims his year of birth to be 1883, on the basis of the handwritten note taken from the diary of Sahib Ditta Mal:

> My seventh child in succession, Madan Lal, was born on Sunday 18 February 1883 (8th Fagun Samvat, 1939) at early morning at 3.15, in Amritsar (the rest of the page is blank).[23]

The Death Certificate issued by the General Register Office, London also claims him to be of 24 yrs of age at the time of execution.[24]

CERTIFIED COPY OF AN ENTRY OF DEATH GIVEN AT THE GENERAL REGISTER OFFICE LONDON

Application No: RS 8409

Registration District Kensington

1909 Death in the sub-district of Lower Holloway in the county of London

When and where died	Name	Age	Occupation	Cause of Death	Signature	When Regd.
17th Aug., 1909 Prison	Madan Lal Dhingra	25	Student	Fracture of cervical Ledbury Rd. vertebra	Certificate received from Geo Da. Ford	17th August, 1909.
Signature Registrar **PANTONVILLE**			Bayswater	Executed by Law	Juomsley Thomas Coroner for London Inquest held **Seventeenth, August, 1909**	

Source: *Martyrs Madan Lal Dhingra, Udham Singh and Vishnu Ganesh Pingale,* by V.R. Joshi, Manorama Prakashan, Bombay, 1991.

Dhingra Building in 1976

Dhingra Building in 2010

In the above certificate, the year of birth is missing, but the age has been mentioned as twenty-five, which confirms to the year of his birth to be 1884.[25] The contemporary literature does not refer to this omission which becomes more glaring when we try to locate the early life of the martyr. Sahib Ditta Mal was a qualified doctor who had noted the birth dates of all his children in his diary. The noted birth date of the martyr Madan Lal Dhingra was 1883.[26]

The second monument which belongs to the Dhingra family in Amritsar is a building known as *Baradari*. It was built by the sons of Sahib Ditta Mal, in loving memory of their father in the heart of Ranjit Singh Palace, popularly known as Company Bagh (Ram Bagh Garden).[27] The site, brings up an important question, why Dhingra family was given the sanction to construct a monument like *'Baradari'* at the most coveted and prized place in the city? Was it a reward to Dhingra family, *in lieu* of their loyalty?

According to his own handwritten diary, Dr. Sahib Ditta Mal Dhingra was born on August 31st, 1845. He served the British Government of India for twenty-three years as a physician. For his services, the title of RAI-SAHIB was conferred upon him by Lord Elgin.

He had eight children—one daughter and seven sons. Madan Lal was the seventh child. His younger brother Bhajan Lal was the youngest of the family.

Here is the list of his family members, with their birthdates, in the handwriting of Dr. Sahib Ditta Mal Dhingra:

Myself born 31-8-1845.

Names	*Dates and Birth*
Kaki Rani	12th Nov. 1865
Kundan Lal	4th May 1867

Mohan Lal	9th April 1871
Bihari Lal	21st July 1873
Ghaman Lal	10th May 1877
Chuni Lal	10th April 1881
Madan Lal	8th Feb. 1883
Bhajan Lal	6th April 1885

Baradari

The *Baradari* is situated in the western side of the palace complex. It is a single storey square structure raised on a high plinth. The roof is flat and it is connected by flights of steps on the all four sides. It has three openings in each side which are flanked by cusped arch formation. Arches are separated by a pillar. Each corner has three plasters. The corner plaster has beautiful serpentine coil or rope design, which is incorporated throughout its body. The façade terminates into projected eave which is supported on decorative brackets and is surmounted by a marble parapet. There is an inscription on the façade of the western side wall stating that the *Baradari* was built by the sons of Rai Sahib Ditta Mal in the memory of their father.

"Presented by the sons of Rai Sahib Ditta Mal in the loving memory of their father".

Born: 30th July, 1846

Died: 29th October, 1916

The edifice of the *Baradari* establishes that the government observed the act of Madan Lal Dhingra in isolation and spared the family, a rare instance of British justice in India. Perhaps, the government had rewarded the family for helping them out from humiliation and embarrassment by openly declaring Madan Lal Dhingra as insane. Madan Lal Dhingra had struck

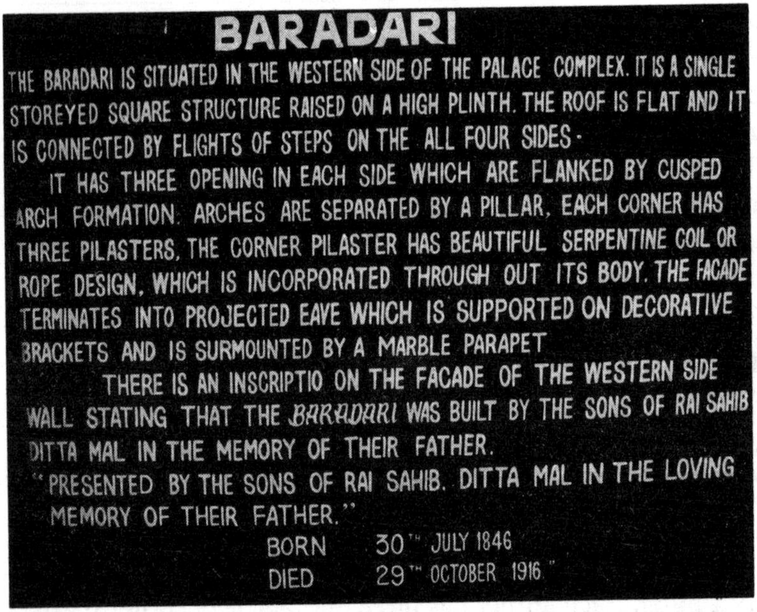

BARADARI

THE BARADARI IS SITUATED IN THE WESTERN SIDE OF THE PALACE COMPLEX. IT IS A SINGLE STOREYED SQUARE STRUCTURE RAISED ON A HIGH PLINTH. THE ROOF IS FLAT AND IT IS CONNECTED BY FLIGHTS OF STEPS ON THE ALL FOUR SIDES.

IT HAS THREE OPENING IN EACH SIDE WHICH ARE FLANKED BY CUSPED ARCH FORMATION. ARCHES ARE SEPARATED BY A PILLAR, EACH CORNER HAS THREE PILASTERS, THE CORNER PILASTER HAS BEAUTIFUL SERPENTINE COIL OR ROPE DESIGN, WHICH IS INCORPORATED THROUGH OUT ITS BODY. THE FACADE TERMINATES INTO PROJECTED EAVE WHICH IS SUPPORTED ON DECORATIVE BRACKETS AND IS SURMOUNTED BY A MARBLE PARAPET

THERE IS AN INSCRIPTIO ON THE FACADE OF THE WESTERN SIDE WALL STATING THAT THE *BARADARI* WAS BUILT BY THE SONS OF RAI SAHIB DITTA MAL IN THE MEMORY OF THEIR FATHER.

"PRESENTED BY THE SONS OF RAI SAHIB. DITTA MAL IN THE LOVING MEMORY OF THEIR FATHER."

BORN 30TH JULY 1846

DIED 29TH OCTOBER 1916."

Baradari

in the very heart and the nerve centre of the British Government, i.e. London. On the one hand, it speaks volumes about the dare devil act of the martyr, Madan Lal Dhingra, and on the other, it exposed the weakness of the Kingdom. If a high profile person like Curzon Wyllie could be targeted and killed so easily then what to talk about the common British man in the country and abroad. It was a clear indication of coming catastrophe. It was out and out the failure of the British intelligence which had failed to detect seditious activities growing under its nose. Internally, they were trying to detect every possible move related with the planned murder but outwardly they were trying to project Dhingra as an insane person who at that spur of moment had acted temperamentally and killed Curzon Wyllie and Dr. Lalcaca. His insanity was fully supported and justified by the family.

The study of the events, which followed the assassination,

provides a suitable clarification to figure out the presence of *Baradari* at such a strategic backdrop. On July 1, the act was committed and on July 3, the news reached public through print, and on July 4, 1909, Behari Lal Dhingra sent a telegram to Dunlop Smith, Private Secretary to Viceroy, condemned the act of his younger brother, Madan Lal Dhingra and emphasized, "He showed eccentricity in childhood and became generally worse. He once ran away from home and worked as *lascar* (sailor)".[28] On July 5, the family telegrammed Bhajan Lal, younger to Madan Lal Dhingra, who was in London at that time:

"Refer Mental Unsoundness from Childhood Express Family Abhorrence, Through Solicitor".[29]

Sahib Ditta Mal, directed his sons, Mohan Lal and Behari Lal, to meet Dunlop Smith and seek his advice regarding the case. They met him in Simla, and after the meeting, as directed, both the brothers addressed a letter to Private Secretary of Viceroy, i.e. Dunlop Smith on July 7, 1909.[30]

"It is an irony of fate in a family like ours, so deeply loyal to Government and so gratefully attached to the British people, a young man should degenerate into a murder.... We felt the deepest agony at the mere thought of the London tragedy, for Sir Curzon Wyllie was one of our kindest friends.... We are anxious to know what exactly the causes of Madan Lal's degeneration into murder have been, we are inclined to believe that, as he was eccentric and subjects to fits of rashness, he was discovered as an excellent tool for evil purposes by Krishna Varma and his lieutenants. He was probably given lectures and taught the use of revolver and daggers...." Madan Lal Dhingra made an exhibition of his eccentricity in London during the very first week—by cutting off the whiskers of the pet cat of the landlady of the lodgings.... Our younger brother left for England last year; and he was taken by Madan

> Lal Dhingra to 'India House'.... It was thereupon decided (by his father) that the best thing would be to write to Sir Curzon Wyllie about the matter (of his being at India House) and invoke his assistance... and in this, Madan Lal's eccentricity and waywardness were alluded to. We believe that the real culprits have cleverly kept themselves in the background. They have succeeded in utilizing a member of a loyal family for their purposes.... But we shall not consider Madan Lal Dhingra as a martyr, as the extremists would desire; we look upon him as a lunatic, who could not be influenced by the traditions and instincts of the family and his act as a detestable act.

After hammering on the loyalty of the Dhingra family to the British Crown, a detailed history of Madan Lal's mental abnormality since childhood was articulated, "He was eccentric and subject to fits of rashness', a cause of much anxiety and embarrassment all these years to the parents who had borne it with patience. He exhibited his eccentricity in London during the very first week—by cutting off the whiskers of the pet cat of the landlady of the lodgings. He became an "Easy tool in the hands of the revolutionaries who used him for their evil designs". The situation becomes clear, when next day the letter was published in the newspapers. Similarly, Sahib Ditta Mal also wrote almost a similar letter to the newspaper *Indian Daily News*, explaining in detail Madan Lal's eccentricity since childhood.[31] The repetition of the incidents can be noticed in all the letters. The family believed in the existence of a deep-rooted conspiracy behind the July event. They alleged that the real culprits had kept themselves in the background and succeeded in utilizing a member of a loyal family to the British Empire for their vicious purpose. The family blamed extremists for infiltrating Dhingra's mind through their sinister propaganda and used him as a tool to fulfil their evil designs. Besides India House, they dragged Shyamji Krishna Varma in this conspiracy and sought his arrest. This leaves no doubt that the letter was officially dictated to them. The government wanted to tighten its noose against all the extremists in one go.

A protest meeting of Indians had been called on July 5, by a representative committee of Indians, at Caxton Hall, in London, and His Highness the Aga Khan, presided it. The members 'expressed indignation at the crime'. Mr. Theodore Morrison, the Secretary of State for India's Council, stepped forward to the platform, leading Bhajan Lal by hand, the younger brother of Madan Lal Dhingra. Acting on Morrison's advice he had come there to tell his countrymen that, though his brother had done the deed, he wanted to join them in repudiating it and thus purge himself before them. The young man was in tears and there was a sympathetic murmur as he was led back to his place.[32] There seems no difference in the press reporting and Mr. Morrison's information. It makes two things quite clear, one that Bhajan Lal was specifically brought to the occasion and secondly, he was unable to express himself as dictated, reasons better known to him, but one can make out that he was being forced to tell a blatant lie which his inner-self did not allow. The meeting was arranged by the British Government to condemn the act of an Indian by Indians, and to invoke abhorrence to the crime and to present Madan Lal Dhingra as a spoilt youth, eccentric since childhood, who had no particular motive in killing a gentleman like Sir Curzon Wyllie. Madan Lal Dhingra was being projected as a villain, his action as mindless, so that no other Indian student should consider him as a hero or martyr. Dunlop Smith's advice to Dhingra brothers and Morrison's action in Caxton Hall to bring Bhajan Lal Dhingra prove beyond doubt, that British Government was trying hard to project the July episode as an act of an individual of an unsound mind.

The story of Madan Lal Dhingra's unsound mind seems to have been cooked up, either to save him from the gallows, or the family's prestige, or above all, to save the British administration from criticism in the Parliament in England. The opposition had been quite vocal in criticizing the repressive policies of the British Government in India. In a speech at Huddersfield, Mr. Victor Grayson[33] had commented, referring to the murderer of Sir Curzon Wyllie, that he had that morning seen a portrait of the murderer, whom they called assassin; and he said to himself, why not put Lord Morley in and say—another assassin? He did not condone the act, but extended his sympathy to the poor Indian, mad and exasperated by the horrors endured by his people. A Member of Parliament was expressing his concern for the martyr and was exposing the misdemeanour and evil plans of the British Government. The reforms of Minto-Morley had come under severe attack in India and England.

The Dhingra family supported the British Government in time of crisis and *in lieu* of that the family was given the privilege to raise a monument in the memory of their father, Rai Sahib Ditta Mal, at the most prestigious site in the city. Otherwise, to imagine a monument of a father whose son was involved in the political assassination of a British Officer raises doubt. It was a reward for the utmost loyalty shown by the Dhingra family in proclaiming their son, Madan Lal Dhingra, as insane. The people feared British wrath. It can be contemplated from the remark made by a bystander after Dhingra had been overpowered, published in *The Tribune* on July 6, "When a military officer, who was standing nearby bluntly exclaimed 'Sorry for Wyllie', one of the Hindu present cried out, 'No, no, be sorry for Indians': We shall all be blamed for this man's wrong doing". The public in general and members of the India House feared government backlash in England and India. Everyone tried to distance and disassociate himself from the martyr. By doing so, the family might have been trying to get reprieve for him, but it provided an *alibi* for the ailing British Empire to wrap up their failure and save itself from humiliation.

It brings in another important question. Was Madan Lal Dhingra really mad? Father's story of his son's eccentricity was duly published in *Indian Daily News* under the heading:

Was Dhingra Mad? [34]

"Madan Lal Dhingra was born in 1883. He showed eccentric disposition from early childhood, and his habits and ways were different from those of other boys of his age. He showed indifference to everything—as regards his own requirements and regarding the pain and pleasures of others. For instance, he would seldom inquire about a sick relative. During one of his mother's terrible and long illness, when distant relatives came to make inquiries he showed absolute indifference, and never once entered the sick room. As another illustration it may be mentioned that on the occasion of the death of his brother's wife, when the whole family was in deep mourning, he was observed promenading and whistling in the street close by in a careless manner."

"On another occasion he shut himself up in a room for an imaginary wrong for over twenty-four hours, and the door had to be forced open."

"When about twenty-two he ran away from home and was not heard of for some months. He went to Burma and other places and then went on board ship to work as a lascar. He came to India after some time and wired for money from Ceylon".

"He returned home and was found to be as eccentric as ever. At times he would get into fits and uncontrollable temper. His behaviour in general was so eccentric that one of his doctor brothers (Dr. Behari Lal Dhingra) induced me to send him to England on medical grounds, as he believed that the English climate and environment, with study for a profession, would be beneficial to him".

Besides his irritant behaviour, historically the letter provides significant information regarding his birth and allows a glance into the early life of Madan Lal Dhingra, about which no other material is available. It becomes crystal clear that he was not having cordial relations with his family members since childhood. The tone of the letter upholds the authoritarian and repressive attitude of the father. The style in which he had framed the letter portrays his authoritarian character quite common among the educated elite of those days. Those who moulded themselves to his whims and fancies could survive in the family and those who detested had to feel the heat. It was one of the rarest instances where an Indian father condemned his ward publicly.

The charges levelled against Madan Lal Dhingra in the above letter were: He had no regard for the pain and pleasure of others, he showed indifference to mother's illness, he demonstrated careless manner at the death of his brother's wife, and he once locked himself in the room. It means he was disregarded in the family from the very beginning. He felt himself detached and isolated since childhood. As far the allegation of his indifference to his mother's illness is concerned, it should be remembered that he once came back home from his exile just to see his sick mother. He loved and respected her. The parental neglect and dictatorian atmosphere in the family played havoc with his emotions and made him stubborn and rebellious. Madan Lal Dhingra was a sensitive child who needed utmost care, tender handling, proper guidance and affection which he could not get. The negligence of the parents in his proper upbringing was reflected in his irresponsive activities. At times, some children feel neglected and unattended in the family and as such they behave indifferently to seek others' attention and that does not mean they are eccentric. Sahib Ditta Mal, in his personal diary, had jotted down few lines for his insane son which turns out to be a befitting tribute to the martyr son. The page of the diary is produced below.

Handwriting of Dr. Sahib Ditta Mal
(Father of Madanlal Dhingra)

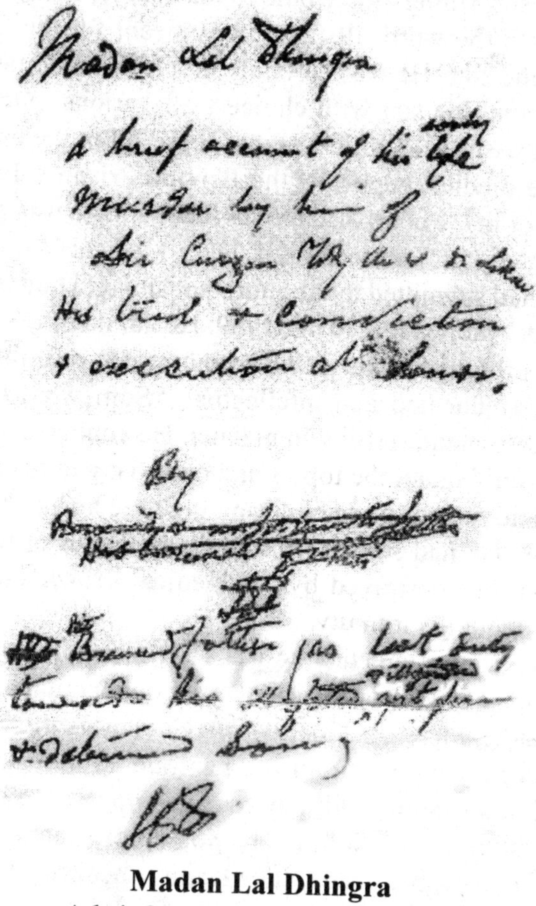

Madan Lal Dhingra
A brief account of his early life,
Murder by him of Sir Curzon Wyllie and Dr. Lalcaca
His trial and conviction and execution at London by
the bereaved father as last duty towards his ill-fated and
ill-guided, yet firm and determined son.[35]

In the above draft, Sahib Ditta Mal, not even once, mentioned Madan Lal Dhingra as an eccentric or of unsound mind. The lines depict the pent-up feelings of a father for his ill-fated and ill-guided son. It clearly indicates that he truly believed that his son was innocent. It appears as if he wanted to write something as a tribute to the martyr, but could not. It looks as if the word 'ill-fated' was meant for the father and not for the son. He was certainly an unfortunate father, who had to label his son with choicest allegations much against his own wishes for which he was regretful in the end.

The medical report of the Brixton Prison submitted by the doctor in the court also proves that Dhingra was physically and mentally fit. The doctor S.R. Dyer, Medical Officer Brixton Prison, had submitted to the court that Dhingra had been under his supervision since July 2, 1909. He admitted to have made several prolonged interviews with him. He informed that he was well educated and intellectual, "Somewhat reticent in conversation and retiring in manner. He conversed rationally and sensibly on all the topics and behaved genuinely in quite a sane and normal manner during the time he had been under my care. He had shown no sign or symptom of insanity".[36] The qualities portrayed by the medical officer clear all the doubts about his insanity.

The accusations that he went to Burma and other places reflect his adventurous spirit. Another allegation against him was that he wired for money from Ceylon. Is there any harm in asking for money from the parents? Moreover, he knew that Dhingra family will pay him for the sake of the honour and prestige of the family. He was a born rebel. His father wanted him to study and settle like his other brothers, whereas he wanted to lead an independent life, father wanted him to be loyal to the British regime, he shook hands with the revolutionaries. Sahib Ditta Mal was always worried about the status of the family, he gave it no importance. Family felt proud to have association with persons like Dunlop Smith and

Sir Curzon Wyllie, while he hated them from the core of his heart. With the help of his family, he could reach London but once he came in contact with the revolutionaries, he tore all ties with his family. During his three years stay in London, he never wrote to his family and if ever he did, it was for money. There existed no love between him and the family. He did what he loved, and loved what he did.

He was a man who loved his country. He wanted to free his motherland from the clutches of the British, a dream which his family could never think. As a born radical, he dared to defy the orders of his father. How a proud and obstinate father could tolerate insubordination from his own blood, as such he did not hesitate to declare him insane. Sahib Ditta Mal admitted in one of his letters that "Behari Lal Dhingra induced me to send him to England on medical grounds, as he believed that the English climate and environment, with study for a profession, would be beneficial to him", as if London was an asylum for the lunatics.

NOTES

1. *The Tribune*, 6 July, 1909, pp. 1, 3. Also see *The Tribune*, 24 Dec. 1976, "How the Tribune covered Dhingra's Episode", p. 3.
2. Born in 1848, Curzon Wyllie had joined the Indian Staff Corpse (later called the Indian Army) in 1869, was selected for service in the Oudh Commission in 1870, and joined the Political Department of the Government of India in 1879. During the Afghan War (1879-80), he served in Kandhar. He was Military Secretary to the Governor of Madras, 1880; Resident in Nepal, 1893-98; Viceroy Agent in Central India, 1898-1900; Agent in Rajputana, 1900-01; Political A.D.C. to the Secretary of State for India, 1901-09; Knighted, 1902. *The Tribune*, July 4, 1909, p. 3 and *The Tribune*, 21 July, 1909. Also see, Martin Gilbert, *Servant of India*, Longman's, 1966, p. 27. For the Assassination of Sir William Curzon Wyllie and Dr. Lalcaca at the Imperial Institute, London see Government of India, Home Department, Political 913, September 1909, No. 66-68.
3. Dr. Cawas Khurshedji Lalcaca, was a prominent medical practitioner from Shanghai originally belonging to highly educated Parsi family

of Bombay. He had a great liking for Europe. A bachelor of forty-eight, dark complexioned and with striking pointed beard. He had come to England for a pleasure trip during the summer, and had been in London since June 8, 1909 *The Statesman*, July 4, 1909. Also see Micro film on Madan Lal Dhingra, No. 1853 at National Archives Delhi.

4. *The Tribune*, July 4, 1909. Also see *The Times*, July 3, London, under the caption "Trial Court Proceedings" had reported: Madan Lal Dhingra, 25 a native of the Punjab described as Engineering student of Ledbury Road, Bayswater was brought up before Mr. Horace Smith at the Westminster Police Court…late in the day (July 2, 1909). The prisoner who gave his age twenty-five years is of light build, of dark olive complexion and has thick black curling hair falling over his forehead. He wore large gold rimmed glasses and was dressed in a darkly well worn ordinary lounge suit. He stood in the dock apparently unconcerned with hands in his pocket: Waraich and Puri, *Tryst with Martyrdom*, pp. 63-64.
5. The letter read "Sir, I am sending herewith for your information copies of two of the letters addressed by the lamented Sir Curzon Wyllie to the address of my eldest son, Mr. K.L. Dhingra, who went to England two years ago for business. The original letters have been sent to Colonel Dunlop Smith. *You will observe how deeply we have been indebted to Sir Curzon, whom my cursed son killed in a fit of madness.* I shall feel grateful to you if you will kindly express in *The Pioneer* the abhorrence of the family at this dastardly crime of my son, who has thus deprived us of one of our kindest friends in London. Thanking you in anticipation, I am yours faithfully, S. Ditta Dhingra, Rai Sahib, retired Civil Surgeon, Dhingra Buildings, Amritsar, July 4, 1909." *The Pioneer*, July 8, 1909, London.
6. Behari Lal Dhingra and Mohan Lal Dhingra to Dunlop Smith, July 7, 1909: Martin Gilbert, *Servant of India*, p. 193.
7. At Home and Abroad *The New Mail's News* (*Telegraph*, Bombay), July 9, 1909 London *The Pioneer* (Sunday), 25 July 1909 Allahabad.
8. Behari Lal Dhingra and Mohan Lal Dhingra to Dunlop Smith, July 7, 1909: Martin Gilbert, *Servant of India*, p. 193.
9. *Pioneer*, July 8, 1909.
10. Malwinder Jit Singh Waraich and Kuldip Puri, *Tryst with Martyrdom: Trial of Madan Lal Dhingra*, Unistar Publication, Chandigarh, 2003, pp. 21-23.

11. Shyamji Krishna Varma in his magazine *The Indian Sociologist* praised his act and declared him a martyr.
12. Earlier, Regent Cinema was known as 'Bande Matram Hall', where political meetings were held.
13. The nephew of Madan Lal Dhingra, Vikram Dhingra, lives there along with his mother, wife and son. His elder brother, Shamsher Dhingra, Manager in Swadeshi Woollen Mills, lives in Shastri Nagar, Lawrence Road, Amritsar. Recently, it was in the news that family had sold the building, to a private owner, who demolished it to reconstruct.
14. *The Daily Milap* (Urdu), 25 November 1975.
15. Kesar Singh, more of a historian than a novelist, started collecting material related with the martyrs and the freedom fighters of India (Punjab) in 1958. The first edition of the novel *Amar Shaheed Madan Lal Dhingra* was published in 1977. In the preface, the writer informs that he went to England to collect the material related with the murder, trial and execution of Martyr Madan Lal Dhingra. In his interview, the author disclosed that he joined law classes with sole aim to get an access to the court proceedings in England. As such his novel provides immense information to understand the psyche of the students studying in England at that time, the emergence of revolutionary movement away from India and helps us to understand the course of events leading to the political murder of Wyllie. V.N. Datta visited Amritsar to get the first-hand information from the members of the Dhingra family. The author tried to weave the early life and career of Madan Lal Dhingra. He attempted to find answer to the question, why he killed Wyllie. The third important work which mainly deals with the court proceedings of Madan Lal Dhingra, held in England was published by Malwinder Jit Singh Waraich and Kuldip Puri, *Tryst with Martyrdom: Trial of Madan Lal Dhingra.* The work is based on the information provided to them by Giani Kesar Singh, the novelist mentioned above. Other works which touch the subjects are, B.S. Maighowalia, *First Indian Martyr: Executed in Pentonville Prison, London*; Brahma Nath Datta, *The Martyrdom of Madan Lal Dhingra: Amur Shaheed Madan Lal Dhingra*; S.C. Mittal, *Vafadar Pita ka Krantikari Putra*; A.K. Deshpande, *Hutatma: Madan Lal Dhingra*; K.K. Khullar, *Madan Lal Dhingra*; Pritam Saini, *Shaheed Madan Lal Dhingra*; Avdhesh Kumar Chaturvedi, *Madan Lal Dhingra*; Jasbir Kaur, *Navalkar Kesar Singh da Jujhhar Manavvad*; Sangeeta Barooah, *Portrait of a Forgotten Hero.*
16. Indulal Yajnik, *Shyamji Krishna Varma*, Arun Coomer Bose, *Indian*

Revolutionaries Abroad, Ram Gopal, *Lokmanya Tilak*, James Campbel Ker, *Political Trouble in India 1907-1917*, S.C Mittal, *Freedom Movement in Punjab (1905-1929)*, V.D. Savarkar, *The Indian War of Independence*, Martin Gilbert, *Servant of India*, Dhananjay Keer, *Veer Savarkar*, M.K. Tang, *Encyclopedia of Indian Nationalism 1800-1918*, Nagendra Singh, *Encyclopedia of Indian Biography*, Vol. I, C-D, etc.

17. Shaheed Madan Lal Dhingra Asthiyan Bharat Layeen Jayen: Amritsar Mein Shaheed ka Makan Tahbil Mein Le Liya. *The Daily Milap* (Urdu), 26 November 1975. Giani Zail Singh was the Chief Minister of the Punjab at that time. The claim to have acquired the building of Madan Lal Dhingra, remained a claim, in the books only.
18. *The Tribune*, December 13, 1976.
19. *The Tribune*, 20 December, 1976.
20. The Memorial to Madan Lal Dhingra, "the platform continues to decay. It is shown no respect by the visitors to the ground. As it is surrounded by a low lying area, it is flooded by rain water. Unless early attention is paid, the brick work will start crumbling". *The Tribune*, 7 September 1990.
21. It was never done so. As informed by Shamsher Dhingra, son of Mukand Lal Dhingra. President Fakhrudin Ali Ahmed, P.M., Indira Gandhi, Chief Minister, Giani Zail Singh, Parliamentary Secretary, Gurcharan Singh Nihalsinghwala, all paid homage to the martyr. Mukand Lal, the nephew of Madan Lal Dhingra, lit the pyre followed by the Chief Minister and others at cattle fair ground, near Youth Hostel, Amritsar. At the same site the statue of the martyr was installed later on.
22. Ashok Sethi, The Tribune correspondent, also provided information and articles related to the subject. G.R. Sethi, a veteran journalist with *The Tribune* and other English dailies of the country, led an eventful career in the media for more than six decades in active journalism, played a pivotal role in Akali Movement and in the Gurdwara Act of 1925. G.R. Sethi, had been tenant of the Dhingra's till 1938 and even his office was also located in the rented accommodation. According to Ashok Sethi (the nephew of G.R. Sethi), "Till partition he stayed in that building and after that he shifted to 5 Rattan Chand Road, The Mall, Amritsar." V.N Datta had also acknowledged the contribution of G.R. Sethi in his work.
23. If we calculate the Samvat 1939, then the year comes out to be 1939 – 57= 1882. Kesar Singh, *Amar Shaheed Madan Lal Dhingra*, p. 7.
24. Malwinder Jit Singh Waraich during his interview insisted on accepting 1883 as the year of Madan Lal Dhingra's birth as per his

father's note in the diary. Waraich and Puri, *Tryst with Martyrdom*, p. 65.

25. According to *The Tribune*, July 6, 1909 (Lahore), Madan Lal Dhingra in 1909 was of twenty-two years of age, which calculates the year of his birth to be 1887.
26. The photocopy of handwritten document of Sahib Ditta Mal regarding the dates of birth of his family was provided by Prof. Malwinder Jit Singh Waraich.
27. The information is gathered from the plate inscription, placed at the site of *Baradari*, at Ram Bagh Gardens, Amritsar.
28. Harichand Chopra, a retired extra Assistant Commissioner, in a letter to Dr. Sahib Ditta Dhingra had written, "I was very sorry indeed for poor Madan Lal's fate. He was really half mad when I met him at Simla in the Tonga Service." Waraich Puri, *Tryst with Martyrdom*, p. 97.
29. "Though everyman responsible for his actions must suffer himself, our whole family is filled with shame and deepest sorrow at Madan's act. He showed eccentricity in childhood and became generally worse. He once ran away from home and worked as *lascar* (sailor). On his return to India I arranged his going to England, my father protesting that he was going mad. Probably he fell into bad hands also. God's will be done." Martin Gilbert, *Servant of India*, p. 193.
30. Martin Gilbert, *Servant of India*, pp. 193-94.
31. *Indian Daily News*, July 10, 1909.
32. Morrison told, "When he came to me to ask what he should do, how he should express his own horror at the crime", I said to him, "Your proper course is to purge yourself before your own countrymen and to tell them that, though the man who committed the crime is your brother, you wish to join with your countrymen in repudiating it." Therefore, this man desires to add his words of support to the resolution. *The Panjabee*, July 6, 1909.
33. Victor Grayson was a Socialist M.P. (1907-10).
34. *Indian Daily News*, July 10, 1909.
35. Kesar Singh, *Amar Shaheed Madan Lal Dhingra*, p. 7.
36. Waraich and Puri, *Tryst with Martyrdom*, p. 85.

□

2

Rebel in the Making

Sahib Ditta Mal, the father of Madan Lal Dhingra, had qualified as an eye surgeon from Medical School, Lahore in 1867. (He was appointed Sub-Assistant Surgeon and got the permission to practice.)[1] He served as Medical Officer in Gurdaspur and as Civil Surgeon, in Hissar. There he developed friendly relations with Dunlop Smith, the Deputy Commissioner. Sahib Ditta Mal also developed cordial relations with Curzon Wyllie and other important British officials. His own status and newly acquired acquaintances, enhanced his prestige in the society and soon he adapted himself to the British attire, and mannerism. For thirty years, he served as Medical Officer and retired as Civil Surgeon. He also served for some time as Honorary. Physician and Surgeon to Maharaja Partap Singh of Jammu and Kashmir. The British Government had rewarded him with the title of 'Rai Sahib' for his meritorious services and loyalty to the Crown. The title had been bestowed on him much before Madan Lal Dhingra committed the act. After retirement, he came back to Amritsar and started his private practice which proved equally successful. For his own residence, he had built a magnificent building known as 'Dhingra Buildings' in Katra Sher Singh near Regent Cinema Hall.[2]

Sahib Ditta Mal had eight children, a daughter Kaki Rani (the eldest), and seven sons: Kundan Lal, Mohan Lal, Behari Lal, Chaman Lal, Chuni Lal, Madan Lal and Bhajan Lal. Kaki Rani was married to a landlord Chetan Das of Sahiwal, who died at an early age.[3] His eldest son, Kundan Lal was widely travelled and had settled down as a successful businessman in textiles in Amritsar.[4] He had developed friendly relations with Sir Curzon Wyllie and had correspondence with him.

Second and third sons, Mohan Lal and Behari Lal after completing their education in medical from London came back to India. Former joined as Health Officer, Municipal Committee, Amritsar. Later on, he joined as Chief Medical Officer of Jammu and Kashmir State. He also wrote some books on Medicine, which were highly appreciated.[5] Behari Lal (M.D. and M.R.C.P.) was appointed as Chief Medical Officer in the erstwhile Jind State (Sangrur PEPSU). The fourth son Chaman Lal passed his Bar-at-Law from London and on return was appointed as an 'Official Receiver' by the Punjab High Court, Lahore (West Pakistan). When Muzzaffarpur bomb tragedy took place, in which Mrs. and Miss Kennedy, wife and daughter of a local barrister were killed, Chaman Lal published a letter in *Civil and Military Gazette*, 11 May 1908, condemning the clandestine act of the revolutionaries. In his letter, he praised the British Rule and prayed for its continuation.

Chuni Lal, was serving as *Munsif* in Jammu.[6] This was the scene of first five sons of Sahib Ditta Mal. Anyone could be proud of such an educated family so well-settled and so well-linked. The seventh and the youngest son of Dr. Sahib Ditta Mall was Mr. Bhajan Lal, Bar-at-Law. He was in London during the trial of Madan Lal Dhingra. After his return to India, he practised for sometime at the Amritsar Bar and afterwards he shifted to Lahore.

Of all the children, Madan Lal Dhingra had been a source of trouble in the family. He was an average student. He passed his Matriculation from Mission High School, and joined Municipal College, and passed his F.Sc. in second division from Amritsar. For his further education, he was sent to the Government College, Lahore and was admitted in Science discipline. After a few months father received the news that his illustrious son was indulging in political activities than studies. Madan Lal Dhingra had never made any secret of his nationalist feelings, although his father was a loyalist to the British Government.[7] Sahib Ditta Mal had no expectations from him. He was the only one who had always disturbed him, may it be on education front or discipline.

What conspired in Lahore that forced Madan Lal Dhingra to give up his studies? As far the facts are concerned, we do not have much information. According to one version, he Matriculated from the Mission High School, Amritsar, and did his Inter in Science from Government College, Lahore. Kesar Singh informs that Sahib Ditta Mal got Madan Lal Dhingra admitted to the Government College, Lahore by utilizing his influence to which latter protested and resented. He further writes that after sometime he left the college, the reasons are wanting.[8] V.N. Datta also informs about his admission to the same college and nothing beyond that. The *Indian Daily News*, July 6, 1909 wrote that Madan Lal Dhingra, a young man of 22, passed his Intermediate in Arts from Amritsar, studied for sometime at Lahore.

Did he take part in politics? Some writers claim that he had joined trade union at Kalka. It establishes that he had inclination for politics and joined the trade union, may be as a beginner, if not at national level. Thus, the view held that he was suspended from the Government College for political activities, seems to carry sense. Otherwise, one finds no other reason for his leaving the college in between the session. The status and influence which Rai Sahib Ditta Mal enjoyed at that time, he could have easily got him re-admitted to the college, but perhaps his uncalled for and obdurate behaviour stopped him to do so. As a reprimand for Madan Lal Dhingra audacious behaviour, which failed to pass the litmus test of loyalty to the Crown, he was made to miss his studies. As a rebel son, Madan Lal Dhingra preferred to be called disloyal to the family than to his country.

Some believe that he was too young to understand the intricacies of politics, but such opinion does not go with his personality and the act he committed afterwards. One can count many young revolutionaries, who were quite involved in politics at a tender age like Bhagat Singh, Udham Singh, Savarkar brothers, etc. Madan Lal Dhingra had defied age, despised wealth, and dedicated his self, for the cause of the freedom of the country, which he had absorbed from the social political set-up prevalent at that time. The study of the political scene in the country as a whole, and Punjab in particular, from 1900 to 1906, the period corresponding to Madan Lal Dhingra's education and stay in the country, will help to comprehend the influence of political beliefs on his impressionable mind.

A well-known, hard-headed imperialist, Curzon on his second term as Viceroy of India, opened up the 'Pandora's Box' culminating in the partition of Bengal on 16 October 1905.[9] The partition of Bengal marked a decisive phase in the history of freedom struggle in India. It sowed the seed of mass movements. Curzon's reactionary rule, and his short-sighted policy to partition Bengal added fuel to the fire and further agitated the revolutionaries in the Congress. The Congress responded by launching Swadeshi and Boycott movements by organizing mass public meetings and processions followed by burning of foreign goods. The social base of the movement was now extended to include, besides the elite class; a certain *zamindari* section, the lower middle class in the cities, in small towns, and students from schools and colleges on a massive scale. Women came out from their home for the first time and joined the procession.[10] Soon the movement spread to the other parts of India and especially the Punjab.

In the Punjab, the Swadeshi and Boycott movements also gained impetus for the national awakening. Punjab was already simmering with discontent against the imposition of *Pre-emption Bill*, the enforcement of Bari Doab water rates, the Canal Colonization Bill and above all the *Land Alienation Bill*. The fear 1906 brought about a clash between the Punjab agriculturists and the government of the province on account of Punjab colonization of Land Bill and the enhancement of the canal water rates.[11] Lahore by the close of the nineteenth century had become a major centre of learning. A small 'Westernized elite', led by such men as Lala Lajpat Rai, Harkishan Lal, Murli Dhar, Duni Chand, Ram Bhaj Dutt, Sain Das, Hans Raj, Munshi Ram, Gokal Chand Narang, Shahbudin, Muhammad Safi, etc., had emerged to safeguard the interest of their brethren. The nucleus of English-educated community vehemently criticized government's arbitrary policies and categorically 'The Punjab Alienation of Land Act (1900)' and made people aware that the Act would create a sharp division at the social, economic and political levels.[12] The marginal educated men, made use of print and public forum to attract the people to educate and awaken them about the high-handed policies of the government and welcomed the Swadeshi and Boycott movements for the cause of nationalism. It was not until 1907, when the Colonization Bill and Land Alienation Amendment Act sparked of political agitation, that the rural populace joined together against the government. It was the economic plight of the rural folk, when pressed through the new legislation, which made them look to the urban political elite for leadership. The Punjab had become the breeding ground for soldiers, producer of wheat for export and as such a British compulsion, to be kept contended at all cost. After the 1857 revolution, British Government was able to exploit Punjab for their economic and military gain, by feeding them with sporadic reforms and pampering their egos, but could not withhold them from the rising storm of nationalism in the country.

The Swadeshi fever raised its head under the leadership of Lala Lajpat Rai and Sardar Ajit Singh.[13] Lala Lajpat Rai thundered, "We ought to be Swadeshi in everything.... Swadeshism is a thing to be taken with mother's milk.... A strong feeling of hatred for everything 'Bideshi' must be impressed upon the younger generation and this is affected by the burning of Bideshi articles."[14] He urged the masses to assist the Swadeshi movement by boycotting all foreign goods, in particular the foreign sugar.[15] He encouraged the school boys to join gymnastic societies and *Akharas,* to keep themselves physically fit.[16] It was a turning point in which for the first time the masses participated actively in the rallies organised by the leaders of Punjab, irrespective of caste, creed and colour.

The launch of Swadeshi Movement gave Lala Lajpat Rai a cause to espouse the national feelings among the people. He utilized his pen and the newspaper *The Punjabee* to promote the cause of India's unrest and government's high-handed policies.[17] About 1,500 strong English-knowing inhabitants of Lahore gathered outside the Town Hall protesting against Lord Curzon's aspersions on Indian character in his address at the Calcutta Convocation.[18] In Punjab, the "fad" of a headstrong Viceroy was decried.[19] Even though a 'small nucleus', these few individuals were prepared for the contemplation of methods of progress, even if invoking troubles and sacrifice. The meetings and demonstrations in some of the major cities illustrated the kind of commotion "not dreamt of a year before" and even the effect of the "Swadeshi Vastu Pracharni" was felt now.[20] In the *Punjabee* newspaper, it was commended, "Boycott is the order of the day in every creek and corner of the land" and meetings were being held everywhere to boycott foreign goods.[21]

In the principal towns of Punjab, particularly in Rawalpindi, Lahore, Amritsar, and Ambala, "Swadeshi Vastu Prachar" gained popularity. *The Tribune* commented: "Swadeshi has brought to fore the exposure of talent which under normal conditions would have remained dormant".[22] S.S. Bhatia (Editor, *Daily Times*) swayed people by his eloquence. Gokal Chand Narang (Professor D.A.V. College, Lahore), M.S. Bhagat (Bar-at-Law, Lahore), Hans Raj Swahney (Lawyer, Rawalpindi), through their speeches convinced many to open Swadeshi Stores in the cities. A company was registered in Lahore as "Punjab Native Stores Limited" dealing exclusively in country-made articles.[23] Schools and colleges formed the focal point of organizing Swadeshi meetings, and even the Hall of the Forman Christian College was used for this purpose.[24] At Raja Dhyan Singh Haveli, Lahore, about three thousand people gathered to hear Roshan Lal (Bar-at-Law), K.P. Chatterji (Editor, *The Tribune*), Mahbub Alam (Editor, *Paise Akhbar*) and Dharam Das Suri (public pleader) all addressed people on movement, Swadeshi. Mahbub Alam pointed out that Swadeshi was of greater benefit for the Muslim community.

At a meeting, held near the water-works reservoir, Lahore, not an inch of space was empty, with about 20,000 people shouting *Bande Matram* along with Vishnu Digamber, (a classical music vocalist) entertaining the audience with patriotic song. Hyder Raza, the Secretary of Swadeshi Association, Delhi, impressed by the Lahore performance gave up his Turkish cap as being foreign. Gokal Chand Narang dilated on the oppression by the British rule in India, and waxed eloquent on the death of 90 million people in ten years (1890-1900) for want of food which he said Swadeshi would provide them.[25] On 23 November 1905, the citizens of Lahore arranged reception for Lala Lajpat Rai at the Railway Station after his return from England, where he had gone along with Gokhale to revoke the partition of Bengal. He shared his experience with the people. He openly declared that British democracy was too busy with its own affairs to do anything for them. He criticized the lukewarm response of the British press which was not willing to champion Indian aspirations. He cautioned the masses to be prepared to fight their own battle for freedom.[26]

The Punjab elite, even though a microscopic minority had reached a stage "If pushed to the wall in repression and unfairness, it would react".[27] With Lala Lajpat Rai's return, Punjab took up again the cause of the 'Swadeshi and Boycott'. Sarla Devi, Ram Bhaj Dutt's wife motivated the whole gathering by her melody, *Bande Matram*.[28] Dunlop Smith wrote to Lady Minto, "One striking feature in the present situation in India is the emancipation of Hindu women. There is an undoubted tendency to relax the rule of *purdah* and even to allow women some part in public life.... The part taken by women in raising funds for so-called 'national' purposes in the Punjab is another sign of the movement".[29] By 1905, the Punjabees started organising political agitation against the *Zalim Sarkar*. The Englishmen were insulted right in the capital, on the Mall; the villagers were approached to stop paying the government revenue and taxes; anti-government leaflets and posters were circulated; efforts were made to incite the police and the soldiery in the name of the country's honour.[30]

There is every possibility that a sensitive person like Madan Lal Dhingra, who had recently entered the educational arena, might have been swayed by the simmering current of discontentment, as Lahore was politically surcharged. Sohan Singh Josh writes that Madan Lal Dhingra was one of the leading participants in the agitation to get these acts annulled. He had begun to take an active part in the political movement of the time.[31] The government was dealing with politically motivated students sternly, and he, as a new entrant in politics must have fallen prey to the government's fury, and thus suspended. Dejected, disturbed and annoyed, the reputed and loyal father Sahib Ditta Mal decided to take back his son Madan Lal Dhingra to Amritsar. Otherwise, a father, so keen to impart best possible education to his children, would not have acted so.[32]

Definitely, Madan Lal's political bent of mind must have disturbed Rai Sahib, who could sense of the approaching troubles. Dhingra family was well aware of the consequences of following the path of loyalty and disloyalty. If loyalty meant reward, then disloyalty meant confrontation with the government, loss of prestige and economic benefits. It was better to make Madan Lal sit back at home, as it would deprive his new born love for politics much needed food for thought abundantly available at Lahore. Sahib Ditta Mal was a man of few words. The entire family feared him and dared not defy his decision. The anglicized, Rai Sahib had created a huge gap between himself and his children and no one had any say in the house, besides him. In such an atmosphere, the feelings and sentiments of the children are sacrificed at the *altar* of family's prestige and status.

Madan Lal Dhingra felt crestfallen and distressed and left his family which was against his thought and action. In the perception of his other brothers, Rai Sahib Ditta Mal was a great man and they were proud of his achievements whereas Madan Lal felt suffocated at the very mention of 'Rai Sahib', perhaps for him, its very connotation meant loyal or *toady*.[33] If he wanted, he could have continued to live along with his wealthy parents. All that was required of him was obedience, discipline and to be loyal to the *mi-baap* British, but it was not his cup of tea. For him, his father's house was just like a cage, though made of gold, yet it was a cage and he decided to give it a call and left his home, to live and earn independently, without caring about the business proposal of his father. He joined as a clerk in Kashmir Settlement Department. He could not stick to the position for long and left it after about six months.[34] He later joined Kalka-Simla *Tonga* Service under the distant relation Rai Bahadur Daulat Ram.[35] After serving there for sometime, he came back home as he got the news of his mother's ill-health. The love and affection which his mother showered on him, provided much needed strength in time of his solitude. At home he could not adjust to the vainglorious atmosphere, where he was the target of attack for his vagrancy. His parents wanted him to pursue studies but he was not ready to go back to the old institution. As things could not be sorted out, once again he left home in search of better opportunities outside. He joined as a *lascar* in a ship, but could not adjust and afterwards went to England, a country more advanced and liberal, where he could breathe afresh.

In July 1906, Madan Lal Dhingra reached England. Who bore the expenditure of his journey? Did he manage the money from his earnings as *lascar* (Indian sailor) or his family supported him. According to one view, he collected money as a *lascar* and managed his travel to England, which seems incorrect. As *lascar*, he went to Burma and Sri Lanka and wired for money from Ceylon.[36] Sahib Ditta Mal gave his final approval for his journey to England and definitely he made monetary arrangements too. After going through the different views and available facts one can conclude, Madan Lal could not find his job as *lascar* interesting and came back to India. He went to meet his brother Dr. Behari Lal Dhingra who was posted as Chief Medical Officer at Sangrur. He welcomed Madan Lal Dhingra with open arms and advised him to pursue his further studies if not in India, then in England. A degree earned there meant better job prospects in India.

Sahib Ditta Mal had a great fascination for England. His other four sons had successfully been educated there and his eldest son, Kundan Lal was a frequent visitor to England for business purposes. As such it was not difficult for Behari Lal to persuade his father to the proposal, who after some hesitation agreed to the suggestion with a hope for his son's better projection. All that required was sufficient money to bear the expenses, and for a rich man like Sahib Ditta Mal, it was not an issue. After meeting the required formalities, Madan Lal Dhingra left for Bombay to board the ship to England in 1906, with the consent of his family. Kesar Singh in his novel laments that nobody came to see off Madan Lal at Bombay. The reasons were obvious, as a rebel he had already cut off his ties with the family.[37] Moreover, Madan Lal Dhingra was well acquainted with Bombay, and as such he must have gone alone thus saving the time and causing unnecessary inconvenience to his brother.

When Madan Lal Dhingra reached England, he was received by his elder brother Kundan Lal, who was already there on business trip. He had made arrangements for his stay in England.[38] During the first three months, he visited all the important sites in England and got well acquainted with its geography. According to the C.I.D. report, "He arrived in London in July, and on October 19, 1906 he joined as a student of engineering at the University College, where he continued to attend up to the last day of June 1909." From 1906 to 1909, he remained in London, studied and passed his diploma in engineering in third division.[39] His certificates prove that he was regular in his college and at studies.

England, by the beginning of the twentieth century, had become the most powerful nation in the world politically and economically. In 1901, Queen Victoria died, and was succeeded by her son Edward VII (1841-1910), who ruled for a decade. .The British Crown was the titular head, as all the powers were vested in the elected house, Parliament. From 1895 to 1905, Conservative Party was in power. To look after Indian affairs, a Secretary of State for India, was appointed, and a 'Council of India', with fifteen members was set-up to help and advise him. In India, the Viceroy, as a personal representative of the Crown, was to act as a *de jure*, head of the State, with an Executive Council to help him. In policy matters, he was advised and guided by the Secretary of State for India. Both were supposed to act in coordination and mutual understanding.[40] Elections in England were approaching and the Congress decided to send a delegation under Gokhale and Lala Lajpat Rai to apprise the British public about the problems and aspirations of the Indians, from British administration. Gokhale addressed group of businessmen, statesmen, politicians, and various institutions and succeeded in creating a favourable impression, personal accomplishment and winning lip sympathy only.

In England, the Liberal Party won the elections and Campbell-Bannerman became the Prime Minister on December 5, 1905.[41] Lord Morley became the Secretary of State for India and Minto (from Conservative Party) was made to continue as Viceroy of India.[42] The hopes and expectations of the moderates in the newly formed Liberal Government in England were puffed up and the party decided, once again, to send Gokhale to strike the final deal. Gokhale reached England on 29 April 1906. He saw about 150 MPs and five times he met John Morley. Morley discussed, conversed in detail, the matters related to the reforms and other affairs, but he never gave his heart nor indicated any inclination to the question of the partition of Bengal, quite dear to the Congress.

The newly elected members of British Parliament supported the cause of moderates and demanded liberal policy to be adopted towards India. Some members like Henry Cotton suggested in "Restoring the old state of things".[43] T. Hart Davies was of the opinion, "It was Machiavellian Policy" framed by the Conservative Government, "The new government should respond to the spirit prevalent in India". Similarly, O'Donnell said, "It is possible to do away with what had been done". Morley reply was a definite 'no' to any suggestion related to the position of Bengal. In his opinion, partition was the "settled fact".[44] He stated that the situation in Bengal was under control and "agitation was subsiding".

Bengali Press had pinned hope on the new government and Morley statement was a shock to their aspirations. The *Indian Mirror* wrote that Morley had been misinformed. *The Dacca Gazette* wrote, "So, after all, the fate of Bengal is sealed".[45] The *Hitwadi* expressed that the authorities must be brought to their senses by a thorough boycott of English goods, suggesting further strengthening of the economic blockade. Morley statement created suspicion in public mind as regards British justice. The *Sandhya* quoted, "The more the *ferangi* will exhibit his true nature, and the closer will the divided parts of Bengal be drawn together in bonds of unity". *The Bengali,*[46] *The Amrita Bazar Patrika* and *The Indian Mirror* urged the government to reconsider the decision and to take into consideration the public opinion. The change of government from Conservatives to Liberals and again to Conservatives in England did not change the stand and the policy of the government towards India. Moreover, the Indians had forgotten that the Liberal Party was meant to be liberal for British only.

In England, Shyamji Krishna Varma openly criticized the mendicant policy of the Congress and tour of Gokhale in his journal *Indian Sociologist.* From the very beginning, he entered into confrontation with Hume and Wedderburn. He was against the way they were manoeuvring the Congress. He also came in conflict with Mahatma Gandhi on the issue of Boer War.[47] Shyamji criticized Gandhi and other Indians who sided with the British in Boer War. He was in favour of adopting mass non-cooperation as a mean and home-rule as an end. He believed that if persuasion fails to get the things done, there was no harm in using force to get the demands accepted.[48] The *garam dal* in the Congress wanted to adopt a stern measure to force the government to accept their demands, as appeals and *dalils* had yielded no results. The split in the Congress Party was avoided in 1906 session but extremists were successful in launching; the Swaraj, Boycott, Swadeshi and National Education as the four cardinal points of the Congress programme. This union based on compromises was short-lived and next year at the Surat session, the split happened.

The government believed that all the mess regarding the

partition of Bengal was a creation of the press. So, the press and its editors had to bear the government's brunt. Tilak, the editor of *Kesari* was sent to Mandalay Jail for six years. Arobindo Ghose was implicated in a revolutionary conspiracy case, later acquitted, gave up politics. B.C. Pal temporarily retired from politics. In Punjab, Lala Lajpat Rai and Sardar Ajit Singh were deported to Mandalay.[49] The extremist dominance in Congress, after Surat fiasco (1907), diminished. The Government of India, lead by Lord Minto, for the time being, succeeded in its mission to divide the Congress, to curtail the political movement of the extremists by adopting every possible fair or unfair means.

The scene of Indian politics after 1907 seems to have shifted from India to England, where the policy of repression was absent and the freedom of expression, speech and of press, triumphed. Men from India had started coming to England, for different purposes, mainly to acquire higher education in Law, Medicine, Engineering and others for business, medical treatment, and for vacations. There were selected few who had political motives behind their visit to England. They utilized the liberal environment of the country, freedom of speech and expression to inculcate the feelings of patriotism among their own people. The main master planner of the revolutionary movement in England was Shyamji Krishna Varma and his pilot was Vinayak Damodar Savarkar and Madan Lal Dhingra was its flag bearer. India House became the platform and the launching pad, wherefrom the plane of revolutionary nationalism took off.

NOTES

1. V.N. Datta writes that Dhingra family had migrated to Amritsar from Sahisral in District Sargada (West Punjab) in about 1850. *Madan Lal Dhingra and the Revolutionary Movement*, p. 1. The title *Rai Bahadur* is mentioned in Baradari of Sahib Ditta Mal, constructed in his memory by his family. Also see M.S. Gill, *Hanerian Ratan Chamakde Tare*, Escort Press, Amritsar, 1997, p. 9.

2. The present occupants at the Dhingra Building, Vikram Dhingra (a grand nephew of Madan Lal Dhingra) has recently renovated the interior of the house. At the enterance of the house the name "Dhingra Buildings" embossed on the wall can still be seen.
3. *The Tribune*, "A Rebel from Aristocracy", 1976.
4. Kundan Lal Dhingra had four sons and one daughter. His eldest son Dr. Hira Lal Dhingra, a dental surgeon, practiced in Delhi. Mr. Mukand Lal, his another son, is living in Amritsar. The Dhingra family had disposed of all of their property in Amritsar. Late G.R. Sethi (*Tribune* correspondent) had developed close relations with the surviving members of the Dhingra family, notably with Kundan Lal, worked as an optician, Dr. Behari Lal, was a famous Prime Minister of erstwhile Jind State and Mr. Bhajan Lal, a barrister with progressive views: *The Tribune*, 1976. "A Rebel From Aristocracy".
5. He qualified as M.D., F.R.C.S., M.R.C.P., D.P.H. from London. After resigning his lucrative job, he migrated abroad, and died in France. Dunlop Smith had mentioned about him in his letter written to Lord Minto, when latter was to pay a visit to the city of Amritsar in March 1909. Dunlop Smith reminded His Excellency, of having met Dr. Mohan Lal at Gwalior. He also praised his work in improving the sanitary conditions of the city, as a Health Officer. Behari Lal and Mohan Lal were joint authors of "Minto Health Pamphlet". Martin Gilbert, *Servant of India*, p. 188.
6. Chuni Lal later joined the erstwhile Patiala State in the capacity of a Judicial Minister. He was married to the Keshab Chandra Sen's granddaughter, niece of Maharani of Cooch Behar. He was survived by a son C.L. Dhingra who retired as Principal of Hindu College, Amritsar.
7. *The Tribune*, 17 December, 1976, "A Rebel from Aristocracy", p. 3.
8. Kesar Singh, *Amar Shaheed Madan Lal Dhingra*, pp. 24-25. Also see, Pritam Saini claims that it was due to his political activities, he was suspended: *Shaheed Madan Lal Dhingra* (Punjabi Eds.), Punjabi University Patiala, 1991, pp. 16-17, and similar view is expressed by K.K. Khullar, *Madan Lal Dhingra*, Ministry of I&B, Government of India, 1983, p. 5.
9. By 1900, the population of Bengal had grown to 78 millions. East Bengal was dominated by the Muslims and West by the Hindus. Assam and Chittagong with fifteen districts of Bengal were united to form the Eastern Bengal with Dacca as its capital, and remaining

part to be known as the province of Bengal, with Calcutta as capital. In reality, the partition was more due to political compulsion than administrative need. Its real purpose of the partition was to thwart the rising tide of nationalism among the Bengali-speaking Hindu *bhadralok*, which was in forefront of the National Movement. D.B. Mathur, *Gokhale: A Political Biography*, Manaktalas Bombay, 1966, p. 88. Ram Chandra Pradhan, *Raj to Swaraj*, Macmillan, New Delhi, 2008, p. 95.

10 For the first time in Bengal, 'Two huge mass meetings' with a gathering of more than 50,000 and 75,000 people respectively were addressed by Anandmohan Bose and Surendranath Banerjee: Bipan Chandra, *India's Struggle for Independence*, Penguin Books, New Delhi, 1989, pp. 133, 137.

11. Ganda Singh (Ed.) *History of the Freedom Movement in the Punjab* (Volume IV), Punjabi University, Patiala 1978, Introduction.

12. The Punjab Alienation of Land Act symbolized British determination to protect the rural and traditional landholder classes and transfer of landed property by mortgage and sale to the urban moneylenders. There was fear of agrarian unrest due to loss of land by hereditary landholders. The Act prohibited the transfer of land from the Punjab agricultural tribes to non-agricultural moneylenders. It widened the cleavage between the urban and educated elite class and the rural masses, with the official patronage for the latter. The Act reflected British policy of divide and rule not only amongst the religious communities, but agriculturlist vs. non-agriculturalist, mainly to strengthen their imperialistic hold: N.G. Barrier, *The Punjab Land Alienation Bill of 1900*, 1966, p. 101. Also see Nina Puri, *Political Elite and Society in the Punjab*, Vikas Publishing House, New Delhi, 1985, p. 78.

13. Ganda Singh (Ed.) *History of the Freedom Movement in the Punjab*, Punjabi University, Patiala, 1978, 9.60-65.

14. V.C. Joshi (Ed.), *Writing and Speeches of Lala Lajpat Rai*, Vol. I, pp. 118-19.

15. Ganda Singh (Ed.), *The History of the Freedom Movement in the Punjab*, 1978, pp. 64-65.

16. Later on, this practice was also followed by the Bengal and other provinces. British Government consider it as an act of treason and the DAV College, Lahore was inspected by the officers to study the actual working of the *Akhara*. Similarly, the *Akhara* at Gurukul Kangri, Haridwar was also kept under surveillance and scrutinized.

The DAV Colleges were the first to include the idea of Swadeshi in their educational programme.

17. Sir Valentine Chirol openly accused Arya Samaj of being a political movement and its ringleaders were Lala Lajpat Rai and Ajit Singh. Ajit Singh was accused of translating the seditious books concerned with the manufacturing of bombs. Lala Lajpat Rai was found corresponding with Shyamji Krishna Varma. Director Criminal Intelligence Departments Report to the government, File-Home Department Political-August 1907, No. 3, Deposit. Bhai Parmanand was found in possession of various formulae for the manufacture of bombs. The same manual was discovered from Manikotla Garden at Calcutta. Michael O' Dwyer had commented, "Wherever there is Arya Samaj, it is the centre of seditious talk", *India as I Know It*, cited in, Radhey Shyam Pareek, Contribution of Arya Samaj in *Making of Modern India, 1875-1947*, pp. 211-12, and 313-15. Also see (Sardar Ajit Singh could not be arrested immediately and a reward of ₹ 500 was offered for his arrest. But according to the Lieut. Governor, "He is infinitely less important and less dangerous than the first (Lala Lajpat Rai)." Also see the Extract from The Confidential Diary of the Superintendent of Police, Lahore for the Week Ending, April 10, 1907: Ganda Singh (Ed.), *History of the Freedom Movement in the Punjab*, (Volume IV), Punjabi University, Patiala 1978, p. viii.
18. *The Panjabee*, April 24, 1905, p. 2.
19. *The Tribune*, July 8, 1905, p. 3.
20. *The Tribune*, November 25, 1905, p. 5.
21. Lala Lajpt Rai wrote in the paper, "The one sole object of Lord Curzon's policy had been to shut all sources of public activity to the sons of the soil, where the latter could possibly learn lessons of self-help and self-reliance and receive the necessary training for the government of their country by themselves", *The Panjabee*, October 10, and 13, 1906; Ganda Singh, *The Freedom Movement of the Punjab*, Vol. IV (History of the Freedom Movement), pp. 61-63.
22. *The Tribune*, November 9, 1905, p. 5.
23. Ravindernath had opened a Swadeshi Bhandar in 1897, Yogesh Chaudhri had opened an Indian Store in 1901 and Sarla Devi started Lakshmi Bhandar in 1903: Sumit Sarkar, *Bengal Mein Swadeshi Andolan* (Hi. Trans. by Adityanarain Singh), *Granth Shilpi*, New Delhi, 2002, p. 36.
24. Meetings were arranged by educated classes in Chiniot, Lyallpur, Kasur, Ferozepur, Gujranwala and Bhera: *The Punjabee*, October 16, 1905, p. 5.

25. *The Panjabee*, November 6, 1905, p. 4.
26. Lala Lajpat Rai, *Young India*, New York (1916), pp. 169-70.
27. *The Panjabee*, November 27, 1905, p. 4.
28. *The Panjabee*, January 6, 1906, p. 4. Sarla Devi had planned to establish a Bengali Red Cross, inspired by Russo-Japanese War: Sumit Sarkar, *Bengal Mein Swadeshi Andolan* (Hi. Trans. by Adityanarain Singh), *Granth Shilpi*, New Delhi, 2002, p. 13.
29. Martin Gilbert, *Servant of India*, pp. 125-26.
30. S.P. Sen (Ed.), *Historical Writings on the Nationalist Movement in India*, K.C. Yadav, Punjab, Basu Printing, Calcutta, 1977, p. 93.
31. Lahore and Calcutta were the centres of this (Bengal partition and Colonization) and anti-British movement in the Punjab and Bengal, and the young students in particular were affected by it: Sohan Singh Josh, *Bhagat Singh and Other Early Revolutionaries*, Communist Party Publication, New Delhi, 1976, p. 76.
32. V.N. Datta, *Madan Lal Dhingra and the Revolutionary Movement*, p. 2.
33. Kesar Singh, pp. 17-18. *Today* was used in bad sense.
34. K.K. Khullar, *Madan Lal Dhingra*, Ministry of I&B, Government of India, 1983, pp. 4-5.
35. *The Tribune*, July 6, 1909.
36. It could not have been possible to purchase ticket from the salary of a *lascar.* Pritam Saini, *Shaheed Madan Lal Dhingra* (Punjabi Ed.), Punjabi University, Patiala, 1991, p. 17. Waraich and Puri, *Tryst with Martyrdom*, p. 95.
37. Kesar Singh, *Amar Shaheed*, p. 17.
38. Kesar Singh writes that Madan Lal Dhingra was received in England by his brother Kundal Lal. Had he come to England without the consent of his father and family, it would not have been possible: Kesar Singh (Hindi), *Amar Shaheed Madan Lal Dhingra*, pp. 60-61.
39. Waraich and Puri, *Tryst with Martyrdom*, see picture gallery.
40. Development after 1858 had in fact considerably enhanced the personal role of the Viceroy-Secretary of State combine through the communications revolution symbolized by the submarine cable and Suez Canal (1865-69). The telegraph lines from Britain to India were successfully connected in 1870. The connection resulted in reduction of existing gulf between the Secretary of State in England and Viceroy in India.
41. He resigned on April 7, 1908 and was succeeded by Henry Asquith (1908-15).

42. John Morley, 1838-1923, Liberal M.P. 1883-1908. Secretary of States for India, 1905-10; historian and biographer and well-known as politician; Viscount 1908, resigned from Cabinet in 1914, being opposed to war with Germany, and explained his action in *Memorandum on Resignation.*
43. Henry Cotton, 1868-1939. Editor of *India*, the London newspaper of the Indian National Congress, 1906-18; author of *New India and India and Home Memories*; Liberal M.P., 1918; President of the Bengal Legislature, 1922-25.
44. Syed Razi Wasti, *Lord Minto and the Indian Nationalist Movement 1905-1910*, Clarendon Press, Oxford, 1964, p. 33. In spite of all opposition and agitation, Curzon had refused to budge from his stand and did not acknowledge the rising public opinion and bluntly asserted "Partition of Bengal is a settled fact and what is settled cannot be unsettled".
45. The early leaders of the Congress had reposed almost undiluted faith in the Liberal patrons in Britain, and this policy was based on the presumption that the government would gradually respond to their legitimate demands. *The Indian Mirror,* 28 February 1906, and *The Dacca Gazette*, Dacca, March 5, 1906.
46. *The Bengalee*, February 28, 1906.
47. In his political career Shyamji came into conflict with the opinion expressed by Gandhiji during the Boer War, Gandhi had said, "We have been proud of our citizenship. Our rulers profess to safeguard our rights because we are British subjects.... It is true that we are helots in the Empire.... It must be conceded that justice is on the side of the Boers, but every single subject of a state must not hope to impose his private opinion on all cases. Our ordinary duty as subjects, therefore, is...to render such assistance as we possibly can." Shyamji criticized those Indians ruthlessly who offered their services to the British to fight against the Boers. Dharamvira, *Lala Hardayal and Revolutionary Movements of His Times*, p. 21.
48. A.C. Bose, *Indian Revolutionaries Abroad 1905-1922*, Bharati Bhawan, Patna, 1971, p. 16.
49. For the publication of seditious literature in the Punjab. For details, see *Government of India*, Home Department, *Political* 967-76, October 1909, No. 145-153.

□

3

India House

India House was established by Shyamji Krishna Varma in London, in 1905. He was a Sanskrit scholar, lawyer, nationalist and a journalist. He got his early education at Elphinstone School in Bombay and went to Balliol College, Oxford for higher studies. On his return to India, he practised Law for sometime; held high offices in native states; Diwan in Ratlam and Junagarh and was a member of State Council in Udaipur. He developed differences with the Crown authority and was dismissed following a supposed conspiracy of local British officials at Junagarh.[1] Soon he left for England. There he founded the Indian Home Rule Society, the *Indian Sociologist* and the India House.

In January 1905, his first English weekly, the *Indian Sociologist*, the organ of the revolutionary was published. Its subtitle *An Organ of Freedom, and Political, Social and Religious Reform*, was published from London till May 1907 and later on its publication continued from Paris where Shyamji had shifted, till 1914.[2] Through the column of his journal, Shyamji regularly advised his countrymen to prepare themselves alone for their political salvation. In its very first number Shyamji announced his decision to start five travelling fellowships of the value of ₹ 2000 each, for enabling Indian graduates to complete their higher education in Britain and to qualify for an independent profession.[3]

Shyamji Krishna Varma launched the Indian Home Rule Society, on 18 February 1905.[4] The proclaimed political objective of the party was to secure Home Rule for India to carry on propaganda in the United Kingdom to that effect, and to spread awareness about independence among the Indians. Muslim students in London by and large kept aloof from the Home Rule for India society.[5]

Shyamji purchased a mansion by spending more than a hundred thousand rupees at 65, Cromwell Avenue, Highgate and named it as India House. It was formally inaugurated in July 1905 by H.M. Hyndman who had made a special study of India's political problems. He advised the Indian youth to be loyal to their nation and not to the Crown. He cautioned them not to be swayed by the false belief that England herself will lead them to liberation. He openly declared that the only method which could bring English Government to its senses was the Nihilists method.[6] Its opening ceremony was attended by prominent leaders like Dadabhai Naoroji, Lala Lajpat Rai, Lala Hans Raj, Anthony Quelch, Madame Deshpard, Sweeny and others. Every Sunday a meeting was held in the afternoon where all Indians were invited to participate in debate and discussion on the topics mostly related to the Indian problems and plans for its liberation.

In Pune, Vinayak Damodar Savarkar read about Shyamji's activities in Marathi newspaper *The Kesari*. He also read Shyamji's monthly *Indian Sociologist*, which contained information about scholarships being offered to Indian students. Shyamji had announced two fellowships—one in the name of Shivaji and another in the name of Guru Gobind Singh. Under its scheme, any Indian graduate could apply for it. The candidate selected was to take a vow that after the completion of his studies in England he will return to his motherland to serve, and will not accept any kind of office, emoluments or service under the British Government. In March 1906, Savarkar applied for the Shivaji scholarship and was selected by Tilak.

A graduate from the Ferguson College Poona, young Savarkar was a first-rate debater, a powerful orator, a rising writer and a leader of a revolutionary organization which was creeping over all villages and towns in the Nasik district Mitra Mela.[7] He was the first Indian leader to make a bonfire of foreign cloth in India and the first Indian student who was rusticated from a government-aided institution for political reasons.

Savarkar and Madan Lal Dhingra arrived at London in 1906. Former was an eloquent speaker who could win the audience by his oration whereas latter was an introvert and rarely entered into any argument. Savarkar was a modest and simple man, while Dhingra was aristocratic in style and manner. Savarkar had come on scholarship while Dhingra had a rich family to support him. For Savarkar educational qualification was a necessity whereas it could have added another feather in the cap of Dhingra family. Savarkar belonged to the family of revolutionaries and got his inspiration from his brother, whereas Madan Lal's family being loyal to the Crown always discouraged and dissuaded him from political activities. Dhingra had come to look for a motive besides studies, whereas Savarkar had come with an undertaking and a plan.

Savarkar believed that through revolution liberation could be achieved. His main objective in London besides studies was to master the techniques of launching of a revolution. Mazzini, the renowned revolutionist was thoroughly studied and translated and his techniques were implied to train and cultivate the young mind as first necessary step for launching a revolution.[8] Madan Lal Dhingra believed that by assassinating a selected few, terror could be struck among the British Officers serving in India and they could be forced to leave. Savarkar, who had the power to convince and command, prepared men to revolt and sacrifice, and Madan Lal Dhingra preferred to set an example by sacrificing himself for the cause of freedom.

Madan Lal Dhingra became acquainted with India House after his admission in the University College, London. He came to know about it from his college friend and visited it. What attracted him to India House? Besides the excellent eloquence of Savarkar, atmosphere, ideology and the simplicity of the working of India House impressed him the most. Outside India, the revolutionaries had their greatest inspiration and support from Shyamji Krishna Varma and his India House. In an interview given to Campbell Green of the *Sunday Chronicle* in March 1909, Savarkar said, "India House is an inexpensive hostel. But for admission as a lodger, one does not need to have any specific political opinion. All that he has to do is to pay one pound (per week) for board and lodge. Political discussions do take place. Persons who consider British Raj as divine dispensation also come here. Those who can convince others by means of truth and logic win the day."

The education system had attracted many young Indians to come to England to qualify in one or the other discipline for their better future perspective. There, they were inspired and attracted to the democratic process prevalent in the country. The system and its applications were not new to them. Republics existed in India. Sabha and Samiti were two bodies of Vedic age where elected and selected few members of the society participated in the formulation of State policies in a democratic pattern. The system got lost in time and space but in England it was in existence. The nationalists desired that the same system of administration should be applied to India also. They wanted Indians to be consulted and included in the formulation and promulgation of administrative policies which concerned them the most. They were against the repressive measures being adopted by the British Indian Government against the radicals.

The interest in Indian politics in England was aroused by the efforts of Shyamji Krishna Varma and his comrades like Madame Vikaji Rustomji Cama, M.B. Godrej, J.M. Parikh, J.C. Mukherji and others. They all were well to do people and had earned a name for themselves. They were rather elderly people, comfortably settled in life and were not prepared to involve themselves for any hardship, but wanted to do something for their country. They provided financial help and encouragement to the youth to join in.

There was sizeable number of Indian students living in London and most of them were likely to hold position of influence on their return home. Men like Krishnavarma, Sardarsinghji Rewa Bhai Rana, Madame Cama, etc., not only provided monetary help to the young revolutionaries but also fully utilized the print media to enlighten the youth to the Indian grievances and to motivate them to the cause of India's freedom. It was necessary, so that when they go back to serve India, they should think serving their own motherland and not the British Crown. Gradually, many Indians were encouraged to join the freedom movement.

Majority of the students from India had come to England with a purpose. Generally, they belonged to well-to-do families who could afford to bear the cost of their study and some had come on merit after earning some scholarship or sponsorship. In England, they felt lonely but at India House they could find a company of their countrymen with whom they could discuss and share their grievances. Madan Lal Dhingra soon started visiting India House at regular intervals. He frequently attended the meetings but rarely took any part in discussion. He resided there for six months from April to October 1908 and also for a month in the early part of 1909. He had become quite friendly to Savarkar whom he admired and respected. Savarkar admired his determination, dedication and concern for the liberation of his motherland. On leaving the India House in April 1909, Madan Lal Dhingra took lodgings with Mrs. Mary Harris at 108, Ledbury Road, Bayswater, in London.

Other important inmates of India House were Pandurang Mahadev *alias* Senapati Bapat, a Mechanical Engineer, wrote a booklet "India Wanted Home Rule" for which Government cancelled his scholarship, Shyamji welcomed him to India House, suspect in Alipore bomb case, served three jail sentences. Waman Vishnu Phadke came to England to qualify for ICS but got interested in nationalist activities and India House. Virendranath Chattopadhyaya, known as Chatto, brother of Sarojni Naidu, aimed to throw British rule through revolution. He was a poet and a fiery journalist and a member of India House. Varahaneri Venkatesa Subramaniyam Aiyer (V.V.S. Aiyer) was a zealous extremist from Tamil Nadu, short-story writer, believed in armed revolution came in contact with India House and worked for the liberation of the country. Dr. Teruvengimalai Sundra Rajan (T.S. Rajan) from Trichnopalli. practiced in Burma, came associated with VVS Aiyer and India House and actively participated in its political activities. Gyanchand Varma was Secretary of Abhinav Bharat, studying law in London and was closely associated with India House. Lala Hardayal was M.A. in English from Panjab University, had come to Oxford for further studies on scholarship, took interest in India House, later on went to America and founded Ghadar Party. Dr. K.P. Jayaswal was the famous author of *Vijay Nagar Empire*. W.V. Phadke, Koregaonkar and Kunte were closely associated with India House and translated *India War of Independence* from Marathi to English. KVR Swami, Mr. Master the correspondent of the paper *The Parsee* was active in India House from July to October 1908 and had to leave due to ill-health. Hemchandra Das (sentenced to *Kalapani* to the Andaman Islands) had also visited India House.

Bipin Chandra Pal came occasionally to India House.[9] His son Niranjan Pal (Nanu) was a close friend of Savarkar and was a frequent visitor. Other visitors included Sikandar Hayat who became the premier of the Punjab; and Shapurjee Saklatvala, Member Parliament in United Kingdom and member of Communist Party. Dadabhai Naoroji, the Grand Old Man of Indian politics, Lala Lajpat Rai, Bhai Parmanand and Mahatma Gandhi all visited India House, the centre of Indian politics in England at that time.

Asaf Ali informs that after enjoying the hospitality of Shyamji and Sardar Rava Singh in Paris, he along with Riza and Rauf reached London in May 1909. Govind Amin took them to India House, a fairly big and well suited for the stay. Asaf Ali informs, "Regular residents were not many; they included taciturn Punjabi, Madan Lal Dhingra and the genial scholar V.V.S. Aiyer of Madras".[10] He further informs that at weekly meetings on Sundays, the gathering at India House would swell to twenty or thirty. One or other would be voted to the chair and somebody could read a paper to deliver a speech, followed by discussion on the topic ending with concluding remarks by the chairperson. India House was a rendezous for politically like-minded Indian youths, and a training ground for perspective public men and revolutionaries.

If the partition of Bengal and the repressive policy of the British was able to ignite the feeling of patriotism and nationalism in India, then the celebrations of 1857's victory in England was very much responsible for fanning the xenophobic fervor in a foreignland among the Indians. Thanks Giving Day was celebrated all over England and especially in London to venerate the victory of 1857, achieved 50 years ago in India from the last Mughal Emperor, Bahadur Shah and his comrades. The warriors, the victors and the people who died fighting for saving the British colony in India deserved acknowledgement and as such there was nothing wrong in remembering and celebrating those glorious moments.

The newspapers carried articles eulogizing the stories of their triumph in 1857. *The Daily Telegraph* wrote, "Warriors have saved British Rule in India". The article carried the story of bravery of the British soldiers and on the other hand decried the cowardice, lassitude and animosity of the Indian soldiers. Whereas the success story and bravery of the soldiers was concerned, it was appreciated by all but the adjectives used for the losers created a wave of discontentment among the Indians who considered them not less than warriors. Had it ended here only, it would have not caused much tension, but the victors were bent upon celebrating the moment in every possible way. On 1 May, a show was staged for the masses, in which Rani Jhansi, Tantiya Tope, Nana Sahib and other Indian warriors were shown as cruel, butchers and blood sucker criminals. This was a move to defame the Indian heroes and weaken the sentiments of the Indians in England. Indians living there were perplexed, annoyed and agitated at the way their war heroes were being misrepresented and projected in the press and the stage shows.

Savarkar organized a meeting in this connection in India House which was largely attended. British celebrations of 1857 were discussed threadbare and its presentation was vehemently condemned. If British soldiers were heroes in the eyes of the British people, then those thousands of Indians who died fighting to save their motherland were no less. Everyone condemned the act of the British and desired to repay in the same tone. The house unanimously decided to counter it by organizing a similar event to commemorate and honour the Indian war heroes of 1857 who died fighting to save Indian Empire from the British. It was decided that on 10 May, a conference should be organized to celebrate and commemorate the first war of India's independence fought in 1857 where the martyrs should be paid befitting tribute and an oath should be taken to fight for the freedom of the country.

In the meeting, it was decided to make badges in memory of the martyrs of 1857. It was decided to observe fast on May 10, and to distribute *chapatis* to the gathering on that day. Different groups were formed each consisting of two members. The major task of the group was to visit the Indian residents to inform and educate them about the coming occasion and celebration. The task of decorating the stage and to organize the conference was given to Madan Lal and Harnam Singh by Savarkar.

Madan Lal Dhingra was full of enthusiasm at his new assignment. He went out and met many Indians and apprised them about the coming celebrations. He was bubbling with energy and actively performed the task assigned to him. Gyan Chand Varma was asked to prepare the report two days before the start of the conference. The invitation letters were posted to inform the Indian students living in England. They were requested to update their respective native places in India about the occasion. Everybody was asked to contribute for the occasion and to reach in large number on the said date. Chattopadhyaya was assigned the duty to meet the Bengali youth. In the day time, they studied and at night they visited the houses of their Indian compatriots. The entire exercise inculcated a feeling of satisfaction and pride among the Indians that there existed an organization in a foreign land to watch their interests.

As the day approached nearer, the Indian became more and more enthusiastic about the celebrations. They began to move from house to house in every lane and street where fellow countrymen resided. It was a delightful activity never experienced before by the Indian residents in England. On 10 May, all roads led to the India House where 51st anniversary of the first war of independence of 1857 was being celebrated. The young revolutionaries of India House had planned to exploit this unique occasion to spread their ideology of revolution and independence.

Emily Brown writes that to mark the completion of the manuscript Savarkar staged an elaborate celebration of the 51st anniversary of the Mutiny, or as he called it, "The Indian National Rising of 1857". The golden anniversary observations a year before had attracted little or no attention, but this time the event received full coverage in the column of the *Times* [11] which provided every minute detail related to the event. It gave elaborate coverage to the invitation card which had been printed in red-ink symbolic for sacrifice and itself considered ominous been printed in red-ink—a fact in itself considered ominous.

Card issued by India House

Bande Mataram*

To Commemorate the anniversary of

The

INDIAN NATIONAL RISING

of 1857

A MEETING OF INDIANS IN

ENGLAND

will be held at

INDIA HOUSE

65, Cromwell Avenue, Highgate N.

On Sunday the 10th of May, 1908,

at 4 P.M. precisely.

You and all your Indian friends are cordially invited to be present.

Oriental Publishers, Delhi (1917 1st edition) 1973, p. 173.

*James Campbell Ker, *Political Trouble in India, 1907-1917*, p. 173.

The observance was the curious mixture of modern day public relations "Gimmicks" and traditional Hindu practices.

On that day, India House was beautifully decorated with flowers and lights. On the red screen, with borders and banners of garlands, panels of names in gold and other colours were hung in frames. Bahadur Shah, Nana Sahib, Rani Laxmi Bai, Raja Kunwar Singh, Maulvi Ahmed Shah, all these and other heroes and martyrs were brilliantly portrayed on the screen. In the hall, flowers and incense created a spiritual atmosphere.

The function commenced with the inspiring national song *Bande Matram* sung by Gyan Chand Varma. Slogan of *Bande Matram* shot through the walls of the hall and boomed beyond. At 4.30 p.m. the President, Sardarsinghji Rewa Bhai Rana, then staying in Paris arrived with a group of selected leaders. He brought a very inspiring message from Paris patriot, 'Beloved Madame Cama'.

After the song V.V.S. Aiyar recited the national prayer. The premises of the India House, even beyond the hall, were packed with men and women. Many had to stand outside as hall was full to its capacity. The song and the prayer enthralled the audience. Savarkar made a spirited speech. While addressing the gathering, he explained the objective of his writing the book *The Indian War of Independence 1857.* He wanted to inspire his people with a burning desire to wage a second and a successful war to liberate their motherland. He considered the war of 1857 to be the first war waged by the Indians against the Crown.[12] Secondly, he wanted to place before the revolutionaries an outline of the programme and action plan of the organization in order to prepare the nation for the future war of liberation. He strongly believed that without fighting war against the usurper freedom could not be achieved. He talked about the sacrifice and sufferings of Bahadur Shah and Nana Saheb for the cause of India and explained the real significance of the War of Independence. At the conclusion of his speech, the whole assembly rose amidst repeated shouts of *Bande Matram.* Then Rafiq Muhammad Khan of Nabha spoke on Raja Kunwar Singh and Hemchandra Das on Rani Laxmi Bai of Jhansi. Mr. Master, a Parsi member of Abhinav Bharat, and other speakers from various communities and provinces of India addressed the meeting which concluded with an inspiring oration by the President. Tributes were paid to the warriors of the Mutiny; Emperor Bahadur Shah, Shrimant Nana

Sahib, Rani Laxmi Bai, Maulvi Ahmed Shah, Raja Kuvar, Kanwar Singh, and other "martyrs". It was followed by declarations of self-denial involving a vow to abjure "pleasures and pass time" and to contribute money to "Fund for the Heroes and Martyrs of 1857". Those taking the vow were given badges to commemorate their commitment. The *Times* reported that more than 100 students from Oxford, Cambridge, and even Edinburg had been present at the observation, which lasted for four hours and was concluded with the distribution of *Prasad*, a ritual offering, in this case, *chapati,* the unleavened Indian bread.

University teachers, doctors, barristers, journalists, merchants, jewellers, women and children spontaneously took the vow to observe a month of sacrifice for the cause of freedom. Special commemoration badges were distributed to all who took this pledge. Some swore abstinence, some abandoned smoking, and some resolved to avoid all pastimes.[13] The objective of 'sacrifice and savings month' was to contribute maximum to the fund for the heroes and martyrs of 1857. The students announced that they would move out with hand in hand to collect donations and also convey to every Indian the message of the great revolt of 1857, and impress upon everyone the necessity of continuing the struggle for the freedom of India. The purpose was to keep the aspiration and desire for the freedom struggle in the masses, a necessary ingredient for the future course of action plan. Madame Cama donated a handsome amount and Rewa Bhai Rana gave away one month's earnings. After the national song the ceremony concluded with the distribution of *prasad* in the form of *chapati* (bread) to symbolize fifty years old war of independence when the *chapatis* were distributed all over the country as a sign of the coming revolution so that people could get ready for it.

Harnam Singh and R.M. Khan, students of Agricultural College, Cirencester, exhibited proudly on their coats the badges of 1857 commemoration. Principal of the institution ordered them to remove the badges but they refused. He publicly scolded them and abused their war heroes and labelled them as murderers. The students could not tolerate the insult and boycotted the college. Some members of Parliament raised the matter in the House and condemned the unwise action of the principal. A patriotic Punjabi lady, Dhan Devi was so impressed by the daredevil act of the students that she invited them over a dinner and offered them the title of *Yar-i-Hind* (Friends of India) engraved upon silver medal. Madan Lal Dhingra too took a fight for the badge and he physically beat up those who tried to take his cherished honour away. The government was alarmed and decided to pacify the students through peaceful means. Instructions were issued and restrictions were imposed on students participating in political activities in educational institutions.

To discuss and pacify the matter, a meeting was convened by the British administration in the Caxton Hall which was well attended by the Indian students. According to the *Daily Chronicle*, a demonstration of disloyalty on the part of the Indian students was observed in the meeting. When Lord Lamington came to the dais to address them, there were repeated loud hissing and deriding laughter creating indiscipline in the hall. The chairman had to call for order. The government realized that the national movement among the Indian students had shaped itself on the pattern of the Russian Nihilists. Similar views were expressed by the secret intelligence in London. The book of Savarkar *The Indian War of Independence 1857*, was considered a great threat by the British intelligence. The book was banned before it could see the daylight. India House also came under their scanner and surveillance. A net of secret agents was planted around it to keep a strict vigil and collect information regarding its activities.

The political activities in the India House, after the year 1907, had intensified. Madan Lal Dhingra stayed there for about six months much against the wishes of his family. This was the time when his association with Savarkar and other members of the India House became intimate to such an extent that he dared to defy his brother's advice to move out of India House. The Punjabi rebel was well fed with intellectual food abundantly available at India House. It was visited by the prominent leaders of that time who delivered their talks and shared their views about the country's future and independence. The discussions after the lecture represented divergent views and the concluding remarks would clarify the misconceptions. Different suggestions were floated to achieve India's cherished dream, liberation. Everyone had his own line of thought and action to achieve the goal. All these discourses one way or the other were leaving a dent on the mind of Madan Lal Dhingra. He too got absorbed in the same thought process ultimately culminating into his action plan, the murder of Curzon Wyllie. The celebrations of May 1908 had further enhanced the importance and prestige of India House and the number of its occupants swelled. This recognition was perhaps short-lived as India House soon became the target of attack by British press.

The *Standard* newspaper was first to come out with news against these meetings and warned the government that Indians in London were preaching revolution. The former Governor of Bombay, Lord Lamington presided over a meeting organized by the British public to condemn the efforts of the extremists in London. Bipin Chandra Pal also delivered a talk and condemned revolutionary methods to achieve liberation. Warner William Leigh, in his speech addressed the Biharis as *Dirty Niggers.* Vasudev Bhattacharya, former editor of *Sandhya* and *Yugantar*, who was present in the audience, could not digest the insult and dared to slap William Leigh Warner. Next day newspapers were filled with condemnation over the 'Daredevil act' of Bhattacharya. The matter went to the court and Bhattacharya was fined twenty rupees. Soon, India House came to be looked upon with suspicion and contempt by the British as a place of seditious activities. Any student, who was associated with it, was looked down upon. The British press targeted India House and its leaders, and started writing against it (often). The main leader who came under their scanner was Shyamji. Scotland Yard Police was asked to keep a strict vigil on India House and provide information about the doings and dealings of the extremists and their sympathizers, residing in London, Paris and other socialist centers and proposed authorization of the Eastern Bengal and Assam Government to communicate directly or through others—with the Commissioner of Police, in London.[14]

The police planted Kirtikar at India House to extract information. As a dental student he entered the House and started delivering information to the police. His actions were noticed by T.S. Rajan and Aiyer and one day he was caught spying for the police. He admitted his crime and apologized. Savarkar, Aiyer and Rajan decided to utilize his services for their own benefits. He was asked to continue with his job, so that police should not get suspicious. He kept on sending the report to the police but under the guidance and surveillance of the senior members of the India House. It was with his help that Aiyer was able to have friendship with other two spies of the Scotland Yard Police. During this time, Mirza Abbas and Sikandar Hayat were able to carry revolvers to India. These activities were perhaps responsible for the fall in the number of members at India House.

Asif Ali who arrived at India House in 1909 informs that the regular members living in India House were not many. The reason for the thin occupancy could be attributed to the political activities of the India House which had become the target of criticism in the press. British public looked at it with suspicion and its inmates as revolutionaries. By the time Madan Lal Dhingra committed the act, very few had been living there and even Savarkar was not staying there at that time. The students coming to England for studies were not interested to be labelled as revolutionaries as it could affect their future career. Moreover, India House was a cluster of people belonging to different castes and communities as such it was not an easy task for everyone to adjust. The kind of food being served in India House also discouraged many to stay.[15]

Savarkar, the mastermind of political activities at India House let no opportunity slip for rallying the forces to the cause of regenerating the national sentiments among the Indian youths. In June 1908, Dr. Desai, a student of London University, delivered a lecture on "Making of Bombs". On 8 November 1908, Savarkar lectured on "Are We Really Disarmed?" and declared that there was ample of war-like material in India which could jeopardize British power provided the support of Indian Army and native states could be enlisted. G.S. Khaparde of Amrote, Lala Lajpat Rai, and Ram Bhuj Dutt from Punjab, and Bipin Chandra Pal of Culcutta, all left India in August and arrived in London in September 1908. On 19 October 1908, a meeting was organized in order to revoke the partition of Bengal. Lala Lajpat Rai presided over the function. Gokal Chand Narang, Bipin Chandra Pal, Gokhale, R.C. Dutt, G.S. Khaparde and Kerantekar delivered the speeches.[16]

On December 20, 1908, another meeting was organized by National Conference with Khaparde as the president, Dada Sahib, Madame Cama and Sir Aga Khan addressed the audience mostly Indian students. Madame Cama raised the motion of boycott of foreign goods, and it was seconded by Gyan Chand Verma. V.V.S. Aiyer congratulated Turkistan on its becoming a republic and Sir Aga Khan supported it. Dr. Kumara Swami raised the issue of Swaraj, and it was seconded by Savarkar. The meaning of the Swaraj was declared to be complete independence. This proposal too was carried by the House. The Minto-Morley Reforms were criticized for being irrational and were much less than their expectations. The members admitted that it was a planned programme of the government to sow the seed of separation among the two major communities in India.

On 29 December 1908, the death bi-centenary of Guru Gobind Singh was celebrated at the Caxton Hall in London.[17] Bipin Chandra Pal presided over the function. The programme started with the song *Amar Desh.* Savarkar sang the Marathi song *Priaykar Hindustan.* Gokal Chand Narang read a paper on Guru Gobind Singh's life and sacrifice. He motivated the audience by citing the examples of his valour and sacrifice, and how he fought against the mighty Mughal Empire. On this occasion, the song *Pagri Sambhal Oye Jattan* echoed in the hall surcharging many emotionally. Savarkar narrated the stories of freedom fighters of the country.

During this time, Kundan Lal Dhingra had come to England on a business trip and he came to meet Madan Lal Dhingra. After exchanging pleasantry he enquired about his studies and latter told him that he need not worry as he had cleared his exams. After some hesitation Kundan Lal came to the main topic for which he had come to meet him. He told Madan Lal Dhingra that father was not happy with his political alliances in England and especially his visit to India House. He wanted him to sever his relations with the revolutionaries. He reminded him that Dhingra family was loyal to the Crown and any wrong act of his could harm the prestige and status of the family. Newly surcharged Madan Lal Dhingra with feeling of patriotism and nationalism was in no mood to fall prey to the family ties and openly declared his intentions to defy. Kundan Lal Dhingra had thought that he will be able to change his mindset but all his efforts failed to change his mind. As a last resort Kundan Lal threatened to cut all ties with him, but even this could not change his stance. The result of this conversation was written by Kesar Singh, that Madan Lal Dhingra disclosed that he had a plan to stay for sometime at India House. Kundan Lal felt humiliated, defeated and left him to his fate. All the cajolery and threats could not deter Madan Lal from his resolution and they parted.

Madan Lal Dhingra had been quite active during these days in the ongoing functions at India House. He was present at the meeting on 24 January 1909, and on 26 February when Naidu read a paper on "How a nationalist views the appointment of the Indian Law Member". A report shows him leaving India House in company of Savarkar and others. Madan Lal Dhingra had brought his brother Bhajan Lal Dhingra to India House when Savarkar and Koregaonkar spoke fervently against the Benchers' decisions to impose restrictions on Savarkar and Harnam Singh. A revolutionary campaign against the British was going on in India House. The venom against the administration and the Crown was being spitted everyday. The Director of Intelligence, C.J. Stevenson-Moore, had written outrage will be committed in London, as a warning to the Commissioner of Police. By April 1909, the anti-British campaign had reached its peak at India House, and Dhingra who resided there was asked by his parents to shift elsewhere. Though he shifted to Ledbury Road, yet his interest in India House never lessened.

The news about the repressive measures of the British Indian Government against the nationalist and revolutionaries was reaching England through the new arrivals. The suppression of the press and its editors by the government was another cause of resentment among the Indian revolutionaries. The news about economic exploitation, the regular outbreak of famines, and spread of diseases like cholera, malaria and plague in India and lack of will and negligence in the efforts of the government to protect the life of the poor, all these happenings were reaching at India House, issues were discussed threadbare and the policies of the government were condemned. This encouraged many settled abroad to do something for their country.

Madan Lal Dhingra's final engineering examinations were over and he had enough time to spare for such activities. The ongoing political activities at India House had left an indelible impact on the nascent mind of Madan Lal Dhingra and had converted him from a mere rebel to a revolutionary. The concept of India's freedom which was planted in his mind during his initial days in India was gradually watered and nurtured at India House to develop into culmination. Here he learnt about the intricacies of the British Administration, its dual faced policies, and profit making plans at the cost of India. He understood the importance of freedom and strived to liberate his motherland from foreign rule. He learnt how British people were plundering the wealth of India in the name of modernization. He held British Government responsible for the appalling condition of the Indians and for the torture and murder of unaccounted innocent people in India.

NOTES

1. He had done favour to an English friend Meconoki who conspired against him and as a result Shyamji was dismissed. He complained to the higher authorities but British officers supported their colleague. Maharana of Udaipur wanted to appoint him as Diwan but Curzon Wyllie did not allow.
2. The title of the journal showed the influence of Herbert Spencer and it carried his two quotes "Everyman is free to do which he will, provided he infringes not the equal freedom of any other man" and "Resistance to aggression is not only justifiable but imperative". *Principle of Ethics*, Section 272, *The Study of Sociology*, Ch. 8. It also contained a note from Henry Mayers Hyndman: "Indians must learn to rely upon themselves and organize themselves apart from their foreign masters for their final emancipation". Sumit Sarkar, *Bengal Mein Swadeshi Andolan* (Hindi), p. 43.
3. In January 1906, Krishna Varma announced six scholarships of ₹ 1000 each for the Indian authors and journalists to visit foreign countries in national interest. Rana also announced three fellowships of ₹ 2000 each, the conditions remaining the same, not to serve the British Government on return to India. Indulal Yajnik, *Syamji Krishna Varma*,

Bombay, 1950, p. 130. Also see A.C. Bose, *Indian Revolutionaries Abroad, 1905-1922*, Bharati Bhawan, Patna, 1971, pp. 16-17.

4. Indian Association, London, was then presided over by Dadabhai Naoroji but it was found lacking in its aim. Against this organization Shyamji had launched his Home Rule Society. Shyamji became its President, J.M. Parikh and M.B. Godrej and S. Suhrawardy as vice-presidents, and J.C. Mukherjee as its secretary. Dr. C.M. Muththu, Mukund Rao Jayakar were also associated with the society.
5. Ziauddin Ahmed, then in Germany had warned Abdullah Suhrawardy against his association with the Home Rule Society, as Vice-President. He wrote, "Do you really believe that the Muhammedans will be profited if Home Rule be granted to India?"
6. Syed Razi Wasti, *Lord Minto and the Indian National Movement, 1905 to 1910*, p. 89.
7. Later the party sprouted into the world famous Abhinav Bharat Society in 1904. The aim of the party was to arouse the passion for independence and hatred for foreign rulers. It encouraged the young revolutionaries to perform physical exercises and mental training, a necessary mode of preparation for a successful revolt.
8. His objective was to educate the Indian students who were pursuing academic career in England. In 1907, there were some 700 Indian students in Great Britain of whom 380 were in London alone: Waraich and Puri, *Tryst with Martyrdom*, p. 12.
9. Bipin Chandra Pal sailed for England on sponsorship by Shyamji. The latter had asked him to deliver forty-five lectures for a sum of rupees one thousand a year to be paid from the *Dash Bhakta Subha* fund and a part of money had been sent to him before he set sail. Pal did not fulfill the expectations of Shyamji. Saral Kumar Chatterjee, *Bipin Chandra Pal*, p. 101.
10. The three—Asaf, Rauf and Riza—had left India in 1909. The first part of Asaf Ali's sojourn in England lasted nearly three years, from May 1909 to January 1912: G.N.S. Raghavan, *Asaf Ali's Memoirs: The Emergence of Modern India*, Ajanta Publication, N. Delhi, p. 69.
11. Emily Brown, *Har Dayal: Hindu Revolutionary and Rationalist*, Manohar, Delhi 1975, pp. 63-64. Also see Dharmavira, *Lala Hardayal*, 1958, p. 115.
12. G.M. Joshi, "The Story of this History" in *Indian War of Independence*, V.D. Savarkar, Phoenix Publication, Bombay, 1947, p. IX. Also see Interception of a book by Savarkar on the Indian Mutiny: Government

of India, Home Department, Political 97, February 1909, No. 13-13A.

13. Kesar Singh, *Amar Shaheed Madan Lal Dhingra*, p. 125. Also see Dharmavira, *Lala Hardayal*, p. 116.
14. Government of India, Home Department, Political Deposit, April 1909, No. 26.
15. Asaf Ali writes, "Within a fortnight of our stay in India House, Rauf and I decided to move out of it. For here food served there defied description. And here there were Madrasis, Maharattas and Punjabis, each so far apart in tastes. Secondly the atmosphere in India House was surcharged with politics, got on my nerves, I wanted to build for myself my own private world". G.N.S. Raghavan, *Asaf Ali's Memoirs*, p. 70.
16. Gokhale was to address the meeting organized by the radicals at Caxton Hall in London, for the release of Tilak, but he refused. Khaparde and Kerantkar had come to appeal for the release of Tilak.
17. Many have mentioned the occasion as Birth Centenary of Guru Gobind Singh, which is not correct. He was born in 1666 and passed away in 1708: V.N. Datta,.*Madan Lal Dhingra and the Revolutionary Movement*, p. 25. Also see Khaparde G.S., Note on doings in England, Government of India, Home Department, Political Deposit, April 1909, No. 21.

□

4

Assassination of Curzon Wyllie

July 1, 1909 was the most absorbing day for Madan Lal Dhingra. It was the day for which he had been waiting and planning. His study in engineering at University College was about to be over, a task for which his family had sent him to England. Qualifying as an engineer in London he had fulfilled the aspirations of his father and the Dhingra family. Now, no one could point a finger at him for not being properly educated, a comparison and an accusation which he had been listening to all through his career in India. In three months time, he would have been sailing back to India, to feel the warmth of mother's affection and see the smile of pride in his father's eyes, but this was not to be so as he had written a different fate for himself, where relations and emotion mattered little, where achievements earned in life paled into insignificance at the *altar* of freedom of motherland.

On July 1, he left his lodgings at about 2 o'clock and by the evening he reached at Tottenham to practice for revolver shooting. The shooting range was near the university where he was studying. Using his personal Colt revolver, he fired

12 shots at the target. 11 shots hit the target which was at 18 feet distance, making a circumference of a man's hand. Dhingra used his personal nickel steel bullets in practice. The revolver ejected the spent cartridge immediately after it had been fired and automatically another cartridge from the magazine would come up taking its place.[1] Normally, the shooters were provided with 320 Webly revolver for practice but Madan Lal Dhingra preferred to practice with his personal revolver. He was satisfied with his practice and accurate aim. He asked the attendant to clean the revolver and after collecting his weapon he came back to his lodging by 7 p.m.

He started making preparation for the evening bonanza, which was arranged by National Indian Association at Imperial Institute in London. The association was under the patronage of His/Her Majesty and it included a number of distinguished officials who had already served in India. The association was launched to provide help and guidance to Indians coming to England for education or any other purpose. It provided them proper information concerning their educational inquiries, boarding, lodging, and any other tribulations. The people coming to England were not ordinary men, and to win their sympathy for the British Crown and faith in British system was a necessity, so that when they go back to serve India they should be Indians in looks only, but a true British in dress, manner, thought and action. It was just another way of infiltrating the minds and hearts of the Indians, through sympathetic and sweet gestures.

Madan Lal Dhingra was well aware of this unscrupulous practice of the association and had no love lost for it. He had recently sought its membership as it was necessary to gain access to it. He admitted that it was through his brother that he had applied for its membership. Miss Beck, the honorary secretary of the association, asked him to see her in the office on following Saturday and on the appointed day he went and got its membership.

Madan Lal Dhingra took out his best shirt and suit from his closet and tied a light silken blue turban on his head. After tying the knot of the tie, he had a look at his appearance in the mirror, and smiled at his own reflection. He was aware of the fact that he would never come back to this room again. He gave a last glance, and checked his pockets, to make sure that whatever he wanted to carry along with was intact or not. He took with him a Colt revolver and a Belgian Pistol loaded with eight and six bullets, respectively. He also pocketed five extra cartridges in his waistcoat pocket, so that he would have material for 19 shots. He took a knife and a handwritten statement explaining his goal. He carefully left a copy of the handwritten statement in the box of his appartment. After having fully satisfied himself about the preparation, he left for the selected destination to fulfil a self-assigned mission.

At about 8.45 p.m. he hired a cab, and left for the selected venue. By 9 o'clock sharp he had entered the Jehangir Hall where the get-together was taking place. "At Home" organized by the National Indian Association for the Indians on Thursday night, was attended by about 200 people. One member of the committee had remarked during the evening that it was perhaps the most successful get-together held under the auspices of the association for some years past. A pleasant feature of the gathering was that a large proportion of Indian ladies and gentlemen had arrived in their national dress. Even Madan Lal Dhingra had come in turban, representing Punjabi culture. Guests were busy in and music items were being played to make the evening pleasant. Sir Charles and Lady Lyall received the guests and among the others present were Sir Stuart and Lady Bayley, Sir Lesley and Lady Probyn, Sir Frederie Candy, Cowasjee Jahangir, and the Princess Sophie Duleep Singh.

Miss Beck saw Madan Lal Dhingra at the entertainment and exchanged pleasantries notes with him. Soon he got engaged in conversation with other Indian guests. He displayed perfectly calm and collected demeanour and maintained it all through the night. It was getting late and guests had started dispersing, but Curzon Wyllie the honorary treasures of the Indian National Association had not yet arrived for whom Madan Lal Dhingra was waiting anxiously. Once again he met Miss Beck and this time they had a long talk, in a friendly and casual way. Though busy in talk, Madan Lal Dhingra eyes were searching for Curzon Wyllie, who was yet to arrive. His delay would have meant, postponement of the mission, which Madan Lal Dhingra never wanted. Miss Beck could not speculate even for a second what was going in his mind.

Sir Curzon Wyllie and Lady Wyllie had almost invariably been present on such celebrations organized by the Indian National Association. On that day they were dining at the Savoy Hotel with Mr. Fazulbhoy Currimbhoy Ibrahim, Chairman of the Bombay Mill Owners Association and his younger brother, who were in the country on a brief visit. After the dinner they all drove to the Imperial Institute. Soon Sir Wyllie, accompanied by his wife and some Indian friends entered the Jehangir Hall where the entertainment was proceeding. Madan Lal Dhingra saw them coming and his mind started planning for the action. His eyes followed Curzon Wyllie wherever he went. He was in search of a right opportunity, to encounter him, if possible, in seclusion. As usual, both Sir Curzon and Lady Wyllie had a busy time giving or receiving introductions and chatting with both Indian and English friends.

The reception was to close at midnight, but already by 11 o'clock the visitors had started leaving. Sir Curzon Wyllie also decided to move out. Mr. Fazulbhoy Currimbhoy Ibrahim escorted the Lady Wyllie downstairs to the cloak-room and Sir Curzon was about to follow, but was stopped to speak to one or two Indians with whom he had no previous opportunity to converse. He was Madan Lal Dhingra, who had sought his attention. Both met near the doorway in the vestibule. Madan

Lal Dhingra engaged him in conversation and they were standing a yard apart from each other.

It was in the midst of this scene that Lady Wyllie had preceded her husband downstairs in order to obtain her wraps from the cloak-room. In between the conversation, Madan Lal Dhingra raised his hand with a pistol in it close to Curzon Wyllie face and fired. He fired rapidly around four or five bullets from the point-blank range. One bullet shattered Curzon's right eye, and another bullet pierced his face below the left eye. Curzon Wyllie fell flat on the floor. Another two shots were fired at the man whom Madan Lal Dhingra thought was about to attack him. He was Dr. Lalcaca from Shanghai, who had come to celebrate his holidays in England. He too fell near the doorway. He had no intention to kill anyone else besides the target. It was perhaps at that spur of moment that he did shot at him. All his anxiety, tension and apprehensions were over, as if he was relieved of a heavy burden. He had accomplished his 'self-assigned' mission. Six rounds of shots had been fired and two cartridges were still left in the pistol.[2] He was happy with the achievement but perturbed due to unintended killing of Dr. Lalcaca, he lowered the pistol to submit. The weapon however was quickly wrested from him, and he offered no further resistance.[3]

Lady Wyllie immediately returned to the landing attracted by the sound of the shots. She realized that someone had been shot but at that time she was not aware of his identity. With a few sympathetic words she bent over the victim, it was then, she realized for the first time that he was her own husband who had met death. She displayed remarkable courage in her agonizing ordeal. She opened his shirt front to see if he was still breathing. She was heard saying "Can't you speak one word to me?" It was obvious to everybody that he was beyond all hope. Lady Wyllie displayed absolute courage and calmness and remained by her husband until the body was removed.

Inquiry was made in the hall for any medical man present. Both Dr. Buchanan, of Vouxhall Bridge Road and Dr. Syed Hassan, Beigrami went to assist the injured. It was relief to all when some Indian screens, which had decorated the platform, were fetched and placed round the bodies, and the guests were persuaded to leave. Dr. Lalcaca was badly wounded but still alive. The only person who seemed to remain unmoved throughout the event was Madan Lal Dhingra. Constable Nicholls, 476 B, who was on duty outside, was called to the Imperial Institute. He saw Madan Lal Dhingra held by some persons. He also saw the body of Sir Curzon Wyllie. He was dead. Dr. Lalcaca was still breathing. A cab was called and Lalcaca was shifted to the hospital, but on the way he too succumbed to the injuries, and died. Madan Lal Dhingra was taken into custody.

Later in the day, Dhingra was brought up at the Westminster Police Court. *The Times* on July 3, had reported, Madan Lal Dhingra, 25, a native of the Punjab, an engineering student of the Ledbury Road, Bayswater, was brought before Mr. Horace Smith, charged with the wilful murder of Lieutenant Colonel Sir William Hutt Curzon Wyllie, K.C.I.E. retired Indian official, and Cowasji Lalcaca, a Parsi physician by shooting at the Imperial Institute. Sir Bodkin appeared for the director of public prosecution, Sir Charles Mathew who was himself present Superintendent Quin from the Political Department of Scotland Yard, represented the Commissioner of Police.

Madan Lal Dhingra, who gave his age as 25 years, was of slight built, dark olive complexion, and had thick black curling hair falling over his forehead. He wore large gold rimmed glasses, and was dressed in a dark well-worn ordinary lounge suit and a blue turban. He stood in the dock apparently unconcerned with his hands in his pocket.

Constable Nicholls, 476 B, stated that shortly after 11 o'clock on the previous night he was called to the Indian

Section of the Imperial Institute. He saw Madan Lal Dhingra being held by some gentlemen and took him into custody. The witness saw the body of Sir William Curzon Wyllie. Dr. Lalcaca who had also been shot was alive at that time.

Superintendent Albert Isaac, B Division, stated that at 12.30 that morning he saw the prisoner detained at Walton-street, Chelsea station. When charged with the murder, the prisoner nodded his head and his lips moved but whatever he said was inaudible, though the witness was only a yard away. The prisoner, speaking good English, though rapidly said "The only thing I want to say is that there is no wilful murder in the case of Dr. Lalcaca. I did not know him. When he advanced to get hold of me I simply fired in 'self-defence'".

Mr. Horace Smith remanded Madan Lal Dhingra into police custody for eight days.

It was noticeable that throughout the entire episode no friend of the prisoner, or any of his countrymen came to attend the proceed. Madan Lal Dhingra chatted unreservedly in an animated way and with a smile on his face, to the police after remand and was later in the day transmitted in a four wheel cab to Brixton prison.

A write up in *The Times* captioned 'A Political Crime', published on 4 July 1909, pointed out that there could not be any ground for affront on the young man's part in respect to any action of Sir Curzon Wyllie. Nothing could exceed the courtesy and consideration which Sir Curzon Wyllie had always exhibited towards the young Indians with whom his duties brought him into contact. He did utmost to fulfil any reasonable request they might make to him and in seeking to help them he went far beyond the strict letter of the requirements of his official position. Hence, it was inconceivable that the motive of the crime should have been mere personal. *The Times* further wrote, "Admittedly the motive was not merely personal, yet at the same time, it is not justifiable to deny that Sir Curzon Wyllie as a person fell in the class of potential targets. What made Curzon Wyllie stand out from the rest of his class was the rapport which he enjoyed with Madan Lal's Loyalist family based at Amritsar."

The paper further reported that Kundan Lal Dhingra wrote to Curzon Wyllie, some two months back, expressing his profound regret that his younger brother, while studying in London, had come under the mischievous influence of Shyamji Krishna Varma's India House and had indeed for a short time been an inmate there. He requested Wyllie to have a word with Madan Lal Dhingra on his conduct, and to use his utmost influence to wean him from the evil company into which he had entered. Curzon Wyllie promptly took the step to carry out the wishes of Dhingra family and wrote a letter to Madan Lal Dhingra requesting him to meet. Probably, Sir Wyllie's letter was never answered.[4]

A meeting of Indian students of the Crystal Palace School of Engineering passed a unanimous resolution expressing horror at the crime and sympathy with Lady Curzon Wyllie. Police enquiries had elicited the fact that Madan Lal Dhingra's brother Bhajan Lal was living in London. He and his family had dissociated themselves from the act, actor, his views and expressed abomination to the crime.

Surendranath Banerjee was present in England at the time of crisis and provides a detailed description related to the event. He informs that he too had been invited to "At Home" but could not attend as he was dining along with the members of the Imperial Press Conference called by Lord Strathcona. On July 2, a newspaper reporter called on him and told about the event of July 1, and inquired about the particulars of Madan Lal Dhingra to which he expressed his astonishment and ignorance. He admitted that it gave him immense relief to discover that the person involved in the crime was not a Bengali.[5] He acted swiftly as he feared its aftermath which could endanger the life of many Indian students living there, and publicly condemned the act and expressed his condolence to the grieved family and hoped that British public and administration will act sensibly to calm the situation. He openly held Shyamji responsible for the episode. *The Pioneer* reported that authorities in London were already communicating with the Paris administration for the arrest and extradition of Shyamji, who had been living there since 1907.[6] The press in England too had expressed similar opinion about India House, its founder and its activities and asked the government to act sternly. They wanted the government to solve the mystery behind the murder which looked more to be an organized crime than an individual act. Some people demanded curtailment on the privileges granted to the Indians in England.

A meeting of Indian residents was held on Saturday, 3 July 1909 at which students were largely represented, and the crime was denounced with befitting warmth and emphasis. Surendranath Banerjee presided and delivered an emphatic speech condemning the act and cautioned young students to keep themselves away from such political influences. He declared that the "Murder is murder no matter what might be the determining motive, and no matter under what specious plausibility it might be sought to be justified by any apostle of any new principle of morality". He added that assassination was not only a crime but a blunder, which had never brought about the changes it was intended to promote.[7]

A resolution was passed declaring detestation of the crime and condoling with Lady Curzon Wyllie and Doctor Lalcaca's family and it was decided to send a wreath to the funeral. A further resolution declared that the reform movement was in no way connected with lawlessness and violence which was fraught with the deepest peril to the best interests of India. Banerjee, who presided, combated the idea of conspiracy and said he was deeply grateful that the British people were not disposed to associate the tragedy with the Indians.

The British Government was already in communication with the French Government for the arrest and extradition of Shyamji

Krishna Varma, the owner of the India House. The chief question was 'on whom to pinpoint the responsibility of the crime' and it was an important query on which the result of the case depended. The idea that had caught favour with the responsible authorities in England was that the deed was no merely an individual act committed on the personal hook but that it was a result of a deep-rooted conspiracy.

The murder of Wyllie had belied all the expectations and reforms carried out by Minto-Morley, the Viceroy and the Secretary of States for India, respectively. The reforms which Lord Morley announced in the House of Lords in December 1908, and which have subsequently been called the 'Minto-Morley' reforms, were debated in the Lords in February and in the Commons in April and May 1909, when they were finally passed. Morley, Minto and Dunlop Smith hoped that the reforms would show Indians that the British were willing to listen to their grievance, and would convince Indians that the continuation of British Rule was entirely in their own interest.[8] What made them thinks so cannot be understood.

In India, the reforms were discussed of debated throughout 1909; and at the end of the year, when they were almost ready to be put in operation, the Indian National Congress passed a resolution against it on the grounds that they fallaciously separated Hindus and Muslims and were thus feebly disguised attempt at the 'Hypocritical imperial policy of Divide and Rule'.[9] The reforms even failed to satisfy the Muslims who were asking that "The Council members should be chosen by direct voting on communal basis, in order to preserve their special identity".[10] The murder of Wyllie in London, A.D.C. to Secretary of States Morley, made the government feel and believe that directly or indirectly the reforms had not been able to satisfy the Indians.

Whereas the assassination was being abhorred by almost every influential and important leader and organization, there was one group of revolutionaries in England which stood like rock along Dhingra and his act. Shyamji Krishna Varma, whom many Englishmen regarded as the chief advocate of terrorism, wrote in an article "Political assassination is not murder…all unprejudiced men treat political assassinators not as criminals anyway, but often regard them as benefactors of their race". The above lines of Herbert Spencer had inspired Shyamji Krishna Varma so much that he had adopted it as motto for the magazine *Sociologist*. In August, following the murder, his monthly journal had published the following as its main headlines:[11]

Indian Martyrdom in England
an Example of Heroic Courage and Patriotism
Humble Tokens of Appreciation

Shyamji Krishna Varma declared Madan Lal Dhingra a patriot and a martyr in a foreign land. Many before Madan Lal Dhingra had died unsung and unrecognized, but Shyamji and Savarkar made it a point to not to let his sacrifice go waste. The British Government tried its level best to treat the murder episode as an act of an eccentric, without any particular rhyme and reason. It tried to keep it in a low profile and not to add any political colour to it, but Indian patriots proved it the other way round.

Lord Curzon had assumed that British rule in India would never die, but within four years of his departure from India, the activities of the revolutionaries in India and abroad had shaken the very faith from its root. The efforts of Minto-Morley to please the selected political parties had failed but it succeeded in sowing the seed of division among Hindu and Muslim unity.

Asaf Ali, who was also in England at that time and was invited to the "At Home" but could not attend as his evening dress was not ready; came to know about the happening of July 1, through the newspaper. Asaf Ali recalls his chance meeting with Madan Lal Dhingra in late June 1909 at India

House where he had gone to attend Sunday gathering.[12] For the first time, he was voted to the chair to conduct the proceedings of the day to which he was not ready and felt awkward and shy and secretly flattered at this compliment little suspecting that it would prove to be the last debate in India House. As usual Niranjan Pal sang a Bengali patriotic song *Our Country* which was even more popular than *Bande Mataram* in those days, comments Asif Ali. Unable to recall the topic, House debated upon, he informs that after the proceedings were over all went out for tea in the garden but he found Madan Lal Dhingra hanging back, and begging Nanu (Niranjan Pal) to sing some other song and play on the organ. He writes, "Dhingra was a most rare bird—a wistful, uncommunicative person who gave you the impression of being cross with life. He attended every meeting, never spoke, and was seldom noticed by anybody. That day he was in a strange mood, and looked hungry for something. I thought that he was feeling terribly nostalgic. As Nanu's Bengali song, for which I stayed on, did not satisfy Dhingra's longing for an Urdu song, he turned to me with his request. I went to the organ, and sang and played an Urdu *Ghazal* and a *Thumri*. He went into a transport of joy, which seemed to me rather extravagant. I left him looking out of the drawing room window in what appeared a far-away state of mind. All this got fixed in my memory by carefully recollecting every detail, when what is to follow called for these recollections."[13] The narration of Asaf Ali, clearly portrayed the mind of Madan Lal Dhingra who was absorbed in deep planning at that time. No one there had the slightest indication of his next move. Madan Lal Dhingra knew well that his moments were short and few and he wanted to enjoy it to the fullest. All were busy in deliberations and argument on how to get 'Independence' whereas he had envisaged action for it, and within a few days he fulfilled the task.

NOTES

1. Waraich and Puri, p. 50.
2. Mention that one round was left in the pistol. Waraich and Puri, p. 77.
3. *The Times*, July 3, 1909, London.
4. The content of the letter read "Your brother Mr. K.L. Dhingra, whose acquaintance I had the pleasure of making in England has written to tell me that you are in London, and asking me to be of any assistance I can to you. I expect to be abroad from 15th to 30th of April but on my return I shall be very pleased to see you at India Office if you can between 11 and 1 or 2.30 and 3.30."
5. The Bengal and Bengalis were well-known for revolutionary activities, whereas the Punjab was considered a peaceful province. *A Nation in Making*, p. 274.
6. *Pioneer*, July 7, 1909.
7. *The Times*, London, 3 July, 1909, "The Assassination of Sir Curzon Wyllie".
8. Martin Gilbert, *Servant of India*, p. 175.
9. *Ibid.*, p. 171.
10. These claims were strongly supported by Chirol and *The Times*, though opposed by Keir Hardie and the *Manchester Guardian* on the grounds that they discriminate between races, and would lead to quarrels and even violence between Muslims and Hindus: *Ibid.*, p. 173.
11. *Ibid.*, p. 175.
12. The author has not mentioned the exact date but from the description it should have been 27 June 1909 as the act was committed on July 1, Thursday.
13. *M. Asaf Ali's Memoirs*, pp. 74-75.

□

5

Proceedings of Inquests

On July 5, two separate inquests were held on Sir Curzon Wyllie and Dr. Cowasji Lalcaca, the victim of shooting outrage at the Imperial Institute on Thursday night July 1. Though both had been shot at Imperial Institute situated in the City of Westminster, Curzon Wyllie died on the spot but Lalcaca had expired in the Hospital which fell under the jurisdiction of Kensington Town Hall. As such two separate inquests were rendered necessary as the jurisdiction of both the deaths had been different. The inquest on Curzon Wyllie was held by Mr. John Troutbeck in Coroner's Court at Westminster.

The Court proceedings started at 10 a.m. The intricacy of the case had attracted a large number of people who had already occupied their seats in the court. The Superintendent Quin Chief of the Political Investigation Department at Scotland Yard, represented the police authority and Sir Benjamin Franklin was present, at the request of Lady Wyllie. Sir William Scott, a personal friend of Curzon Wyllie, and late Accountant General at the India Office, was also present. Lord Morley, the Secretary of State for India, was represented by Mr. Hertzell his Private Secretary.

New statue of Madan Lal Dhingra installed near Town Hall Amritsar

At the very start of the proceedings, the Coroner said "The case, so far as the Coroner's Court was concerned, would be so clear and simple in itself that he did not anticipate any difficulty with regard to the léngth of inquiry. The person accused of committing the crime had been communicated with, but had decided not to attend the inquest."

The very first flaw in the functioning of the two separate inquests held on July 5, to record the statements of the witnesses in murder of Curzon Wyllie and Dr. Lalcaca were conducted without the presence of Madan Lal Dhingra, the main accused in the case. At the very start of the proceedings, Coroner had remarked "The case, so far as the Coroner's Court was concerned, would be so clear and simple in itself...." How far it was justified, for the Coroner to give his opinion regarding the nature of the case at the very start of the proceedings? How could he decide and declare such an opinion without listening to the witnesses?

It clearly reflects the bias of the Coroner towards the victims and creates doubt about its proceedings.

Mr. John Troutbeck further informed the court "The person accused of committing the crime had been communicated with, but had decided not to attend the inquest."

Was Madan Lal Dhingra in a position to refuse the court orders? Neither he nor the Brixton Prison authorities could dare to disobey the court orders, if the court had actually desired so.

It was a planned more of the government in connivance with the court to keep Madan Lal Dhingra away from public approach. The inquests proceedings were conducted without the presence of Madan Lal Dhingra to speed up the trial. Otherwise if the court had followed the normal course, the trial could not be held till Madan Lal Dhingra was in police remand. His presence in the court at the time witnesses recorded their statements was very much necessary and legally obligatory.

The question arises, why Madan Lal Dhingra had refused to appear in the Coroner's Court. Rather such an opportunity would have provided him an excuse to be away from the police clutches, though even for a short while. Perhaps, the police interrogation had rendered him incapacitated to attend the court. As such it was better to make an excuse that too on his behalf. To declare in the court that Madan Lal Dhingra had refused to attend the proceedings was the part of the plan, to project him as an arrogant and tarnish his image. As such, the entire Coroner's Court proceedings conducted in the absence of the main accused, Madan Lal Dhingra, was unlawful and generates distrust in the entire legal process.

Why the court overlooked the legal process? Perhaps the government wanted to settle the case and punish the accused at the earliest possible as delay could have given the event of July 1 and its actor Madan Lal Dhingra much publicity which government wanted to avoid. Coroner had admitted in the beginning that the case was so simple in itself that he did not anticipate any difficulty with regard to the length of inquiry.

Mark his words "With regard to the length of inquiry" which clearly expose the actual intention of the court which was working at the behest of the government.

Was the case as simple as Coroner had claimed? At first glance the case looks simple. The accused who committed the crime had been caught, the weapon used in the crime, dead bodies of the victims, Sir Curzon Wyllie and Cowasjee Lalcaca, too, had been recovered from the scene of crime. There were about five witnesses who had seen Madan Lal Dhingra committing the 'act'. Moreover, the accused had been arrested and identified, an important prerequisite in a murder case. Thus, every requirement for the court proceedings to fix the accused in the case had been fulfilled. As such the case seems crystal clear and leaves no space for accuse to escape the punishment. But the government knew well that if they followed the regular legal process, it could stretch the case which government wanted to evade. The normal legal process could involve a number of court hearings which would mean exposing Madan Lal Dhingra to public and press, thus providing him undue publicity. It preferred to give it a hasty and peaceful demise. The event of July 1 had already exposed the weakness of the British administration, belied the myth of invincible British might.

Manmohan Sinha, a student of the Middle Temple; William Thorburn, a journalist; Charles Rolleston, a retired officer of the English Army; John Buchanan Hutt M.R.C.S. (Doctor); Robert Salisbury Trevor (Surgeon); and Emma Josephine Beck, Honorary Secretary of National Indian Association, Frederick Nicholls, Constable R.C. 476 B Division, who was first to enter the Imperial Institute and take Dhingra in his custody; Frank Eveleigh, a Sergeant B Division who helped him; Charles Glass, Signal Inspector, B Division; and Albert Draper, Detective Inspector, B Division, all appeared as witnesses in the Coroner's Court. The original copies of the statements duly signed by the witnesses were made available by Prof. Malwinder Jit Singh Waraich and they are being produced here without any alteration.

Manmohan Sinha

I live at Maida Hill West. I am a student of the Middle Temple. I didn't know the accused. I was at the "At Home" at the Imperial Institute on July 1, 1909. I was here by an invitation from the National Indian Association of which I am a member. There were a good number of people present. We were invited from 9 o'clock. I came about 9.20 p.m. nothing unusual had occurred.

I was in the Hall almost 11.10 p.m. when I heard shots coming from the ante room. I looked out and saw Sir Curzon Wyllie standing by Madan Lal Dhingra. They were only a yard apart. Curzon Wyllie was standing facing the man, he was on the right. The man was exactly facing him. I saw him took a revolver and shoot. I saw the flash. This shot was aimed at the left side of Sir Curzon Wyllie's face. I rushed to the man, while I was rushing Sir Curzon Wyllie dropped. There were certainly more than four shots. The shots were fired in very quick succession. I did not see Dr. Lalcaca, nor did I saw him fall. I did not hear Dhingra say anything.

There was no dispute, nor disturbance before the shots were fired. I got hold of the man. He was still holding the revolver. He first levelled the revolver at me and then put the muzzle in his right ear. I heard the click of the trigger but there was no explosion. I pushed him down.

I saw revolver taken out of his inside pocket, also a hunting knife. The only thing he said was that he wanted his glasses. His manner was very calm. He was the only person not agitated or excited. I saw Dr. Lalcaca writhing in agony about two or three yards from Curzon Wyllie. Dr. Lalcaca had been on the other side of Sir Curzon Wyllie. I had not seen the man come up to Sir Curzon Wyllie.

William Thorburn, sworn saith

I live at the National Liberal Club. I am a journalist. I was present at the "At Home" on July 1, at the Imperial Institute.

I was standing in the Hall just four feet inside the folding doors. I was looking around me and happened to glance out over the vestibule. I saw Sir Curzon Wyllie, whom I didn't know at that time, standing facing a young Indian. Sir Curzon Wyllie was sideways to me with his face rather towards me. I didn't think he wore a decoration. The Indian stood facing him. Almost at the instant the Indian raised his right arm and fired a revolver full into Sir Curzon's face. The muzzle of the revolver almost touched the face.

I am certain there were four shots fired to begin with, very rapidly, all directly at his face, and so rapid that they were before he had time to collapse on the floor. Thus, after a comparatively short interval, there were two more shots. In the short of the moment, I could not say in what direction they were fired. As far as I could collect myself I rushed forward and at the same time I had the impression of someone else falling. I directed my attention to restraining the Indian. He made no remark. I asked him while I was holding him, "Why have you done it or what have you done or something to that effect." But he looked quietly into my face and said nothing at all.

Charles Rolleston, sworn saith

I live at Broadhurst Gardens, Hampstead. I am a retired officer of the English Army and now engaged in literature. I was "At Home" I was standing at a raised platform at one side of the Hall.

Suddenly, I heard a noise which I thought at first was of fireworks, about five explosions. I looked towards the door leading into the vestibule and then a young man dressed in English costume but with a light blue turban came in front of the door and took a deliberate aim with the revolver at an Indian gentleman dressed in English Evening Clothes. They were about four feet apart facing each other.

When I just saw them the Indian gentleman (the deceased), he was standing with his hands down, not doing anything. The

Indian fired and Dr. Lalcaca dropped forwards at once. I was about 16 yards off. Only one shot that I could see was fired at Dr. Lalcaca. He was then standing upright straight facing the Indian.

There may have been a previous shot at Dr. Lalcaca. The shot I saw seemed to have hit Dr. Lalcaca in the middle of the body. I then saw it was a case of assassination. I went to the open door and found Sir Curzon Wyllie lying dead close to the door. With a large pool of blood on his left side.

I saw Dr. Lalcaca about a yard away from Sir Curzon writhing on the ground. I then found two or three men holding the Indian. I went over to assist them in holding him. I suggested that he should be searched. One gentleman put his hand into the man's left hand side pocket and produced a small revolver and a dagger. I searched the breast pockets. I pulled out a role of papers—one apparently foolscap folded into four and also a number of small slips of paper. I kept possession of them and later handed them to a policeman. I also found a pen knife, some money, about 6 or 7 shillings, a pair of spectacles in a case, several loose keys, a handkerchief and a pair of gloves.

These were all handed by me to the police. I spoke to the man he gave his name as Dhinagri (Dhingra). I asked him what could be his motive for committing the crime. He said in a slow measured tone of voice "I will tell the police". I then questioned him in Hindustani.

He would give no information. He seemed perfectly composed. He had a half-dazed dreamy manner which made me suspect he, in fact, has taken *bhang.* I saw a bullet almost a foot and a half from the foot of the Indian which I handed to the police. I think five shots were fired in quick succession and then one, making six in all.

Buchanan, sworn saith

I live at 259, Vauxhall Bridge Road. I am M.D. of Glasgow and M.R.C.S. England. I was a guest "At Home". I was on the far side of the reception hall. There I heard six shots. One, two, then a very short pause, three, four, a distinct pause, then five, six. My impression was they were fireworks.

Very soon there was a cry some one was hurt and was there a doctor present. I replied I was a doctor and made for the door into the vestibule. In getting through the crowd here was an interval of at least three minutes.

In the vestibule, I found one Sir Curzon Wyllie. I attended to him first and found he was dead. Over in front was a chair upon which the prisoner was seated with four or five men holding him. Another Indian gentleman in evening clothes was lying on his back with his feet under the same chair. I knew he was unconscious and wriggling in pain. He did not speak. I took him by the shoulders and saw him about two yards. I tried to revive him. He could not swallow. He was slightly sick and made no reply to any question. I saw a mark on his shirt in the right side of the lower ribs over the region of the liver. On removing the shirt I saw the mark of a bullet wound. The man was apparently dying. In no moment he was put in the ambulance just as he was breathing his last. The place of death is most probably the Imperial Institute.

Robert Salusbury Trevor, sworn saith

I am pathologist and curator of the museum at St. George's Hospital. I am in B. & B.S. of Cambridge. I made a post-mortem examination on July 2 at 1.45 p.m. The body was that of an Indian gentleman of short-built. On the front of the report chart 2 and half inches below the right nipple 3/4 inches internal to a vertical line drawn through the nipple was an oral bullet wound half an inch in diameter which was vertically placed with regard to the body.

The wound was filled with blood clot and showed no actual opening at the time of examination. On gently probing it, it was ascertained that the direction of entrance was from above downwards. The probe would pass about half an inch. In the back on the right side 6 inch inwards from the back of the right shoulder was a small wound bullet hole with sharply pointing edges and through which blood was exuding.

I could find no other mark of injury on the body. Upon internal examination the right chest was full of blood and through the 4th rib behind was bullet hole. In a line with this was another hole from the top of the lower lobe of the right lung. This lobe was found to be penetrated by the bullet from top to bottom. This bullet had then gone through the diaphragm to the right lobe of the liver, the attachment of the small intestine, the small intestine in the five places. The attachment of the large intestine and after a prolonged search was found smashed ¼ inch in the left side of the pelvis—I produce the bullet. It is unaltered in shape.

The abdominal cavalry was full of blood and contained free gas with the exception of the injuries mentioned caused and the passage of the bullet, the abdominal organs were healthy. In examining the other bullet hole in the front of the chest a short blood stained track about ¾ inch in length was found leading downwards and inwards on to the ribs. The track was entirely lost after this. A most prolonged search failed to find a record bullet. There were some old adhesions to the left lung, but the organs were otherwise healthy. The death is due to haemorrhage and shock from injuries produced by a bullet wound entering the body in the back. I think it was hit by two shots. The record shot in the front did not injure any vital organ. The deceased must have been stooping forward. The shot went diagonally downward.

I saw the dead man's clothes. There was a bullet hole in the waist-coat shirt and vest corresponding to the wound in the right chest in front. There was a hole through the coat, waist-coat and two holes in the wrist and one in the rest over the bullet hole in the back.

Emma Josephine Beck, affirming saith

I am single and live at 160, Kingston Park Road. I met man Dhingra. He wrote to me that his brother in India wished him to come and see me that was in March last. I asked him to come and see me. I think he is twenty-six years old. He came to England in 1906. He lived during the last few months at 108, Ledbury Road. He was a student of Engineering at University College.

I saw him four or five times. He never mentioned Sir Curzon Wyllie's or the deceased's name. He never said anything to suggest he had any idea of crime. I saw him last in April. I was "At Home" on 1 July. I saw him come in soon after 9. I spoke to him later on in the evening. I had a conversation with him about half an hour before the tragedy.

I noticed nothing peculiar about his condition. He remained quite normal. I asked him what he had been doing in his work recently. He said he had first finished his work at University College and intended to go up for the A.M.I.C.E. Examination in October after which he would return to India. I asked him if he had friends "At Home". He said he knew several. He seemed quite calm. He was a member of the association and had received an invitation to the "At Home".

Frederick Nicholls, saith

I am R.C. 476 B. At eleven p.m. yesterday night I was on duty in Institute Road. I heard several blowing police whistles and shouting police. I went into the Indian section of the Institute and went up to the first floor into the landing staircase. I saw two bodies lying on the floor. I enquired if there was a doctor there. I asked who did it. A man named Sinha said, "This Man" meaning Dhingra who was being held by two or three gentlemen. Sinha being one of them.

I told Dhingra I should take him into custody. He made no reply. He was then holding a revolver in a crouching position and the gentlemen were trying to get it away. I searched Dhingra and found a revolver in the right hand pocket of the inside of the coat.

There was a dagger in the inside pocket of his coat on the left side. I took charge of Dhingra and took him to the police station with a detective sergeant. Dhingra soon spoke. He was charged and made no reply. He was very quiet.

Frank Eveleigh, sworn saith,

I am detective sergeant, B Division. I was called to the Institute at 11.20 p.m. on 1 July. In the Institute on the ground I saw two gentlemen lying. The accused Dhingra was being held by the constable and Mr. Sinha. Sir Lesley Probyn handed one pistol, a Colt automatic and Captain Rolleston handed me a Belgian pistol. I subsequently examined them. The Belgian pistol was loaded with six cartridges. It is a magazine pistol which could eight cartridges. The Colt contained one cartridge in the barrel.

There were signs of the pistol having been recently fired. The bullet Dr. Trevor produced could have been fired from the Colt. I went to the station with Dhingra.

Charles Glass, sworn saith

I am signal inspector, B Division. At 3 a.m. second trial; I was present at Walton St. Police Station and took the charge against Dhingra for the willful murder of Sir William Hutt Curzon Wyllie and Dr. Lalcaca. I read the charge over to the prisoner and he nodded his head and said "Yes". I said "Do you wish any of your friends to be communicated with?" He said "I do not think it necessary tonight but they will know it later on." He was then placed in the cell.

Albert Draper, sworn saith

I am detective inspector, B Division. At 3 a.m. second trial: I went with three officers to 108, Ledbury Road, where I saw Ms. Harris. She pointed out to me the room occupied by Dhingra. I found there 63 loose cartridges and a magazine-containing seven cartridges. The magazine would fit the Belgian Pistol. I found a gun license in the name of Dhingra taken...in January last. Also a book of records of shooting, showing the prisoner had been practicing during May, giving the dates and the results. I was present at Westminster Police Station on the second trial: When Dhingra was charged, and in reply to the question whether he had anything to say, but by the magistrate he said "The only thing I want to say is that there was no willful murder in the case of Dr. Lalcaca. I did not know him. When he advanced to get hold of me I simply fired in self-defence." I am the detective inspector in-charge in this case. There is nothing known to me to suggest that any person beside Dhingra is concerned in the crime which appears to be his own initiation....

> **The above written information**
> **were respectively taken and**
> **acknowledged before me.**
> **Troutbeck**
> **Signed by Coroner**

On the same day another inquest on the body, of Dr. Lalcaca[1] was held at Kensington, Town Hall, London where once again the witnesses appeared to give their statements.

The first to appear was Sir Cowasjee Jehangir, an Indian gentleman resident in Bombay now staying at the hotel Cecil, gave evidence of identification. The written statement of Cowasjee Jehangir is being presented here as to the letter.

Cowasjee Jehangir, sworn saith

I got inquiry at the hotel Cecil, London. I live in Bombay. I have seen the body, I identify it as that of Dr. Cowas Lalcaca. I have known him about 23 years. He resided in Bombay and later in Shanghai. He practiced as doctor of medicine. He has been in England since June 8 staying at the Grand Hotel, Northumberland Avenue. Northern Island Arena, I was at the "At Home" on evening of 1 July at the Imperial Institute. I saw Dr. Lalcaca at the "At Home". I heard shots about 11.10 p.m.

I was in the main hall just behind the folding doors. I saw the deceased five minutes after. I saw he had been seriously injured. He could not speak. He was taken to St. (George) Hospital in an ambulance. I think he died at the Imperial Institute while being put into the ambulance. I am certain the deceased did not know anything about the man who shot him.

Manmohan Sinha repeated the evidence which he had given at Kensington. He said that after four shots have been fired in quick succession. He noticed Dr. Lalcaca lying on the ground about two and half yard from Curzon Wyllie and writhing in agony. Mr. Thorburn also repeated the evidence he had already given at the other inquest. He added that while holding the prisoner he asked, "Why did you, do it? What have you done?" But he received no answer.[2]

Captain Charles Rolleston, of Broadburn Garden, Hempstead, who was also present at the Institute and had already given his statement earlier in the day, said, there were about five explosions.[3] On looking towards the vestibule he saw a youngman dressed in English clothes but wearing a light blue turban came in front of the door and took a deliberate aim with a revolver at the Indian gentleman whom he afterwards discovered to be Lalcaca. The two men were about four feet apart facing each other. Dr. Lalcaca dropped to the ground. There might have been a previous shot at Dr. Lalcaca, without the witness seeing it. The shot struck Dr. Lalcaca in the middle of the body. The witness went to the vestibule and saw Sir Curzon Wyllie lying dead close to the door, and Dr. Lalcaca lying close by him. The witness asked the man what his motive was in committing the 'crime'. And he said in a slow measured tone of voice "I will tell the police". The witness questioned him in Hindustani but he would give no information. He appeared to be in dreamy-dosed condition which made the witness suspect the possibility that he had taken a drug, probably *bhang.* The shots must have been fired by an expert. No one who had not practiced with a revolver could have fired as quickly as he did.

Medical Evidence

Dr. Buchanan repeated his previous evidence. Dr. Lalcaca, he said, was not dead when placed on the ambulance at the Institute but must have died within two or three minutes. Mr. R.S. Trevor of St. George Hospital who had made a post-mortem examination, said he found in the right breast an oval bullet wound half an inch in its greater diameter, the direction of the entrance of the bullet being downwards. There was another bullet hole in the top of the lower lobe of the right lung. That lobe of the lung was penetrated by the bullet. One bullet, unaltered in shape, was found imbedded in the left side of the pelvis. He failed to find the reported bullet. The cause of the death was haemorrhage and shock from injury produced by a bullet wound entering the body by back. The bullet entered the back of the right shoulder when Dr. Lalcaca was stooping forward. Thc second shot did not injure any vital organ.

Miss Beck, Honorable Secretary of the National Indian Association, having again given evidence. Mrs. Mary Harris, of

Ledbury Road, Bayswater, said the man Dhingra had lodged with her since Easter Monday. He was a man of regular and steady habits, and seldom went out in the evening. She did not know that he possessed any firearms. On Thursday he had an early lunch and no dinner. She did not think he took drugs. She saw him leave the home at about half past one. He had never said anything which led her to think that he contemplated an act of the kind which had been committed.[5] The jury returned the verdict of "Willful Murder" against Madan Lal Dhingra.

NOTES

1. *The Times*, July 6, 1909, London, "The Scene at the Imperial Institute", p. 5.
2. *Ibid.*, "The Inquest on Dr. Lalcaca", p. 6. Also see Madan Lal Dhingra, Micro Film, No. 1853, National Archives New Delhi.
3. *The Times*, July 6, 1909, London, p. 6.
4. *Ibid.*
5. *Ibid.*

□

6

Court Proceedings

On July 2, 1909, Madan Lal Dhingra was given eight days police remand by Horace Smith and was sent to Brixton Prison. The two inquests on the murder of Sir Curzon Wyllie and Dr. Lalcaca were held on July 5, where the statements of the witnesses were recorded in the separate courts. As Dhingra had been under police remand for eight days, he was not presented in the court during the entire proceedings. By July 10, 1909, the police remand of Dhingra was over. He was brought to Westminster Police Court, before the Magistrate, Mr. Horace Smith. Sitting by the Magistrate were Sir Edward Bradford, late Commissioner Metropolitan Police and Sir Charles Mathews, Director of Public Prosecution.

Mr. A.H. Bodkin started the prosecution by stating the charges leveled against Madan Lal Dhingra by the previous Inquests held on July 5. He informed that accused had been charged with "Willful Murder". After stating the charges, Bodkin gave detail of the Dhingra's life in London. He told the court that he had been an Engineering Student at University College, London for the last three years and successfully passed various examinations and received certificates. He further told that since Easter last, he had been lodging at the house of Mrs. Harris at 108, Ledbury Road, Bayswater.

The first date he had to mention, said Counsel, in connection with the tragedy was January 26 of the present year, when the prisoner went to the Hatton-Garden Post Office and obtained the necessary license to carry a revolver. Later he purchased at Gamage's a very powerful Colt revolver, and this was the one used on July 1, the date of the tragedy. It would be shown that the prisoner had the regular practice with this weapon at an establishment known as 'Fun-Land' in Tottenham Court Road, and attained a considerable degree of proficiency. On the afternoon or evening of July 1, he was at this place, and had the weapon cleaned and returned to him. In addition to this revolver, the prisoner had another, of Belgian make, the action being practically identical with that of Colt. He also possessed a dagger and it was clear that with these three weapons he went to a concert or entertainment given in connection with the National Indian Association at the Imperial Institute. Mr. Bodkin proceeded to relate the details of the crime as brought out at the Coroner's Inquest, and then went on to say that certain documents and photographs found on the prisoner and his belonging would be produced, with a statement which bore upon the crime. From this it was clear that the prisoner for sometime before July 1, premeditated some terrible crime; that he intended to commit with a revolver; and that with regard to his action on July 1, he gave some opinions which he had formed as to India and as to the position of India, which clearly threw light upon the reasons which prompted him. The report of police investigation on Dhingra might have provided this information.

Sir Lesley Probyn of Onslow Square, South Kensington was first called. He was appearing for the first time in the court to test as a witness to the July 1 case. He did not appear in the first two inquests held on July 5, earlier.

He said that he had known Sir Curzon Wyllie for many years, and saw him, with Lady Wyllie, at the Imperial Institute on the evening of 1 July. As he was about to leave he heard several shots fired—three or four first of all, then another, and finally another. He saw prisoner—after the first three or four shots—holding a revolver, but pointing it at no one in particular. Again it was fired, and instantly the prisoner turned it around and put it to his temple. The witness rushed at him and caught his two hands, and managed to get hold of the revolver, and he retained possession of it until he fell. Other gentleman came to his assistance he remembered Mr. Sinha, an Indian gentleman, did so. Sir Lesley added that he supposed the prisoner resisted to some extent: the witness remembered that he injured his nose and ribs through falling. The next thing he recollected was some conversation between the prisoner and Mr. Sinha. On the arrival of a constable the witness said, "Here's the man".

Asked if he desired to question the witness, the prisoner replied, "I object to the use of the word 'Murder'. It was a thing that any Englishman would have done and was quite justified".

Mr. Sinha, an Indian Law student, repeated the evidence he gave at Inquest. This man is a traitor to my country said Madan Lal Dhingra, as Mr. Sinha's evidence was read over.

Mr. D.W. Thorburn, a journalist, gave similar testimony. The witness with others, rushed at the man and asked, "Why did you do this? What have you done?" But received no answer.

Captain Charles Rolleston of Broad Hurst-Garden, Hampstead said, "Suddenly I heard a noise which I thought at first was of fireworks, about five explosions. I looked towards the door leading into the vestibule and then a young man dressed in English costume but with a light blue turban came in front of the door and took a deliberate aim with the revolver at an Indian gentleman dressed in English evening clothes. They were about four feet apart facing each other.

When I just saw them the Indian gentleman Dr. Lalcaca was standing with his hands down, not doing anything. The Indian gentleman fired and Dr. Lalcaca dropped forwards at once. I was about 16 yards off. Only one shot that I could see was fired at Dr. Lalcaca. He was then standing upright straight facing the Indian.

There may have been a previous shot at Lalcaca. The shot I saw seemed to have hit Dr. Lalcaca in the middle of the body. I then saw it was a case of assassination. I went to the open door and found Sir Curzon Wyllie lying dead close to the door with a large pool of blood on his left side.

I saw Dr. Lalcaca about a yard away from Sir Curzon writhing on the ground. I then found two or three men holding the Indian. I went over to assist them in holding him. I suggested that he should be searched. One gentleman put his hand into the man's left hand side pocket and produced a small revolver and a dagger. I searched the breast pockets. I pulled out a role of papers—one apparently foolscap folded into four and also a number of small slips of paper. I kept possession of them and later handed them to a policeman. I also found a pen knife, some money, about six or seven shillings, a pair of spectacles in a case, several loose keys, a handkerchief and a pair of gloves.

These were all handed by me to the police. I spoke to the man he gave his name as Dhingra. I asked him what could be his motive for committing the crime. He said in a slow measured tone of voice 'I will tell the police'. I then questioned him in Hindustani. He would give no information. He seemed perfectly composed."

Miss Emma Josephine Beck, the Honorary Secretary of the National Indian Association, said, that she had known the prisoner for some four months, and sent him an invitation ticket to the concert. It was not in response to a request from him. The witness had some conversation with the prisoner about his work. He wrote to me that his brother in India wished him to come and see me that was in March last. I asked him to come and see me. I think he is twenty-six years old. He came to England in 1906. He lived during the last few months at 108, Ledbury Road. He was a student of Engineering at University College.

I saw him four or five times. He never mentioned Sir Curzon Wyllie's or the deceased's name. He never said anything to suggest he had any idea of crime. I saw him last in April. I was "At

Home", on 1 July. I saw him come in soon after 9. I spoke to him later in the evening. I had a conversation with him about half an hour before the tragedy.

I noticed nothing peculiar about his condition. He remained quite normal. I asked him what he had been doing in his work recently. He said he had first finished his work at University College and intended to go up for the A.M.I.C.E. Examination in October after which he would return to India. I asked him if he had friends "At Home". He said he knew several. He seemed quite calm. He was a member of the association and had received an invitation to the "At Home".

Mr. Cowas Jehangir of Bombay, said Dr. Cowas Lalcaca was also from that place, but practiced at Shanghai. They came to England by the same boat on June 8. He was present at the Imperial Institute, and after hearing some shots fired, saw his friend dead. He had earlier told the court I got inquiry at the Hotel Cecil, London. I live in Bombay. I have seen the body, I identify it as that of Dr. Cowas Lalcaca. I have known him for about 23 years. He resided in Bombay and later in Shanghai. He practiced as doctor of medicine. He has been in England since June 8 staying at the Grand Hotel, Northumberland Avenue. Northern Island Arerra. I was at the "At Home" on evening of 1 at the Imperial Institute.

I saw Dr. Lalcaca at the "At Home". I heard shots about 11.10 p.m. I was in the main hall just behind the folding doors. I saw the deceased five minutes later. I saw he had been seriously injured. He could not speak. He was taken to St. George Hospital in an ambulance. I think he died at the Imperial Institute while being put into the ambulance. I am certain the deceased did not know anything about the man who shot him.

Buchanan repeated his earlier statement: I was on the far side of the reception hall. There I heard six shots. My impression was they were fireworks. Very soon there was a cry someone was hurt and there was a doctor present. I replied I was a doctor and made for the door into the vestibule. In getting through the crowd there was an interval of at least three minutes. In the vestibule I found one Sir Curzon Wyllie. I attended to him first and found he was dead. Over in front was a chair upon which the prisoner was seated with four or five men holding him. Another Indian gentleman in evening clothes was lying on his back with his feet under the same chair. I knew he was unconscious and wriggling in pain. He did not speak. I took him by the shoulders and saw him about two yards. I tried to revive him. He could not swallow. He was slightly sick and made no reply to any question. I saw a mark on his shirt in the right side of the lower ribs over the region of the liver. On removing the shirt I saw the mark of a bullet wound. The man was apparently dying. In no moment he was put in the ambulance just as he was breathing his last. The place of death is most probably the Imperial Institute.

Mr. John Stanton Morley, of 'Fun-Land' at 'Tottenham Court Road', said he had a rifle and pistol range there. He recognized the prisoner as a young man who had been practicing at the range with his own pistol for two or three months. He always used his pistol and ammunition. He noticed at times the prisoner fired more rapidly than others, the pause being the shots being shorter. He improved slightly after a time. On the evening of Thursday, July 1, the prisoner was at the range and fired 12 shots at one of the ordinary targets. Before he left he asked that his pistol might be cleaned.

The target the prisoner used on the occasion of his last visit was produced. There were 11 hits and seven or eight of these could be covered by a man's hand. Dr. R.S. Trevor, pathologist at St. George's Hospital, spoke as to the injuries sustained by Dr. Lalcaca, and the post-mortem examination. He told the court: I made a post-mortem examination on July 2 at 1.45 p.m. on the body of an Indian gentleman of short built. On the front of the report chart two and half inches below the right nipple ¾ inches internal to a vertical line drawn through the nipple was an oral bullet wound half an inch in diameter which was vertically placed with regard to the body. The wound filled with blood clot and showed no actual opening at the time of examination. On gently probing it, it was ascertained that the direction of entrance was from above downwards. The probe would pass about half an inch. In the back on the right side six inch inwards from the back of the right shoulder was a small wound bullet hole with sharply pointing edges and through which blood was exuding.

I could find no other mark of injury on the body. Upon internal examination the right chest was full of blood and through the fourth rib behind was bullet hole. In a line with this was another hole from the top of the lower lobe of the right lung. This lobe was found to be penetrated by the bullet from top to bottom. This bullet had then gone through the diaphragm to the right lobe of the liver, the attachment of the small intestine, the small intestine in the five places. The attachment of the large intestine and after a prolonged search was found smashed ¼ inch in the left side of the pelvis—I produce the bullet. It is unaltered in shape.

The abdominal cavalry was full of blood and contained free gas with the exception of the injuries mentioned caused and the passage of the bullet, the abdominal organs were healthy. In examining the other bullet hole in the front of the chest a short blood stained track about ¾ inch in length was found leading downwards and inwards on to the ribs. The track was entirely lost after this. A most prolonged search failed to find a record bullet. There were some old adhesions to the left lung, but the organs were otherwise healthy. The death is due to haemorrhage and shock from injuries produced by a bullet wound entering the body in the back. I think it was hit by two shots. The shot in the front did not injure any vital organ. The deceased must have been stooping forward. The shot went diagonally downward.

I saw the dead man's clothes. There was a bullet hole in the waist-coat shirt and vest corresponding to the wound in the right chest in front. There was a hole through the coat, waist-coat and two holes in the wrist and one in the rest over the bullet hole in the back.

Dr. Thomas Neville, police divisional surgeon, said he saw the prisoner at the Walton Street Police Station at 11.55 on the night of 1 July. His condition was normal, and he said he was not hurt in any way and did not want the service of a doctor. A post-mortem examination of the body of Sir Curzon Wyllie showed that death was due to injury to the brain.

Mrs. Harris, of Ledbury Road, Bayswater, said the man Dhingra had lodged with her since Easter Monday. He was a man of regular and steady habits, and seldom went out in the evening. She did not know that he possessed any firearms. On Thursday he had an early lunch and no dinner. She did not think he took drugs.

Mrs. Harris, the landlady said she remembered that on 1 July the prisoner left the house at about 2 p.m. in the afternoon and returned at 6 p.m. The witness had never seen any firearms in the prisoner's room, but once she saw a bullet and had told the police about it. She saw him leave the home at about half past one. He had never said anything which led her to think that he contemplated an act of the kind which had been committed.

Frank Eveleigh told the court

I was called to the Institute at 11.20 p.m. on July 1. In the Institute on the ground I saw two gentlemen lying. Dhingra was being held by the constable and Mr. Sinha. Sir Lesley Probyn handed one pistol, a Colt automatic and Captain Rolleston handed me a Belgian pistol. I subsequently examined them. The Belgian pistol was loaded with six cartridges. It is a magazine pistol contains eight cartridges. The Colt contained one cartridge in the barrel. There were signs of the pistol having been recently fired. The bullet Dr. Trevor produced could have been fired from the Colt.

The witness received this pistol with a dagger and several papers from the Captain Rolleston. In the prisoner's waist-coat pockets were five cartridges.

Madan Lal Dhingra – there were also two newspaper cuttings:

Sergeant Eveleigh – Yes.

Mr. Bodkin produced them, and said they could be handed in if the prisoner wished it.

Dhingra replied that he did not.

Detective Inspector Draper said that he visited 108, Ledbury Road early in the morning after the murder and searched the prisoner's room. I went with three officers where I saw Miss Harris. She pointed out to me the room occupied by Dhingra. I found there 63 loose cartridges and a magazine containing seven cartridges. The magazine would fit the Belgian Pistol. I found a gun license in the name of Dhingra taken in January last. Also a book of records of shooting, showing the prisoner had been practicing during May, giving the dates and the results. I was present at Westminster Police Station on the second trial: When Dhingra was charged, and in reply to the question whether he had anything to say, but by the magistrate he said "The only thing I want to say is that there was no willful murder in the case of Dr. Lalcaca. I did not know him. When he advanced to get hold of me I simply fired in self-defence." There is nothing known to me to suggest that any person beside Dhingra is concerned in the crime which appears to be his own initiation. Detective Inspector Mac Brian produced a photograph removed from the prisoner's cabinet in the room.[1] (This was produced but was kept face downward.)

After the evidence to the purchase of a pistol at Carnage's, and also of identification of the prisoner's handwriting by a clerk from the University College, Mr. Bodkin said this completed the case, and he asked for the 'prisoner's committal'.

Mr. Horace Smith in committing the accused gave the customary caution, and asked him if he had anything to say regarding the case.

He is on record to have said, "Whatever else I have to say is in my statement which is in the court." He was referring to the papers, one which had been taken by the police and other which he had left in his apartment and was now lying with the court. Both these papers had been kept "sealed" by the orders of the court and its contents were never officially disclosed.

Magistrate repeated if he had anything to mention in the court.

Dhingra again said, "My papers had been taken by the court."

Magistrate said, "Do you wish to say something?"

Dhingra again said, "Another statement on foolscap papers."

The judge insisted "If there was anything else you wish to say you must say it now".

Dhingra shot back, "The paper was taken from my pocket".

"I don't care what was taken from your pocket" retorted the judge impatiently.

"Anything else you have to say you must say to the jury. What you have written on a previous occasion is no evidence in this case."

Ultimately Dhingra said, "No".

After the witnesses had been testified and their statements noted in the court, the name of Madan Lal Dhingra was announced and the charges were read:[2]

> **Madan Lal Dhingra stands charged before the undersigned, one of the Magistrates of the Police Courts of the Metropolis sitting at the Westminster Police Court, in the Metropolitan Police District, this tenth day of July in the Year of our Lord One Thousand Nine Hundred and Nine as herein before set forth, and the said charge being read to the said accused, and the said witnesses for the prosecution being severally examined in the presence of the said accused, the said accused is now addressed by me as follows.**

Magistrate once again asked Madan Lal Dhingra, "Having heard the evidence do you wish to say anything in answer to the charge? You are not obliged to say anything unless you desire to do so, but whatever you say will be taken down in writing, and may be given in evidence against you upon your trial, and if you desire to call any witness, you can now do so."

Till now Madan Lal Dhingra had been insisting on the written statement, taken from his pocket and house, to be read in the court but when his repeated appeal was not accepted, he made the following declaration:

"I don't want to say anything in defence of myself, but simply to prove the justice of my deed. As for myself, I do not think that any English Law Court has any authority to arrest me or detain me in prison or to pass sentence of death on me. That is the reason I did not have any counsel to defend me. And I maintain that if it is patriotic in an Englishman to fight against the Germans if they were to occupy this country it is much more justifiable and patriotic in my case to fight against the English; I hold the English people responsible for the murder of 80 millions of my countrymen, Indians I mean, in the last 50 years. And they are also responsible for taking away £ 100,000,000 every year from India to this country. I also hold them responsible for the hanging and deportations of my patriotic countrymen, who do just the same as the English people here are advising their countrymen to do; and an Englishman who goes out to India and, say, gets £ 100 a month; that simply means that he passes sentence of death on 1,000 people who can very easily live with those £ 100 which the Englishmen spend mostly in his frivolities and pleasures.

"Just as die-Germans have got no right to occupy this country. So the English people have no right to occupy India, and it is perfectly justifiable on our part to kill an Englishman who is polluting our sacred land.

"I am surprised at the terrible hypocrisy, farce and mockery of the English people, when they pose as champions of oppressed humanity as the people of Congo and the people of Russia, when there is such terrible oppression and horrible atrocities committed in India, for example, killing two millions of people every year, and outraging our women. In case this country is occupied by Germans, and an Englishman not bearing to see the Germans walking with the insolence of conquerors in the streets of London, goes and kills one or two Germans, then if that Englishman is to be held as a patriot by the people of this country, then certainly I am a patriot, too, working for the emancipation of my motherland. Whatever else I have to say is in my statement which is in the Court.

"I made this statement not because I wish to plead for mercy or anything of that kind. I wish that the English people should sentence me to death; for in that case, the vengeance of my countrymen will be all the more keener. I just forward this statement to show the justice of my case to the outside world, especially to our sympathizers in America and Germany. That is all."[3]

Taken before me as aforesaid on the day years above mentioned.

Horace Smith

(10 July, 1909)

As per the press report the prisoner was then removed. Throughout the lengthy hearing he had maintained an exceedingly calm demeanor.

NOTES

1. They recovered from his lodging a picture postcard of the original painting of the great Russian painter Verastchagin depicting the blowing of Indian rebels from the muzzles of the field gun in India, 1857-58, and the other portrait of Lord Curzon on which was penciled "Heathen Dog". *Indian Sociologist*, 21 July 1909.
2. Waraich and Puri, *Tryst With Martyrdom*, pp. 61-62.
3. Waraich and Puri, *Tryst With Martyrdom*, pp. 61-62.

□

7

Accusations and Analysis

In the Coroner's court held on July 5, 1909, the witnesses leveled three accusations on Madan Lal Dhingra: first, he tried to commit suicide; second, he was under the intoxication of *Bhang*; third, it was not his plan.

Manmohan Sinha, a student was the only person to present the story of suicide attempt on July 5. No other witness supported his statement on that day. Let's examine his statement.

Sinha told the court: There was neither dispute nor disturbance before the shots were fired. I got hold of the man. He was still holding the revolver. He first leveled the revolver at me and then put the muzzle in his right ear. I heard the click of the trigger but there was no explosion. I pushed him down.

Sinha got hold of Madan Lal Dhingra, who had already shot two to the ground and was still holding the revolver! A rare daredevil action mostly seen in the movies but rarely in real life. No logical person will accept such a story. Very difficult to believe and digest.

The immediate thought that comes to the mind after reading Sinha's statement is that Sinha might have been standing very close to Madan Lal Dhingra at the time of crime and might have witnessed the entire bloodshed before his eyes on the midnight of July 1 and he must have reacted to the situation without caring for the consequences. In such a situation, it can be possible not otherwise. Was it so? Let us examine.

Sinha said: I was in the Hall almost 11.10 p.m. when I heard shots coming from the ante room. I looked out and saw Sir Curzon Wyllie standing by Madan Lal Dhingra. They were only a yard apart. Curzon Wyllie was standing facing the man, he was on the right. The man was exactly facing him. I saw him took a revolver and shoot. I saw the flash. This shot was aimed at the left side of Sir Curzon Wyllie's face. I rushed to the man, while I was rushing Sir Curzon Wyllie dropped. There were certainly more than four shots. The shots were fired in very quick succession. I did not see Dr. Lalcaca, nor did I saw him fall. I did not hear Dhingra say anything. Let us analyze the statements of the witnesses.

- Manmohan Sinha was in the Hall when he heard the shots while the murder took place in the ante room. By the time he would have looked toward the ante room, Curzon Wyllie must have succumb to the shots as it happened in seconds. At the most he could have seen Curzon Wyllie falling and not more. But the scene which Sinha narrates was prior to the shots had been fired. He looked out and saw Sir Curzon Wyllie standing by Madan Lal Dhingra. They were only a yard apart. Curzon Wyllie was standing facing the man, he was on the right. The man was exactly facing him. "I saw him took a revolver and shoot." This kind of description was narrated by only one witness Mr. William Thorburn because he happened to look out before the shooting and he was standing near the entrance of the Hall.
- **Thorburn told the court:** I was present at the "At Home" on 1 July at the Imperial Institute. I was standing in the Hall just four feet inside the folding doors. I was looking around and happened to glance out over

the vestibule. I saw Sir Curzon Wyllie, whom I didn't know at that time, standing facing a young Indian. Sir Curzon Wyllie was sideways to me with his face rather towards me. I didn't think he wore a decoration. The Indian stood facing him. Almost at the instant the Indian raised his right arm and fired a revolver full into Sir Curzon's face. The muzzle of the revolver almost touched the face.

- Otherwise at first instance, no one could recognize the sound of the shot. Most of them there thought it was a firework. Charles Rolleston told: Suddenly I heard a noise which I thought at first was of fireworks, about five explosions. Buchanan told: There I heard six shots. My impression was they were fireworks.
- The other surprising comment of Sinha's statement was that he saw the flash of fire. Again very strange and unbelievable comment of Sinha. Other three witnesses, Rolleston, Buchanan and Thorburn, were too in the Hall but they did not see "the flash of fire" perhaps they were not as blessed as our Sinha who had some extraordinary eyesight.
- Let us agree that Sinha being an extraordinary person recognized the sound and acted swiftly but even then all he could have seen would have been Curzon Wyllie being shot at and falling dead, as he had admitted "I was in the Hall when I heard the shots coming from the ante room." Definitely, he could not have seen Curzon Wyllie being shot but he would have seen Lalcaca being shot if he had stayed inside and kept looking outside but he claimed, "I saw Dr. Lalcaca writhing in agony about two or three yards from Curzon Wyllie. Dr. Lalcaca had been on the other side of Sir Curzon Wyllie. I had not seen the man come up to Sir Curzon Wyllie." It should have taken him a minute

or two to come out of the Hall and by that time the act was over. It must have taken him another few seconds to understand the whole situation outside and act. In that case it was not possible for him to attack an armed Madan Lal Dhingra.

- The only other person who supported the story of Sinha was Lesley Probyn. He did not appear before the inquests held on July 5, but came to testify to the court on July 10. He told: I saw prisoner after three or four shots, holding a revolver, but pointing it at no one in particular. Again it was fired, an instantly Madan Lal Dhingra turned it around and put it to his temple. I rushed to him and caught his two hands and managed to get hold of the revolver and retained the possession of it until I fell.
- Probyn told the court that he saw Madan Lal Dhingra put his revolver to his temple. Probyn held both his hands and did not leave till he got the revolver wrested. Sinha said Madan Lal Dhingra tried to kill himself but the trigger did not click. Who was right Sinha or Probyn. No other witness supported their story which was weaved with a purpose to defame and project Dhingra as a weak person which was totally false.
- After Madan Lal Dhingra had shot Dr. Lalcaca he realised that he had overstepped his plan. He had no intention to kill any other person besides Curzon, the selected target. Dhingra was not a criminal but a revolutionary who had come to Imperial Institute to set an example by killing a high British official. By doing so he wanted to show his young Indian friends a way to get freedom for India at the earliest possible time. He believed, if like him, the budding Indians started killing targeted British high officers serving in India, the Britons will leave their motherland out of sheer fear. He had developed this idea in India House and executed it to set an example for the others.

- Dharmavira writes: "Dhingra, after committing the act, now threw away the revolver; the crowd drew near him.[1] Either he threw it or lowered his hand suggesting he had surrendered. The bystanders immediately pounced upon him."
- An interview given by another eyewitness on the happening of July 1 provides a little relief to the above controversy. Mr. C.A. Colman informed a representative of the *Times*, that he was present at the Imperial Institute. He said there were between 150 and 200 people present, and the guests included many well-known Anglo-Indians and natives of India, whose highly coloured oriental costumes made the spectacle unusually dazzling. It was the fact that visitors were expected to wear either evening dress or native costume which particularly attracted my attention to the man who is now in custody, as he was the only person present who was not so attired. Whether he was acquainted with anybody else I am unable to say, but he was certainly in the Hall while the concert was in progress. At about 11 o'clock I was preparing to leave the hall, and had almost reached the folding doors leading to the landing when a revolver shot rang out. I was inclined at first to attach no importance to the incident, as I had some vague impression that it might be a way of signalling the close of the proceedings, and I did not realize what had happened within a few inches of where I was standing until the shot was followed, after a slight pause, by three or four others in quick succession. The guests who were on the landing drew back in horror, but I at once ran out, and saw Sir Curzon Wyllie stretched at full length on the ground. His face was covered with blood, and it was obvious that he was beyond any assistance we could render. In the meanwhile the assassin had been

seized, and his captor called for help, as he was unable to hold him down. I ran forward, and caught him by the wrist, determined at all cost to keep the revolver pointing to the ground as I was under the impression that five barrels had only been fired and that he would use the last either upon his captors or himself. The revolver however was quickly wrested from him and the prisoner offered no further resistance while I was present.[2] Not even once Colman mentioned that Dhingra tried to shot himself. It was his impression that he might do so. It was Colman's thinking and not Dhingra's doing. What was common factor noticeable in the statements of the witnesses was that everyone was trying to project himself as the saviour of the situation. Colman did not mention the suicide theory much publicized by Probyn and others.

- They wanted to tie his hands. Dhingra smiled in derision and remarked: "Please let me place my specs properly. Then you tie my hands!" A physician, who was present in the hall, found that when everyone there, was breathing heavily Dhingra alone was cool and unperturbed. He behaved as nothing had happened. Had his plan to commit suicide been unsuccessful, he would not have been sitting clam and quiet.
- Madan Lal Dhingra had objected to only one person in the court when he appeared for the first time on July 10 and that was none other than Manmohan Sinha. When Sinha had finished his statement in the court Madan Lal Dhingra said "This man is traitor to my country" sufficient to prove how far Sinha was true to his statement. His statement lacked coherence and he fumble in narration in the court.

A careful study of the above statements of the witnesses, one finds plentiful ambiguities and misrepresentation of the facts, which forces one to doubt the statements of the witnesses.

As no one bothered to question their authenticity and as such the statements were considered to be true. His refusal to hire a lawyer further strengthened the allegations and accusations as there was no one in the court to counter the false charges levelled against him. He himself did not bother to object to the statements of the witnesses. His attitude towards the British witnesses was totally indifferent. He was perturbed to hear the comments of Sinha and had objected to it. Besides that he never raised any objection to the allegations of others. His silence was taken as yes to all the charges. That does not mean that the charges levelled against him were correct as we have just seen and analysed above.

If we look into the statement of Dhingra, he was again and again insisting, that he had no wilful intention to kill Dr. Lalcaca. It was done in self-defense. It shows that he was not happy at his death as he had never planned it. It all happened in a fraction of seconds and did not give him enough time to think. But after he had accomplished the task, he realized his mistake. He had killed an Indian in self-defense. He had not come to harm anyone else except his selected target and he gave up. Otherwise, no one like Sinha or Probyn could have dared to touch him or to go near him. Madan Lal Dhingra did not object to Probyn who had narrated the same suicide story. He even did not bother to look at him while he was narrating the scene, perhaps because he was a foreigner, a part of the ruling family, it was expected of him. But when Sinha tells the blatant lie he could not resist to use the harshest word, 'traitor'.

Had Madan Lal Dhingra committed suicide, his sacrifice would have completely been wasted. He was the mastermind of his plan and the only person to know what he was doing and why. Suicide was never the part of his agenda otherwise no one could have dared to stop him from its execution. The story was concocted to malign his image and project him weak which was quite contrary to his life-size image.

Let us look at the second charge levelled by Charles Rolleston, a retired officer of the English Army stated, "He seemed perfectly composed. He had a half dazed dreamy manner which made me suspect, he in fact has taken *bhang*". Perhaps he had heard the word *bhang* during his service in India.

Had Madan been under the intoxication of *bhang*, he would have been lying in the hospital and not committing murder. *Bhang* is an extract of a cannabis plant abundantly found in India.[3] It is a well-known fact that consumption of *bhang* makes a man coward and not bold enough to commit murder. Moreover, Dhingra was not an addict to any kind of intoxicant. To such a person, the dosage of *bhang* or any other intoxicant could have caused a negative effect.

Our Indian historians accepting the statement to be a categorical truth forwarded a lengthy explaination detailing its properties. V.N. Datta wrote, "The consumption of *bhang* relieves the tension and conflicts to which the human mind is susceptible, particularly in crucial matters, weakens the hold of rationality, almost destroys, though temporarily, the sense to discriminate between good and evil, and creates that state of mind when rational instincts are overpowered by passions of indifference, when theirs not to reason why, theirs but to do or die".[4] Such rare qualities of *bhang* like enslaving the mind of a person to get a desired task accomplished, even a murder, were not known earlier, till Datta Sahib explained. If such result could have been possible then God forbid the consequences. How our worthy historian discovered it or perhaps experienced it could not be collaborated and experts expressed their apprehension and refused to accept it. Its effect on beginners starts after a few minutes of its intake and one begins to behave strangely. Many a time repetition of act, expression of unknown fear yelling, and withdrawal symptoms have been noticed. The consumption of *bhang* generates depressing emotions and one feels sluggish, apprehensive and timid. One of the addicts said, "One fears his own reflection, forget killing." No doubt the rationality to decide what is good and bad is gone but what is left in the mind is not to commit murder at least, but to find a corner in the room to hide as it generates tranquilizing effect.

V.N. Datta writes, "The consumption of *bhang* relieves the tension and conflicts to which the human mind is susceptible...."

What kind of conflict was there in the mind of Madan Lal Dhingra? Does it mean that latter was being forced to commit a crime for which he was not prepared mentally or he was afraid to commit murder and was scared of its consequences? It is not true. The facts present altogether a different picture which even an ordinary man can see but not our historian who was perhaps over obsessed with Charles Rolleston comment and had more faith in British intelligence reports which had stated that Dhingra took *bhang* as a part of a plan, to leave nothing to chance, and to expel even the remotest possibility of running away from the duty of killing an Englishman. As if *bhang* was a remote control. Madan Lal Dhingra had no conflict either about the target or about its consequences. He himself had selected the target and accomplished the task without the knowledge of any other person. Not even for a fraction of a second, anyone could read or judge his mind. As such there was no question his being double minded or being under any kind of intoxication.

Yes, he was addicted with patriotism. Stung by the virus of independence, he wanted to have even at the cost of his life. Madan Lal Dhingra was not an ordinary individual but an entity in himself. He was born with a silver spoon, and got his degree in engineering. Soon destiny would have smiled upon him—good job, handsome salary and family life, for which every man aspires. All this would have been at his footsteps, but he left it for his cherished bride, 'Independence'. Such men need no intoxication to fulfill a desired dream.

Emma Beck, who talked to him for about half an hour at the "At Home", could not make out if he was under the influence of any drug. Had he consumed *bhang*, he should either have been stammering or confusing the conversation, which she did not report. She told the court, "I had a conversation with him about half an hour before the tragedy. I noticed nothing peculiar about his condition. He remained quite normal. I asked him what he had been doing in his work recently. He told that after finishing his studies at University College he intend to apear in A.M.I.C.E. Examination in October after which he would return to India. I asked him if he had friends 'At Home'. He said he knew several. He seemed quite calm." She had admitted that the conversation lasted for half an hour, enough time to judge a person, whether he is in senses or not.

V.N. Datta illustrates the scene of the Imperial Institute where the party was on. At the function, light snacks and tea were served, and some musical items presented. All this must have strained Dhingra's tense nerves and, possibly, he could not enjoy that evening the charms and delights of lively female company and conversation. His mind was elsewhere, his thoughts wandered, but probably the mild effect of intoxication had a soothing effect on him, though it had warmed his blood, and as usual, he was polite, courteous and impeccable in manners. But he seemed basically disappointed for he was not sure who to pick, and who to kill; disappointed because there was neither Morley, nor Curzon or any other high official who had acted as a red rag to the Indian bull.[5]

What was going in the mind of Dhingra at that particular moment of time only he could tell and that he disclosed through his action when he shot dead Curzon Wyllie. No other person was aware of his move, not even Savarkar, to whom he was considered to be very close. The reason of such secrecy is not difficult to guess. A minor leakage could have jeopardized the whole plan and would have forced many to face its aftermath at British hands, the very thought of which could make one shudder in dreams. As such he preferred to go alone with it alone without fearing the consequences.

Even his polite, courteous and impeccable mannerism had been attributed to *bhang*. Pity Dhingra, whom not only his family disowned but even the historians failed to provide justice. It tantamounts to undermine his sacrifice and projects him as a puppet under the command of the revolutionaries who forced him to commit murder under the intoxication of *bhang*. It presents Dhingra as directionless, who had no mind of his own, who was a puppet in the hands of the conspirators.

These are mere assumptions that he had come for Morley or some other big-bull. From the literature and the photograph found in his lodging, it leaves no doubt that he had already selected his target and was waiting for Curzon Wyllie and none else. Definitely, his delay might have caused him worry, but after meeting and talking to Miss Beck he had become sure of his arrival. It could be possible only because he was under no obligation and compulsion, either of any individual or group. It was his personal resolution and plan in which no one else was involved and as such he was answerable to none.

His calm and silent manner at the Imperial Institute made Rolleston doubt that he might have consumed *bhang*. Let us accept it to be true. On July 1, he remained calm because of *bhang*, but what about July 10. There was hardly any change in his behaviour in the court. Let us look at the *Times* reporting, "Throughout the lengthy hearing he had maintained an exceedingly calm behaviour."[6] Does this prove that Madan Lal Dhingra had been intoxicated a dosage of *bhang* by the police to project such a posture. Captain Charles Rolleston was the only person to have made such a comment. Court never took it seriously. If this was the case then why Dhingra was not medically examined? It was the part of the plan to label him an addict, of criminal temperament and lower caliber who committed the act without any particular cause.

Varinder Sharma, Commissioner Police informed that he had not come across any case during his entire career where a person, after consuming *bhang*, had committed a murder.[7]

It clearly proves beyond doubt that the purpose was to project Madan Lal Dhingra as insane, coward, who under the intoxication of *bhang* committed a crime. The intake of *bhang* produces a depressing effect. Many a time, it has been noticed that the person who takes *bhang* behaves illogically. If he starts laughing or weeping, he continues doing so. After consuming *bhang* one looses control over his senses and thinking, cannot act as planned because logical thinking dies down. *Bhang* is considered a passive intoxicant which leaves the consumer lathargic. Unlike alcohol it does not excite, agitate or arouse but makes one lethargic and inactive. As such, one finds the entire energy of the witnesses concentrated in establishing Curzon Wyllie as the most humble and ill-fated person, whereas Madan Lal Dhingra as the most ill-guided individual.

There is no resentment and reservation against the British Captain Rolleston who blamed Dhingra of consuming *bhang*, because in doing so he was serving his nation, but what about the Indian historians who accepted the indictment literally and went beyond their means and competence to prove it. It will be a sheer accusation to portray an ordinary, simple and diligent student an addict, coward and dud, who acted as carrier of someone's dictates, which was never the case. When Dhingra was arrested why he was not medically examined at that very moment? It should have been the prior duty of the investigating team. It was not done so as no one had suspected him under any intoxication. It was just a blame game in which many were taken for a ride.

Was it a planned conspiracy? V.N. Datta believed that it was a planned conspiracy. He opines, "Sir Curzon Wyllie entered Jehangir Hall about 9.30 p.m., almost half an hour after Dhingra's arrival. Koregaonkar was also present in the hall, and he had been sent by Savarkar to make sure that Dhingra did not flinch from the assigned task—Rajan and Dhingra had earlier visited Koregaonkar at his residence."[8] When Wyllie entered the hall, Koregaonkar is reported to have told Dhingra, "Look out". His eyes fell on Wyllie who had incurred the Indian student community's wrath because of his sinister design of shadowing their movements. Dhingra had also felt humiliated at his hands—Wyllie had been meddling with his private affairs on behalf of his family. It seems that in the hall he was still untask maybe due to intoxication, irresolution, or diminishing hopes of finding Morley or Curzon. He wanted to strike off the heads of tall poppies, but Lord they were not to be found there. After a delightful evening, people were streaming out, and Wyllie too was leaving the hall when Koregaonkar said to Dhingra, "*Aji Jao na, Kya Karte ho.*" (Well, go on, what are you doing?) Dhingra moved up, engaged Wyllie in conversation as he was coming out of the door in the vestibule, fired four shots from close range of three or four feet, and Wyllie fell dead.[9]

Similar assertion were made by Dharmavira who penned Hardayal biography. He informs that Madan Lal Dhingra, Koregaonkar and Gyan Chand Varma decided that to avenge Ganesh Savarkar (elder brother of V.D. Savarkar), sentence besides those of Khudi Ram Bose, Kanai Lal, Barindra, Bhupendra and Hem Chandra Das it was decided to shoot Curzon in the very heart of the British Empire. They began to practice revolver shooting at a range.[10] Dhananjay Keer also presented somewhat similar story, on the last day of June 1909, Madan Lal Dhingra came to Savarkar in the student's hostel kept at the residence of B.C. Pal in Sinclair Road, where Savarkar had been staying since April 3, 1909. There they had a talk. Then Savarkar and Niranjan Pal accompanied Dhingra to Notting Hill Gate Station. Savarkar gave him a nickel-plated revolver and while bidding him farewell he said, "Don't show me your face if you fail this time."[11] Next day Savarkar sent Koregaonkar and G.C. Varma to the Imperial

Institute to keep Dhingra to the resolve. Dhananjay Keer does not mention the presence of Rajan whereas V.N Datta had mentioned his presence.

The following extract from the *Weekly Report of the Director of Criminal Intelligence, Simla, 7th August 1909,* is being presented here which will clear many ambiguities.

London—The following information received from the Scotland Yard under date July 16th confirms as far as it goes, the account given by our correspondent, as to the complicity of Dr. Rajan, V.V.S. Aiyer and Koregaonkar in Dhingra's crime:-

On the evening of the murder Dhingra and another Indian described as a 'pock-marked man' visited H.K. Koregaonkar's lodgings at 47, Coram Street, W.C., and were with him for half an hour. Dhingra and the pock-marked man left Koregaonkar's room together. Dr. T.S.S. Rajan was thought to be the man who corresponded to the description of the 'pock-marked man' and his photo has been shown to Koregaonkar's landlady, but she failed to identify him. His movements subsequent to the above visit have not, up to the present, been established.

Koregaonkar is said to have been present in the Imperial Institute on the night of the murder, but was not seen to hold any conversation with Dhingra, and his action after the crime was not such as would justify his being cognizant of Dhingra's intention to commit the crime.

However, Rajan and Koregaonkar have been making attempts to see the prisoner in Brixton Jail, and have sent letters to him offering to get the solicitor for his defence. V.V.S. Aiyer has also associated himself with Rajan and Koregaonkar in the efforts to see and write to Dhingra.

In this report it is again stated that the evidence obtained so far regarding the murder of Sir Curzon Wyllie

does not indicate that there was any actual conspiracy to commit this crime.[12]

British Prime Minister Asquith had a few days back said in Parliament that there was evidence of widespread conspiracy in India against the British Empire. The positive aspect was that it was confined to a small group of people, who were desperate and determined to act.[13] On July 4, 1909, the meeting of New Reform Club was held where Indian students had gathered to contemplate on July 1 event. Surendranath Banerjee addressing the gathering challenged the Prime Minister's assertion that there was a widespread conspiracy in India; the implication being that Dhingra belonged to this gang. Though a strong critic of India House and its founder Shyamji Krishna Varma, Surendranath Banerjee never accepted the theory of a collaborated conspiracy in Curzon murder case. Similarly, Bipan Chandra Pal bitterly criticized Madan Lal Dhingra's killing of Wyllie and Lalcaca in a public meeting at London, but nowhere had he mentioned it as a part of the planned conspiracy. He also condemned the revolutionaries as "Immature, impatient and irresponsible men."[14]

There was widespread fear among the Indian students that soon they will be harassed for the misdoing of someone else.[15] *The Times* supported Prime Minister Mr. Asquith's assertion. Many in England were apprehensive of a planned conspiracy and every move of the government was to detect if such plot existed. So much so, Morley had cautioned Minto to keep a strict vigil on the activities of the extremist outfits, to detect every possible move related to the conspiracy and deal with it severely. It was the question of England's prestige, which had been shattered due to the spirited effort of an individual. This clearly proves that these theories were being propounded by those who wanted the India House and its activities to be sacked, along with its leaders, no doubt prominent among them being Krishna Varma, Savarkar and their comrades. Had it been a planned conspiracy, every other accomplice would have been fixed and punished. "Dhingra was sent for eight days police remand where even hardened criminal do spell." It was enough time for an ordinary student like him to divulge the truth. But the trial subsequent made it clear that Madan Lal Dhingra stood alone in his deed, and had acted on his own impulse and initiative.

Had it been a planned conspiracy, Savarkar would have never stayed away from the scene of action. His love and liking for Dhingra was well-known and need not be elaborated here. Rather, Dhingra's action had caught him unaware. Perhaps, it was never a part of their plan to indulge in killing in England, as the country had provided them enough opportunity to propagate and support their revolutionary brothers in India. India House, with passage of time had earned a great reputation among the Indians coming to England, as the most reasonable place to stay. India House was performing as a parallel organization to the National Indian Association in winning over the Indian students to their cause. The purpose it was serving for the Indian students cannot be measured in terms of killing.

As it had been noticed, Savarkar was alone to defend Dhingra in the gathering, at Caxton Hall on July 5 to condemn latter's act. By doing so he was openly inviting the attention and wrath of the British public and the administration, but he was least worried about it. To think that such a man could hatch a conspiracy and throw someone else into the fire and stay out to watch his hanging does not go with his character. He was the one who could dare to enter England in the heat of opposition and get arrested for life imprisonment. He could, like others, have stayed back in France and enjoyed the freedom for the rest of his life, but he chose the other way. Throughout his life he admired the sacrifice of Dhingra without mentioning his role in it.

To understand these revolutionaries, one will have to enter their mind and study their psyche. They have different attitude and aptitude towards life. For a common human being, it looks unintelligent and unimaginable that how a young man belonging to such an affluent family, well educated, could sacrifice his life for the sake of freedom of his country. His family declared him mad, others must have accepted it to be true. Captain Rolleston gave him the tag of *bhang* others made it sure that it remained intact to his character. Madan Lal Dhingra was least bothered what people would say about him or his act. He had done what he thought was right.

Writers have failed to do justice to the valour and chivalry of Dhingra and had cast aspersions without verifying the facts. Similarly, other writers, writing the biographies, preferred to attribute Dhingra's daredevil act to their hero's, thus undermining his role in history. Truth cannot be suppressed for long, one day it has to come out and raise its head and stand high and alone. No one can undermine the sacrifice of Madan Lal Dhingra and his contribution towards freedom movement.

NOTES

1. Dharmavira, *Lala Hardayal and Revolutionary Movements of His Times*, Indian Book Company New Delhi, 1970, p. 120.
2. *The Civil and Military Gazette*, Narratives of Eyewitnesses, Lahore, July 20, 1909. Also see, B.S. Maighowalia, First Indian Martyr: Executed in Pentonville Prison, London, p. 87.
3. *Bhang* is made from the leaf and flower of a cannabis plant abundantly found in India. Its leaves and seeds are rubbed vigorously in between the palm of the hands till it turns into black thick solid paste and then it is consumed sometimes directly, or mixed with some soft drink or in some eatables according to the taste.
4. V.N. Datta, p. 54.
5. *Ibid.*, p. 56.
6. *The Times*, London, "The Murder of Sir Curzon Wyllie", July 12, 1909, p. 6.

7. Police Commissioner Varinder Kumar Sharma was interviewed on July 22, 2009 at 4.15 p.m. at his office in District Courts, Amritsar.
8. According to the information received from Scotland Yard, he accompanied a "pock-marked man" (later identified as T.S.S. Rajan) to H.K. Koregaonkar lodgings. Some of Dhingra's close friends were there, but not Savarkar who had preferred to keep himself away, and people were in a light mood exchanging pleasantries: V.N. Datta, p.55.
9. *Ibid.*, p. 56.
10. Dharmavira, *Lala Hardayal and Revolutionary Movements of His Times,* 1970, pp. 119-20.
11. Dhananjay Keer, *Veer Savarkar*, Bombay, 1950, p. 53.
12. Weekly Report of the Director of Criminal Intelligence, Simla, 7 August 1909: Government of India, Home Department Proceedings, August 1909, No. 47.
13. *The Times*, London, July 3, 1909.
14. J. Keir Hardie, *India-Impression and Suggestions*, pp. 57-58.
15. Surendranath Banerjee had come to England on the invitation made by Lovat Fraser, formerly editor of the *Times of India*, and at the time on the staff of *The Times.* Banerjee was a staunch critic of Krishna Varma and his ideology and openly criticized it: Surendranath Banerjee, *A Nation in the Making*, 1925, p. 257.

□

8

Trial and Verdict

Central Criminal Court, July 23; Before the Lord Chief Justice of England: On July 23, 1909, two cases had come up before the Lord Chief Justice of England, in the Old Bailey Court for hearing; first was of Arthur Fletcher Horsley, indicted for unlawfully, maliciously, seditious, printing and publishing in *Indian Sociologist* a wicked scandalous and seditious libel concerning the government of the King of and in the Indian Empire, and second case on agenda was of Madan Lal Dhingra, the assassin of Sir Curzon Wyllie and Lalcaca. Mr. Horsley, the printer of *Indian Sociologist* was sentenced to four months imprisonment for having published material justifying political murders.[1]

After that the Dhingra case was taken up by Lord Chief Justice. The Old Bailey (Court) was crowded when the trial of Madan Lal Dhingra took place. Lord Averstone presided. The Attorney General described the crime as long pre-meditated, with an obvious motive.[2]

Madan Lal was not defended, and refused Counsel.

His sole defence consisted in reading again his Police Court statement.

The Central Court Proceedings

The trial began with the introduction of the accused and pronouncement of the last verdict of the court proceedings, trial held on July 10, 1909.

Dhingra, Madan Lal (25, student), was indicted for, and charged on the Coroner's inquisition with the wilful murder of William Hutt Curzon Wyllie and Cowasji Lalcaca.

On being called upon to plead to the indictment for the "willful murder" of Sir W.H. Curzon Wyllie, Madan Lal Dhingra said, "First of all I would say that these words cannot be used with regard to me at all. Whatever I did was an act of patriotism and justice which was justified. The only thing I have to say is in the statement which I believe you have got."

The Clerk of Arraigns: The question now is whether you plead "Guilty" or "Not guilty" to the indictment?

Dhingra: Well, according to my view I will plead "Not guilty". Whatever I want to say is in the statement that was taken from my waist-coat. Madan Lal Dhingra again insists the court to read his earlier paper taken from him at the time of crime. He might have thought that as it was his last appearance in the court and as the judge was new, his request might be accepted. But judge ignored his request.

The Lord Chief Justice directed a plea of not guilty to be entered.

To the indictment for the willful murder of Dr. Cowasji Lalcaca, Dhingra pleaded "Not guilty".

Asked whether he had any counsel to defend him, Dhingra replied that he had not.

The Attorney-General (Sir William Robson, K.C., HP.), Mr. Bodkin, Mr. Rowlatt, and Mr. Leycester prosecuted the witness.

Mrs. Harris, 108, Ledbury Road, Bayswater. Dhingra came to lodge at my house on Easter Monday; he occupied a ground floor front room. On July 1 he left the house about two in the afternoon, returned just after eight and shortly afterwards went out again. He was then dressed in ordinary clothes, with a blue turban; he left in a cab.

The Lord Chief Justice asked Dhingra if he wished to put any questions.

Dhingra: No, I do not want to ask any questions; I want to say something.

The Lord Chief Justice: You can say what you like afterwards. Do you want to ask any questions now?

Dhingra: No, I don't want to ask anything.

William Burrow, an assistant at Gamage Limited, Holborn, proved that prisoner on January 26 purchased a Colt's automatic magazine pistol for £ 35*s*. He produced a gun licence taken out in the name of Madan Lal Dhingra, of University College.[3]

Henry Stautout Morley. I am proprietor of an exhibition of automatic machines and a shooting range at 92, Tottenham Court Road. About three months ago prisoner commenced to frequent the range for revolver practice; he attended two or three times a week, bringing his own revolver, an automatic Colt, and his own ammunition. He used to fire 12 shots on each visit. He took a lot of care in his shooting and acquired considerable proficiency. On July 1, about 5.30 p.m., he was at the range, and I saw him fire 12 shots at a target distance of 18 ft. (The target was shown to the Jury; there were 11 hit.)

Police constable Frederick James Palmer, D Division, produced a plan to scale of the Jehangir Hall and other portions of the Imperial Institute.

Miss Beck, 168, Kensington Park Road. I am Honorary Secretary of the National Indian Association. Her Majesty the Queen is patron of the association; Lieutenant-Colonel Sir William Hutt Canon Wyllie was a member of the Council and Honorary Treasurer. The object of the association was the promotion of social intercourse between the English people and the Indian people in London, one of the methods being entertainments or conversations. I first knew of prisoner in

March last. In May, I sent him an invitation to call upon me; he did not call. I sent him an invitation for our entertainment at the Jehangir Hall of the Imperial Institute on July 1. I attended that evening and saw prisoner there. About half past ten I spoke to him, asking him what he was doing in his work; he said he had finished his course at University College and that he would be taking the examination for A.M.I.C.E. in October, and then going home. I asked him whether he knew many of those present and he said he knew some.[4]

Douglas William Thorburn, journalist. I was present at the entertainment at the Imperial Institute on July 1. About 11 o'clock I was in the main hall. On looking through the doorway of the vestibule, I saw prisoner apparently speaking to Sir Curzon Wyllie. Prisoner raised his arm and rapidly fired four shots in Sir Curzon's face—into his eyes. Sir Curzon collapsed at the fourth shot. After a short interval, there were two more shots, but I did not see in what direction they were fired. I ran to prisoner to prevent anything further being done, and others also rushed to the spot. Prisoner had his right hand free and he placed the revolver to his own temple, but there was merely a click. With assistance I got him down. I asked him, "What have you done? Why did you do it?" Prisoner looked at me quietly but did not say anything. He later on said, "Let me put my spectacles on."

Sir Leslie Probyn. I was present at this entertainment. About 11 o'clock I was in the Jehangir Hall, going towards the exit door, when I heard the sound of three or four shots. On going forward I saw the prisoner, who fired another shot; he then held the pistol straight in front of him and apparently fired another shot. He next turned the pistol round to his own temple. I immediately went at him, held his arms, and got the pistol from him. There was a struggle, and I hardly know what happened, as I fell down and injured my nose and ribs. I handed the prisoner over to a police constable, also the revolver.

Captain Charles Rolleston, another guest at the entertainment, spoke to hearing five shots. One shot was fired deliberately by prisoner at a native Indian gentleman in evening dress. The gentleman Dr. Lalcaca fell backwards. The body of Sir Curzon Wyllie was lying three or four yards away. Witness asked prisoner his name and address, and he gave them as "Dhingra, Ledbury Road". Witness, speaking to him mostly in Hindustani, asked what could be his motive for the crime. He replied, "I will tell the police."

Evidence of the prisoner's arrest was given by the police:

Police constable Frederick Nicholls, 476 B said that on being called to the Imperial Institute he found prisoner being held by several gentlemen, and he took him into custody. On his being searched there were found in prisoner's waist-coat pocket the pistol and the dagger produced.

Detective Sergeant Frank Eadley, B Division, who was with Nicholls, explained to the arrest and the finding upon prisoner of the second revolver and cartridges.

Superintendent Alfred Isaac, B Division. On the early morning of July 2, I saw prisoner at Marylebone Police Station. The charge was read over to him and he nodded his head.

Sub-Divisional Inspector Charles Glass, B Division. At the police station I took the charge against prisoner. On its being read over he said, "Yes", nodding his head. I said, "Do you wish any of your friends to be communicated with?" He replied, "I do not think it necessary tonight, they will know later on."

Inspector Albert Draper, B Division. I was present at Westminster Police Court on July 2. Just before being remanded, prisoner said to the Magistrate, "The only thing I want to say is that there was no wilful murder in the case of Dr. Lalcaca; I did not know him; when he advanced to take hold of me I simply fired in sclf-defence."

Dr. Thomas Neville, 123, Sloane Street. On July 1, I went to the Imperial Institute and there saw the dead body of

Sir Curzon Wyllie. Later that night I saw prisoner at the police station; he seemed quiet, calm, and collected. I asked him whether he was hurt, and he said "No". I felt his pulse; it was quite regular and normal. On making a post-mortem examination of Sir Curzon Wyllie, I found a bullet entrance wound on the right eye, with an exit wound at the back of the neck; another two wounds on the left eye and at the back of the neck; two other wounds, one below the left ear, the other over the left eyebrow, the bullets being found in the head. The cause of death was injury to the brain; death must have been instantaneous.[5]

This concluded the case for the prosecution.

The Lord Chief Justice (addressing the prisoner): Do you wish to give evidence in the box or say what you have to say there?

Dhingra: I have nothing to say. I admit that I did it. This evidence is all true. I should like my statement read.

The Lord Chief Justice: Do you wish your statement read that you made at the police court?

Dhingra: Yes.

The statement was then read by the Clerk of Arraigns as follows:[6]

> "I do not want to say anything in defence of myself...no English law court has got any authority to arrest and detain me in prison, or pass sentence of death on me. That is the reason I did not have any counsel to defend me. Whatever else I have to say is in the paper before the Court I make this statement,... 'I wish that English people should sentence me to death, for in that case the vengeance of my countrymen will be all the more keen'. I put forward this statement to show the justice of my cause to the outside world, and especially to our sympathisers in America and Germany." [7]

The Lord Chief Justice: Do you wish to call any evidence?

Dhingra: No. I only want the statement to be read.

The Lord Chief Justice: Do you wish to say anything more?

Dhingra: There is another statement on foolscap paper.

The Lord Chief Justice: Any other statement you must make now yourself.

Dhingra: But I don't remember it now.

The Lord Chief Justice: If there is anything you wish to say to the Jury say it now. You can say anything you wish.

Dhingra: It was taken from my pocket among other papers.

The Lord Chief Justice: I don't care what was in your pocket. The question of what you have written before has nothing to do with this case. You have got to say anything you wish to the Jury. What you have written on previous occasions or what was in your pocket is no evidence in this case. If you wish to say anything to the Jury in defence of yourself say it now. Do you wish to say anything more?

Dhingra: No.

The Lord Chief Justice, in summing up, said, "It was not necessary for him to detain them for more than a few seconds, because he was sure that they had followed the evidence which was, of course, absolutely conclusive. All he had to say to them was that they had nothing to do—as they already knew—with any suggestion that there was any justification for this crime on political grounds."[8] They had nothing to do with the suggestion made that he was as justified in killing Sir William Curzon Wyllie as some other person might have been in killing some foreign subject who was walking about the streets of London. They had here got to deal with the case of an ordinary crime, by which as far as we knew a blameless man, who had given his life to the public service and had done an immense deal for the natives of this country of India, had lost his life. It was quite plain on the evidence before them that there had been considerable premeditation. They would remember that the only communication made by the deceased man to the prisoner was one of friendship, offering him kindness, having received a letter from his brother. They had heard the evidence given before them—not one particle of which was questioned by the prisoner, for he had not asked a single question, although he was a man perfectly competent to ask any questions if he could have thrown any doubt upon the facts—that he purchased the revolver some weeks before and had been regularly practising at shooting gallery and had acquired considerable skill with revolver. They had heard that he went to the Imperial Institute that night having upon him two loaded revolvers, one with eigth cartridges and other with six, and five other cartridges in his pocket and a dagger—a dangerous weapon, which had been produced before them. They had heard on the evidence of the eyewitnesses that he was seen speaking to Sir Curzon Wyllie, to draw revolver upon him, shoot at the distance of a few inches, four shots—one in one eye, one in the other eye and the other two by the ear and left temple, the last two bullets remaining in his body. Death, as they had heard, was absolutely instantaneous. It was not suggested, nor it could be suggested, that there was anything which could reduce the crime from murder to manslaughter. It was not suggested that the prisoner did anything in self-defence.

On the contrary, with regard to Sir Curzon Wyllie, the prisoner, having fired two other shots which killed another innocent gentleman, said, as they had heard proved today, "I did not intend to kill Dr. Lalcaca. I only fired at him in self-defence when he came to take hold of me",—indicating as plainly as possible the distinction that he drew in his mind between the two cases. It was not suggested by him that he was not sane, and not in his right mind. The deliberations of his movements before showed that he was so. The statements that he made afterwards, also showed that he knew perfectly well that he had done. It was no part of his (the Lord Chief Justice's) duty again to recall to their minds the evidence, because they had heard it from the witnesses on the oath in the last hour and a half. They had proved it before them, that this man drew this deadly weapon and fired, intending to kill and did kill, that poor gentleman who was his friend, and against whom he had no right to have the slightest feeling of resentment. He need only tell the Jury that which they knew perfectly well, that the suggestion that there was justification found no place in our courts of justice. If there were anything of the kind to be considered, it might be considered with reference to other matters—as for the instance the carrying of the sentences into fact, but the Jury had nothing to do with that. If, on this evidence, which was absolutely uncontradicted, the Jury was satisfied that the prisoner fired the pistol at that poor gentleman and killed him, they had but one duty to perform, and that was the duty which they were sworn on their oath to perform—to return a verdict in accordance with the evidence, and he told them that, if they believed this evidence, the only possible verdict was one of wilful murder.[9]

Verdict and Sentence

The Jury after a short consultation in their box, found the prisoner guilty.

The Clerk of Arraigns asked the prisoner if he had anything to say why sentence of death should not be passed on him.

Dhingra—"I have told you over and over again that I do not acknowledge the authority of the court. You can do whatever you like. I do not mind at all. You can pass sentence of death on me. I do not care, but remember that one day we shall be all powerful, then we can do what we like. That is all I want to say."

The Lord Chief Justice having assumed the black cap addressing the prisoner, said, "Madan Lal Dhingra, no words of mine would have the slightest effect on you; nor do I intend to say anything more than point out that you have been convicted on the clearest possible evidence of the brutal murder of an innocent man. The law enforces me to pass the only sentence which is possible in such a case.[10]

The Lord Chief Justice proceeded to pass sentence of death on the prisoner in the usual form. The prisoner, making an oriental salute to the judge, said, "Thank You My Lord. I don't care. I am proud to have the honour of laying down my life for the cause of my country."

Madan Lal Dhingra was then removed.

Mr. Tindal Atkinson, K.C., addressing the Lord Chief Justice said, "I have been instructed to watch this case on behalf of the family of the man who has just been convicted. I have been instructed to say that they view this crime with the greatest abhorrence, and they wish to repudiate in the most emphatic way the slightest sympathy with the views or motives which have led up to the crime. Further, I am instructed to say, on behalf of the father of this man and the rest of his family, that there are no more loyal subjects of the Empire than they are.[11]

The Lord Chief Justice: Mr. Tindal Atkinson, although the course may have seemed somewhat unusual, having regard to the nature of this crime and the wicked attempt at justification in some quarters, I am very glad you should have said that on behalf of the members of the family.[12]

Madan Lal Dhingra, the young Indian student who murdered Sir Wyllie and Dr. Lalcaca at the Imperial Institute suffered the extreme penalty of the law for his crime at Pentonville Prison on Tuesday.[13] On Saturday (14 August), an official intimation reached the Governor of Pentonville Prison from the Home Office to the effect that Home Secretary, after careful consideration of all the facts, had decided that law must take its course in case of the condemned student.

During his imprisonment, the Indian had expressed a desire to see Mr. M.S. Master, an Indian Lecturer of Archway Road,

High Gate. Mr. Master on Monday (16 August) made application to the Home Office for admission to the prison and received the following reply:

"The Under Secretary is directed by the Secretary of State to say that he regrets that Mr. M.S. Master's request to be allowed to visit Dhingra cannot be complied with." According to the English law, the body of a murderer must be buried within the precincts of the prison and the authorities refused to deviate from the usual practice.

Mr. Master of Hyderabad who described himself as having come to England as the Edmund Burke Indian Lecturer, applied to the authorities to be admitted as a witness to execution but his request was firmly refused. Dhingra seemed to have maintained the same callous indifference to his fate that he displayed at the trial and after he was sentenced.[14] Some of Dhingra's friends endeavoured at the last moment to get the body of Dhingra cremated. They were prepared to bear the cost of cremation.

The convict maintained the same stolid demeanour that he evinced at the trial after the conviction, and expressed no contrition for the crime. Facilities were afforded of communicating with, or receiving visits from either relatives or friends, but with the exception of two visits from one of the fellow compatriots the condemned man did not see anyone.[15]

At 9 o'clock on 17 August (Tuesday) 1909 morning Madan Lal Dhingra breathed his last.[16] Stolid and defiant to the end, Madan Lal Dhingra, Indian student was hanged yesterday morning in Pentonville Prison for the assassination of Sir Wyllie and of Dr. Lalcaca at the Imperial Institute on July 1.[17]

Outside the prison a large crowd gathered to await the news that the execution had taken place, but there were very few Indians among those present.

The sentence was carried out of course with the strictest privacy, only the Under Sheriff of London, Mr. Metcalf, the prison officials, and the Chaplain Rev. L.J. Hudson being present. Mr. Hudson took no part in attending the condemned man, Dhingra having refused to see him, or to accept any ministrations.

Madan Lal Dhingra, it was announced, made no statement before death.[18] Dhingra's application to the Home Secretary to allow his body to be cremated was refused, and it will be buried, in accordance with the usual custom within the walls of the prison.

There was no demonstration outside the prison, although the authorities had taken all precautions in case there should have been several hundred people assembled, but only one of the Dhingra's compatriots was among the number. After the bell was tolled and the notice was posted the crowd quietly dispersed.[19]

Asaf Ali informs that "Dhingra had on his person a written statement which the police confiscated. Savarkar made available a copy to the *Daily News* of London, which published it on the morning of 16 August 1909—a day before the sentence of death passed on Dhingra was carried out at the gallows."[20]

An idea struck Savarkar. "I must do something to get this historic statement published in all the papers of important countries before Madan Lal Dhingra breathes his last. That will give him some consolation at the time of his death", he thought.

Savarkar called his revolutionary friend Gyan Chand Varma and told him to get the statement printed in all the important papers of European countries. Gyan Chand Varma took it and went to Paris secretly. There he printed thousands of copies of the statement. He sent it to the leading newspapers of several important countries like Germany, Italy and America. The *Daily News* was an important newspaper published from London. An English friend of Savarkar was working in the *Daily News*. While the paper was being printed at night, he inserted Dhingra's statement; no one else knew what he was doing. So on

16 August, a day before Dhingra's death, the statement appeared in the *Daily News.*

After a trial, which was concluded in one hour, Dhingra was sentenced to death and hanged on August 17. Some suspense was engendered when the police refused to introduce in evidence a prepared statement which Dhingra had carried on his person, along with the guns and the cutlery. After Dhingra was hanged, the statement appeared in the *Daily News*, placed thereby young David Garnett at Savarkar's behest.

The Challenge

"I attempted to shed English blood intentionally and of purpose, as a humble protest against the inhuman transportations and hangings of Indian youth.

In this attempt I consulted none but my own conscience; conspired with none but with my own duty.

I believe that a nation unwillingly held down by foreign bayonets, is in a perpetual state of war. Since open battle is rendered impossible I attacked by surprise since canon could not be had I drew forth and fired a revolver.

As a Hindu I feel that the slavery of my nation is an insult to my God. Her cause is the cause of freedom. Her service is the service of Sri Krishna. Neither rich nor able, a poor son like myself can offer nothing but his blood on the altar of Mother's deliverance and so I rejoice at the prospect of my martyrdom.

The only lesson required in India is to learn how to die and the only way to teach it is by dying alone.

The soul is immortal and if everyone of my countrymen takes at least two lives of Englishmen before his body falls the mother's salvation is a day's work.

This war ceases not only with the independence of India alone, it shall continue as long as the English and Hindu races exists in this world.

Until our country is free Sri Krishna stands exhorting, if you are killed, you attain heaven; if successful you win the earth.

It is my fervent prayer, may I be reborn of the same mother, and may I re-die in the same sacred cause, till my mission is done and She stands free for the good of humanity and to the glory of God."[21]

"It was generally assumed that Dhingra had not been the author, but no one has been willing to say that Savarkar was."[22] The extremists regarded Dhingra's act as one of supreme courage and self-sacrifice and his statement a stirring patriotic cry. The moderates, with Gokhale as their spokesman, disassociated themselves from what they considered both shocking and reckless act.

Those who contest and protest the wording of 'The Challenge' one can wonder at the poverty of their thought and mind. They forget to realize that Dhingra was not dud and dumb, as they think or project. He was highly educated and had successfully passed Diploma in Engineering. The last statement of Dhingra had been challenged as it is not original. Campbell Ker writes, "The 'India House' party made strenuous but unsuccessful attempts to have it published, in the course of trial, in the English newspapers, and afterwards printed it as a leaflet and posted large number of copies to India. The style suggests that it was probably Savarkar's and certainly not Dhingra's composition."[23]

We should not forget that Savarkar had met him in the gaol and Dhingra must have disclosed to him the content of his letter which he had written before the assassination, and which was not produced in the court even after his persistent insistence. Savarkar as a true comrade, nationalist, succeeded in publishing it definitely, he might have added certain words on his own, as it usually happens when someone presents the opinion of the other.[24]

But we should not forget that Dhingra went to kill Wyllie in a Sikh attire (he was wearing blue turban), which clearly identified him as a true Punjabee Hindu Sikh. It was unfortunate that his family refused to recognize his contribution and abhorred his act publicly and declared him insane. So much so, the members of the family stopped using the surname Dhingra along with their names.[25] Sahib Ditta Mal in his registered will made it clear that none of his family member could claim financial assistance from his trust for proceeding to England. Why? Perhaps he feared that London was the breeding ground of the political thinkers or he wanted to disassociate his family from the infamous place where his son had gone astray.

Before Dhingra it was only Bengal which was known to have produced martyrs for the freedom of the country. His act surpassed them all. He was first Indian to commit such a daring act in a foreign land.

A more complete text of Hardayal's tribute to Dhingra, as follows:

Dhingra has behaved at each stage of his trial like a hero of ancient times. He has reminded us of the history of medieval Rajputs and Sikhs who loved death like a bride. England thinks she killed Dhingra: in reality he lives forever, and has given the death blow to English sovereignty in India....

In time to come, when the British Empire in India shall have been reduced to dust and ashes, Dhingra's monument will adorn the squares of our chief towns, recalling the memory of our children to the noble life and noble death of him who lived on his life in a far off land for a cause he loved so well.[26]

Although the British were outraged publicly, admiration for Dhingra's act had been privately expressed by David Lloyd George and Winston Churchill, who is reported to have called Dhingra's statement "The finest ever made in the name of patriotism."[27] W.S. Blunt, the supporter of the Egyptian, Irish, and Indian Nationalist movements, and opponent of British imperialism expressed admiration for Dhingra's action, and wrote: "No Christian martyr ever faced his judges more fiercely or with greater dignity."

Shyamji Krishna Varma acknowledged Dhingra's act and declared him a 'Martyr' for the cause of Indian's Independence.[28]

After Dhingra's assassination of Curzon Wyllie, India House was closed and it ceased to be a resort for Indians, Later Krishna Varma sold it.[29]

While authorities searched for the remain of Udham Singh, Dhingra's body was accidentally found and repatriated to India on December 13, 1976. Both the martyrs belonged to Amritsar, Today Dhingra is widely remembered in India. His dare gave inspiration to revolutionaries like Bhagat Singh and Chandrashekhar Azad.

NOTES

1. Lord Chief Justice, in giving judgment in the first case said, "Arthur Fletcher Horsley, you have certainly adopted a very proper course, so far as what you have done since this charge was made against you, and I am quite willing to take the view that you did print this very terrible and wicked article without taking sufficient care, and without knowing, it may be, exactly what the contents were." "I believe that you honestly said that you would stop the publication if there was any objection to it, the reply given by the police…and the warning which ought to have made you more watchful." "I believe you were careless and had no direct criminal intention in publishing this article. But it must not be forgotten that the intention may be gathered from the article.... I cannot pass over the matter without some punishment, I think it would be of the worst example if that were done, because, as I have said, what has happened—it may be in consequence of such articles as this—is patent to all of us at the present moment...a person convicted of seditious libel; are ordered to be treated as first-class misdemeanants…as such…I must sentence you to four months imprisonment as a first class misdemeanant." *The Times*, Central Criminal Court, July 23, London, July 24, 1909. Also see *Proceedings of the Central Criminal Court*, 'Old Bailey Online' pp. 460-61.

2. Madan Lal was not defended, and refused counsel. His sole defence consisted in reading again his police court statement.
3. *The Times*, Central Criminal Court, July 23, London, July 24, 1909.
4. *Ibid.*
5. *Ibid.*
6. The complete statement can be seen in Chapter VII, pp. 115-16.
7. *The Times*, Central Criminal Court, July 23, London, July 24, 1909.
8. *Ibid.*
9. *Ibid.*
10. *Ibid.*
11. Waraich and Puri, *Tryst with Martyrdom*, p. 85.
12. *The Times*, Central Criminal Court, July 23, London, July 24, 1909.
13. *The English Mail*, "Execution of Dhingra: Callous to the End", 20 August 1909.
14. There was no demonstration outside the prison, although the authorities had taken all precautions in case there should have been several hundred people assembled, but only one of the Dhingra's compatriots was among the number. After the bell was tolled and the notice was posted the crowd quietly dispersed: Waraich and Puri, *Tryst with Martyrdom*, Unistar, Chandigarh, 2003, p. 85.
15. *Note: It is a misrepresentation of facts in view of preceding press.* During the period of his incarceration at Pentonville, the convict spent most of his time in reading principally magazines supplied from the prison library: Waraich and Puri, *Tryst with Martyrdom*, pp. 87-88.
16. Until within a few days of the execution the Home Office declined to make a definite announcement as to the murderer's fate but it was never seriously supposed that the government would decide to reprieve him. There was no public suggestion that the ordinary course of law should be altered. Indeed, it was felt that any show of such feelings would have been a lamentable expression of national weakness which would have done much harm to the always delicate position in India. The affair was in a double sense a great tragedy and nearly everyone, whatever his views, is agreed that the terrible affair has been ended in the least unsatisfactory way: *The English Mail*, "Execution of Dhingra", 20 August 1909. Madan Lal Dhingra was punished by death for the dastardly assassination of Sir Curzon Wyllie. He bore his fate with the same strange indifference which has characterized his conduct ever since the moment of the crime. He appeared to be still quite convinced of the innocence of his motives and to believe that he had performed an act of glory on behalf of his country: Waraich and Puri, *Tryst with Martyrdom*, Unistar, Chandigarh, 2003, pp. 86-87.

17. *The Daily Chronicle*, "Execution of Dhingra: Assassin of Sir Curzon Wyllie dies Unrepentant", August 18, 1909.
18. The Deputy under Sheriff informed a press representative that death was instantaneous and that Dhingra made no statement whatever: *The English Mail*, "Execution of Dhingra", August 20, 1909.
19. Waraich and Puri, *Tryst with Martyrdom*, p. 85.
20. G.N.S. Raghavan, *M. Asaf Ali's Memoirs*, p. 74.
21. James Campbell Ker, *Political Trouble in India, 1907-17*, pp. 179-80.
22. Emily C. Brown, *Har Dayal: Hindu Revolutionary and Rationalist*, p. 72.
23. James Campbell Ker, *Political Trouble in India, 1907-17*, p. 179.
24. The article in the *Tribune* read: "Most people get their facts wrong, and the very witness offered a picture that was twenty-five per cent fictions. Human being can't actually describe an event of great importance that they have just witnessed with their own eyes. The more certain witness the more wrong they were". *The Tribune*, "Mistakes: Our Life Long Companion", September 15, 2010, Punjab, p. 11.
25. The information is provided by Asaf Ali in his memoirs. He informs that he went to Simla in 1912-13. There he met Maya Roy (Bengali), his old acquaintance in England. She introduced him to Mr. and Mrs. Chaman Lal. At that time the Law Minister of Patiala, Chaman Lal was brother of Madan Lal Dhingra, the revolutionary assassin of Curzon Wyllie. The family had in those days dropped the surname 'Dhingra'. Mrs. Chaman Lal was granddaughter of Keshab Chandra Sen, the Brahmo Samaj leader. She was one of the pioneers to lead the way to inter-caste and inter-provincial marriage, a rare in those days. I was invited to join their table, and soon became one of the groups: G.N.S. Raghavan, *M. Asaf Ali's Memoirs*, p. 93.
26. Indulal Yajnik, *Shyamji Krishna Varma*, p. 275.
27. Blunt added, again we sat up till later. Among the many memorable things Churchill said was this: Talking of Dhingra he said that there had been much discussion in the Cabinet about him. Lloyd George had expressed to him his highest admiration on Dhingra's attitude as a patriot in which he (Churchill) shared. Dhingra will be remembered 2000 years hence, as we remember Regulas and Caractacus and Plutarch's herpes, and Churchill quoted with admiration Dhingra's last words as the finest ever made in the name of patriotism. Blunt, W.S., *My Diaries (1900-1914)*, Vol. II, London, 1919, *op. cit.*, pp. 262, 277-78. Also see, Emily C. Brown, *Har Dayal: Hindu Revolutionary and Rationalist*, Manohar, p. 72. V.N. Datta, *Madan Lal Dhingra and the Revolutionary Movement*, p. 77.

28. *The Times*, London, July 17, 1909. Also see V.N. Datta, *Madan Lal Dhingra and the Revolutionary Movement*, p. 75.
29. As a consequence of murder of Jackson, the District Magistrate of Nasik, Savarkar sought refuge in Paris on January 6, 1910: returned to England on March 13, was arrested and sent to India. Also see File: Government of India, Home Department, Political 849-850, August 1909, Nos. 23-27; for interception under Section 26 of the Indian Post Office Act, 1898 (VI of 1898), and prohibition of the entry into India under Section 19 of the Sea Custom Act, 1878 (VIII of 1878), of a book or pamphlet: V.V.S. Aiyer and Varindra Chattopadhyaya shifted to Paris, H.K. Koregaonkar and Chatturbhaj turned approvers in the Nasik conspiracy case, Harnam Singh had already deserted his friends under domestic pressure, Bapat was in India. Henceforth, Paris became the centre of the revolutionary activities. Harnam Singh was refused the permission to practice law: Proposal to oppose the application of Harnam Singh for enrolment as an advocate of the Chief Court of the Punjab see File Government of India, Home Department, Political 885-887, August 1909, Nos. 135-137. Similarly, V.D. Savarkar was also refused to practice, and Ganesh Savarkar had been sentenced to transportation on life under Section 124 (Sedition) for publishing and distributing revolutionary pamphlets causes which encouraged Dhingra to act.

□

9

Reaction and Response

The chapter covers the various meetings organized in England after July 1, to condone and condemn the 'Act of Dhingra'. It also highlights the reaction and response of the people in general, besides Indian leaders and administrators, present in England, which took the shape of public debate and was duly published in various newspapers, and especially in the *Times*.

Dhingra's act was strongly criticized in Indian political circles. A meeting was held in London on July 3, 1909, denouncing the crime. Surendranath Banerjee, Bipin Chandra Pal, J.M. Parikh and G.S. Khaparde all spoke against the 'act of Dhingra'.[1] The Eighty Club members met at the Westminster Palace Hotel to discuss the political scenario—England of India. Among those present were: Mr. Silcock, M.P. The Hon. E. Montagu, M.P. Wiles, M.P. Mr. Mackarness, M.P., Mr. Morrell, M.P. and several Indian gentlemen.[2]

Mr. Lehman M.P. presided and said, "It had become impossible to carry out the object of the gathering with any success.[3] The dreadful crime which was committed on Thursday last had entirely altered the circumstance. As they were still reeling under shock of this terrible tragedy, it was impossible to discuss with necessary calm and deliberation on the subject which stood on their agenda". But they could not however let the occasion pass without giving some expressions both to the horror and to the sympathy aroused in their minds by these causeless and infamous assassinations.

On July 5, a meeting was organized at Caxton Hall and was attended by a number of Europeans and Indians.[4] The room originally hired was soon seemed to be utterly inadequate for the gathering, and adjournment was made to one of the largest rooms in the building. This also proved insufficient for the present gathering. The seats rapidly filled, the gangways were blocked with late-comers, and the audience overflowed to the ante-room and even to the corridor. The meeting was representative of all shades of Indian opinions.

The meeting was organized to condemn the act of Dhingra. This meeting was arranged in order to express the indignation of the Indian community in London. Aga Khan presided the meeting. His Highness, the Aga Khan, was loudly cheered as he took his seat on the platform. In addition to those who took part in the proceeding, included the Maharaj Kumar of Cooch Behar, the Maharaj Kumar of Bobili, Sir Din Shah, Mr. Fazalbhoy Currimbhoy (Chairman of the Bombay Mill Owners Association), Khan Bahadur, Sahib Zada Abdul Qayam, C.I.F., Mr. Syed Hassan, Bilgrami, and Mr. K.G. Gupta (Members of the Indian Council), Mr. S.G. Khaparde and Mr. J.M. Parikh, together with a few English friends including Sir Arthur Wollaston and Miss Beck, the Honourable Secretary of National Indian Association. Sir M.M. Bhownagari read message of sympathy with the objects of the meeting.[5]

(1) That the general meeting, consisting of the representatives of all the communities of India and the bulk of Indian residents in Great Britain expressed their horror and indignation on the dastardly crime committed by an obscure and ill-conditioned Indian youth, last Thursday, which resulted in the death of Sir William Curzon Wyllie and also of Dr. Lalcaca.

(2) The British public will accept the feelings expressed

by the Indian community in London, and they will realise that it was an act of Fanatic and it had aroused the deepest indignation of all the people of India.[6]

Aga Khan read the Presidential note. He said that they were meeting under the shadow not only of a personal or public bereavement, but of a national disaster.

By one foul hand, one of the best friends of Indian people was done to death in an assemblage and amid a scene illustrative of his sterling worth, sweeping as it were into oblivion all the noblest traditions of the people of India, all their credit for gratitude, loyalty and devotion to the Imperial Crown. The humiliating sense of that discredit was upon them, and they had met to see how they could rehabilitate themselves among their fellow subjects of the Empire in face of that dastardly act.

President expressed his grief and sympathy to Mrs. Wyllie and prayed to the Almighty, to comfort and assuage her grief in that hour of dire distress. To him, it was a source of melancholy satisfaction, both on public and personal grounds, to be called upon to preside over that influential gathering. From long and intimate acquaintance with Sir Curzon Wyllie, he had formed the highest opinion of his sterling worth, his sincere and sympathetic friendship for the Indian people and the tact with which he performed his delicate duties.[7]

He also paid tribute to Dr. Lalcaca and said that the country had also suffered a heavy loss by the death of Dr. Cowas Lalcaca. A prominent member of the Parsi community, he had carved out for himself a highly successful career in Shanghai in the heroic manner of his race.[8] The crowd loudly cheered the President. It reflected the mood of the people gathered there. Many had come to show their sympathy with the departed souls and to condemn the 'Act of Dhingra'. This was the appropriate platform to enlist themselves in the category of British sympathizers and the supporters, as per the situation demanded.

Sir M.M. Bhownagari proposed the first resolution— "That this general meeting, consisting of representatives of all communities of India and of the bulk of the Indian residents in Great Britain, desire to express the horror and indignation with which they, in common with the whole of the people of India view the terrible crime committed by an Indian youth last Thursday, which resulted in the deplorable death of Sir Curzon Wyllie and also of Dr. Lalcaca".[9] The crime had destroyed, he hoped not for all time, the noble traditions of the Indian people not only for loyalty but for peaceful pursuits. The tragedy had cast a gloom upon two continents, indeed upon the whole civilized world. Nothing could be said in defense of so atrocious an act, some explanation of the motives of the crime would be conceivable, but considering the noble nature of the man upon whom the assassin's pistol was first turned, there could be no explanation of the slightest extenuation of so dastardly a crime.[10]

Mr. Amir Ali, in seconding the resolution, said that they had gathered to mourn the loss of a man who had made himself beloved by his deeds of personal friendship with Indians, and to express their indignation to the crime which had deprived the state of so distinguished a servant and the people of India of such a valued friend. For his part he felt that the occasion was not one for perfect eloquence; indeed, he could not himself find words to give expression to his sorrow and to his indignation in regard to a crime committed in state that could hardly be considered without emotion. But he might be permitted to say, without offending any person, or giving rise to any criticism, that at that moment there rested a great responsibility upon politicians and publicists both in India and England to weigh the language they used and to beware of exaggeration in questioning matters of state or in alluding to British rule in India in a manner likely to excite the feeling of hysterical youths.

At this stage Mr. Theodore Morrison, member of the India Council, stepped upon the platform holding by the hand a young

Indian, Bhajan Lal, the younger brother of Madan Lal Dhingra. He openly condemned the act of his brother and disassociated himself from the murderer. He was so overcome by emotions that he could hardly speak. Thereafter, Mr. Morrison said he wished to ask their sympathy for the youth who stood at his side. He was the younger brother of the student who committed the terrible crime on Thursday last.[11] When this youth went to him that day to ask what he should do in the dreadful circumstance and how he should express his own horror of a brother's crime, he replied—"Your proper course is to come and purge yourself of all sympathy with the crime before your own countrymen at the meeting tonight, and to tell them that, though the man who committed the deed is your brother, you wish to join with others with all Indians who will be gathered there, in repudiating sympathy and expressing horror in respect to the tragedy." Mr. Morrison added that the youngman had asked him on his behalf to say with what depth of sincerity he supported the resolution. Aga Khan read out the resolution.

The resolution being put to the meeting was carried with hearty applause. The chairman declared it unanimously passed, whereupon there was a cry from the middle of the room, "No not at all" and amid much uproar a young man rose to oppose the resolution.[12]

"Your name please".

At this, some lost their cool, and shouted, "Pull him down, and drive him out".

"It is me. My name is Savarkar".

At that moment Sir Mancherjee Bhownagari jumped from the platform and ran in the direction of the voice. In the heat of the passion an Eurasian, swooped down upon Savarkar and struck him a blow on the forehead. Savarkar's face was besmeared with blood. His clothes were dripping and his spectacles broken to pieces. "With all this I say I am against the resolution." He said standing as firm as rock to maintain his opinion to the last drop of blood. As he was saying this Tirumalacharya, who was standing by Savarkar, thrashed the head of the fanatic, one Mr. Palmer and down went Palmer reeling. Aiyer was about to shoot Palmer but Savarkar winked at him and restrained him.[13]

Surendranath left the hall protesting against Savarkar. Sir Aga Khan too did not like the rashness of Sir Mancherjee Bhownagari. At last at the instance of Sir Mancherjee Bhownagari, the police interfered, but seeing that the truth was on Savarkar's side, they let him go.

A few chairs were brandished, and an East India gentleman Mr. Palmer received a blow upon the cheek. Mr. Savarkar was expelled in spite of the crowded state of the hall. Mr. Palmer advancing to the platform, made a brief speech, with blood streaming from his face. He said that he had ancestors who helped build up the British Empire in India and when a man deliberately came to that gathering of Indians of all castes and communities to raise his voice against the resolution, he felt that they would not be men if they did not with one consent expell him from there midst. The Indians in that country were enjoying the hospitality of the British people, at the present time constitutional privileges were being granted to India. The man who could in such circumstances, go to that meeting and object to condemnation of the dastardly crime of last Thursday was not worthy of any consideration at their hands.[14]

On the motion of Bhagwandin Dube, seconded by R.N. Mukherjee (of Messer's Martin and Co.), the second resolution was passed as follows:

"That this meeting considers it due to the British public to ensure them that they deplore with feelings of humiliation an act of this heinous character, committed in the metropolis of the British Empire, and beg that they will realize that it is the act of a fanatic or madman which has aroused the deepest indignation of all the people of India".

At this point Dr. Bhattacharji, who was summoned last February for assisting Sir W. Lee Warner, came forward and told that he had had no connection whatever with the Indian anarchist movement in London. He felt that it was fitting that he should express his heartfelt sympathy.

On the motion of Mr. D. Sen, seconded by Mr. Ghine, C.I.E., of Burma, a resolution was passed conveying to Lord Morley respectful sympathy the loss of so-trusted and efficient a officer as Sir Curzon Wyllie, "Who by his great courtesy and tact, had won the hearts of the princes and people of India during their visits and residence in Europe".

Cowasjee Jehangir proposed, and Mr. Senatihi Raja of Trivendrum, seconded, a vote of respectful condolence with Lady Wyllie. A similar vote of condolence with the family of late Dr. Lalcaca was submitted by Bipin Chandra Pal (who repeated the condemnation of the murderous outrage he had expressed at Saturday's meeting), and seconded by Dr. Abdul Majid.[15]

The resolution was supported by Mr. Cowasjee Jehangir, who spoke of his close friendship with Dr. Lalcaca. Mr. Syed Hassan Bilgrami proposed that copy of the resolution be forwarded with the suitable covering letter to Lady Wyllie, and also to the family of Dr. Lalcaca.[16] Major Sinha suggested that a memorial fund to Sir Curzon Wyllie should be raised, and should take the form of affording provision for assisting Indians in this country when in strained circumstances. The meeting closed with a vote of thanks to the chair proposed to Mr. J.M. Mullah and seconded by Mr. Abdul. Thus, the meeting organized at the Caxton Hall to abhor and condemn the 'Act of Dhingra' and to pass a resolution paying floral tribute to Sir Curzon Wyllie and Lalcaca ended.[17]

Dhingra's 'act' had encouraged a widespread condemnation and denunciation against him in England and India.[18] His family was the first to join the chorus of admonition. His younger

brother, Bhajan Lal, gave a lengthy interview to the press, expressing his abhorrence to the 'Act of Dhingra' which was duly published in the *Daily Chronicle.*[19]

Last night a representative of *The Daily Chronicle* had an interview in London, with Bhajan Lal, the younger brother of Madan Lal Dhingra. A quiet, smooth-cheeked, slimly-built youth, he offered a striking contrast to the rugged-faced Indian who now lies in Brixton Prison charged with the assassinations at the Imperial Institute.[20] His only resemblance to his brother, indeed, was that he wore a pair of gold-rimmed spectacles.

His eyes grew dim (writes our representative) as he spoke of the crimes.—"It is terrible", he said, with evident distress. "I cannot understand it at all. I feel it very, very keenly."

I asked him how long he had been in England.

"About a year", he said. "My brother, you, know, has been here for over two years. Have you seen him frequently since your arrival?"

"No, we have met very, very seldom. I have seen scarcely anything of him. He met me on my arrival in England, but since then we have been almost like strangers to each other."

Why did you not live together? "Because he did not want me—that is all."

"Do you know of any reason for this?"

"Well, he always liked to be by himself. When we were in India together he never made a companion of me. He was very reserved—exceedingly so. Altogether he was very peculiar in his habits".

"When did you see him last?"

"About two months ago".

"What did he say?"

"We did not speak".

"Has he written to you from time to time?"

"No, he never wrote. So I have seldom known what he has been doing. In my letters, I have occasionally mentioned him, but I have never had very much to tell."

"So I may take it that you do not know whether he has had any companions or not?"—"No, I do not know at all."

"Did you know that your brother in India had written to Sir Curzon Wyllie regarding Madan?"

"No. I don't know."

"Not at the 'At Home'".

"You were of course not present at the Imperial Institute last Thursday night?"

"Well, I had an interview to the 'At Home' but I was unable to go".

I then asked him how he first heard of the assassination.

With quivering lips he replied, "When I went out after breakfast on Friday morning.

I saw a placard that there had been some assassinations by an Indian in London. With just ordinary curiosity I went into a shop and bought a paper. I was horror-struck as I looked at the account which it gave. I saw my brother's name; it was misspelt, but clearly Madan was referred to. I did not know what to do. I felt helpless. I spoke to a friend, but there was nothing that he could advise me to do. I was beside myself with grief."

"You had no idea what were the political views of your brother?"

"I can't remember that I ever heard him talk very much about politics. I, myself, am not very much interested in them. He was, as I have said, exceedingly reserved. He was also somewhat excitable. I cannot think what made him do this—unless it is lunacy."

"Have you heard from your brother since his arrest?"

"No not a word—".

Finally, said that he was anxious to, go to the Caxton Hall to show—silent though his testimony was—that he himself was a loyal subject, and that the assassinations were abhorrent to him.

Again, however, his eyes moistened, as, maybe, he thought of his brother lying in a prison cell. Thus, do the innocent suffer with the guilty?[21]

How far these meetings of condemnation were important and necessary? It was definitely a necessary exercise required to win the sympathy and confidence of the British Government and its people, who after the 'Act of 1 July', considered all the Indian students as anarchists. The leaders feared that the 'act of Dhingra' might jeopardize the career of many such students in England. There was a common feeling among the Indian youths, what if the government retaliates? What will happen to them if the British people refused to accept them as paying guest? Above all it was feared that the situation ought not to effect ongoing reform efforts for India, as at that time government was considering of granting constitutional privileges to the Indians.

C.A. Elliott had written to *The Times*, expressing his concern over the present situation. He wrote: "The assassination of Sir Curzon Wyllie has been a severe blow, not only to the estimation in which Indian students are held in England, but also to the aspirations of many Anglo-Indians who have done so much to befriend them and to make their lives here pleasant and beneficial to themselves. They come to England in most cases without any introduction or references of any sort, and they have been received with open-handed kindness and hospitality by many private persons. The three main associations in London—the Northbrook, the National Indian, and the East Indian—have welcomed them as members on payment of slight subscriptions, and admitted them to their receptions and discussions in large numbers". Mahatma Gandhi, who had gone to England to study Law at Inner Temple, one of the Four Inns of Court in 1888, had praised the British hospitality.[22]

Elliott further wrote, "Many persons are asking, can this state of things continue? What security have we that those whom we admit among our wives and families are not imbued with the same anarchical sentiments and involved in the same conspiracy as the murderer Dhingra?"[23] He informed, "It is only a few days ago that I invited more than 100 of these students to an entertainment in my garden; and I candidly confess that I should not feel justified, for the sake of other guests, in repeating such an invitation, except to those of whose loyalty and non-complicity in anarchical plots I had obtained some conviction."[24]

After July 1, the Indian students were under strict surveillance of the British intelligence and doubtful glare of the common Briton. The major fear of the Indian leaders in England was that the 'Act of Dhingra', might not disrupt the process of on-going constitutional reforms under Morley, the Secretary of State, for India. This fear was also expressed even by the members of British Parliament. Mr. Ramsay Macdonald said—"In the maze of every political movement there are persons whose minds are overbalanced. The murder of last night is the work of these persons. This is a time for statesmanship and not for panic. I am deeply grieved at the crime which has been committed, but I should be more deeply grieved if the crime stopped the progress of political reform in India."[25] Dr. B.H. Rutherford, who had associated himself with the reform movement in India, expressed similar views. "Such crimes", he said, "do an enormous amount of harm. They jeopardize genuine and good movement. I abhor them, but I hope this one will not be allowed to stand in way of the legitimate aspirations of the people of India."[26]

Similar concern was cxpressed by Mr. Banerjee in the meeting, hastily summoned and attended by the most influential Indians residing in London on July 2.[27] He said, "I deplore the incident on every ground. It is calculated to do a lot of harm. I hope that it will not be allowed to retard the work of reform in anyway. Those in authority know that the bulk of people have nothing whatever to do with it".[28] He pointed out that it was an act of an individual and common man was not involved in it.

"This is a stray incidence altogether", he wrote, "I have been meeting your youngmen in various parts of the country, and I have told them that they must set their face against violence and murder, and have been loudly cheered. There is, of course, some excitement among our youngman, but there is absolutely no sedition."

It was an appropriate move on the part of some intelligent and seasoned politicians to organize such meetings to pacify the tension, and to clear the doubts, created in the minds of many in England, about the sincerity of the Indian students. The meeting of July 5 was organized by the Indians, along with the British members; to show solidarity with the British Government, to condemn the assassination of Sir Curzon Wyllie, and to project as a gentleman, a true friend of the Indians and to discourage other Indian youth, lest they considered Dhingra as their role model. But the meeting did not conclude the way the organizers had wanted. Savarkar with his 'No' to the resolution of Dhingra's condemnation, not only disrupted the smooth conduct of the proceedings, but also succeeded in registering his protest and dissent. Why he acted so, is a big question. He could have kept quiet, the way many other Indians did that day. Did he try to seek the public attention? No, as such recognition, he knew it well, could land him into more troubles with the British Government. Perhaps, he could not control his emotions and the only obeisance he could pay at that moment to his great hero Madan Lal Dhingra, was, by protesting. The outcome of his 'No' was very much expected; just as the result of the 'Act of Dhingra' would lead to wide condemnation was anticipated. He was thrown out of the meeting, being held in the Caxton Hall. The things did not end here, soon a cold war started between the Indian revolutionaries and the British administrators in the columns of the newspapers, especially in *The Times*, which continued to dominate the political arena in England, till the final verdict on Dhingra was announced. The following letters of the various people pleading for and against the 'Act', omissions, and repressive policies of the British Government in India, presented an interesting picture and help the reader to understand and have a look into the psyche of the British Rule in India.

The letters to the editors which had started at personal note soon engulfed other questions related to India and the problems of the Indians. The newspaper published letters which questioned the legality of the British Rule in India challenged, and deplored the working of the administrative machinery of the government and its agents in India. The effect of those letters to the editors could be well noticed when the questions raised and discussed in the newspapers, were raised in the Parliament making the cause of Indian grievances and distress part of British Parliament. This was the major impact and outcome of the 'Act of Dhingra'. A careful study of the letters to the editors published in *The Times* would help in understanding their views and opinion about the Indian leadership and general people, it will help to comprehend the political state of affairs in England, from where all the legal matters and policies to govern and control the Indian State originated.

Savarkar had been thrown out of the meeting held at Caxton Hall on July 5, for his big 'No', and to clarify his stand on the issue, he wrote to *The Times*:

"The fact is that when the President put the resolution before the meeting and asked those in favour of the same to raise their hands, and he acknowledged the right in accordance with the invariable practice in all public meetings of everyone who was present to vote according to his choice. The resolution was explained by those who proposed and seconded it so as to presume the criminality of the man who is accused of having committed the murder. It seemed to me an encroachment upon the authority of the law course to declare a man criminal, who is still under trial. The man accused of the murder has made no confession. So, it seemed to me more just and appropriate to omit the word crime and criminals from the resolution. As the proceedings had advanced too far to affect this I simply voted against the resolution as it stood and wanted to bring to the notice of the President the fact that the resolution could not be declared as passed unanimously. I was perfectly within my right as a voter, and the only proper way for the President was to account the votes against and for and declare the results. But some excited spirits forgot themselves so much as to shout eject him and even went so far as to threaten me with physical force. I stood perfectly calm simply asserting my right and without giving the least provocation. In a minute or two one man, Mr. Palmer by name reached to the place where I was standing and attacked me while I was actually in the act of explaining the meaning of my opposition in clear terms, thought, they were drowned in the cry of the excited few. The man who committed this unprovoked assault upon one who simply insisted upon either being heard or ejected will soon be brought before the courts. Meanwhile I hastened to write this letter to you to explain my conduct at the meeting and to prevent any misunderstanding or misinterpretation."[29]

From legal point of view, Savarkar was right in his assertion, that such meetings have no right to pass aspersions on Dhingra, as his case was still pending in the court and could affect the judgment. Savarkar's action in the Caxton Hall, further highlighted the 'Act of Dhingra' and forced many to delve deep into the basic causes responsible for his action. Had the former not objected to the resolution, the things would have sailed smoothly, and the 'Act of Dhingra' won't have received the public attention which soon followed after that incidence.

The letter of Savarkar prompted Palmer to post his reply to clear his stand on the July 5 incident. He immediately wrote to *The Times*, "Savarkar, either for purposes of notoriety or from a spirit of fiendish vindictiveness, protested against the resolution, and attempted to make the meeting an absolute fiasco. Springing forward at the reiterated request of the gentlemen on the platform, I endeavoured to put the man out. A partisan of his, standing on a chair, struck me on the head with his stick. I stepped back, and feeling that I must act promptly, I planted a truly British blow between the eyes of Savarkar who had raised a chair to fell me. Others hustled him and his companions out of the room and the meeting proceeded without any further interruption."[30]

He justified his act and commented, "I am not sorry for what I did. I am an Indian amongst Indians. The traditions of my descent are glorious and I could not and would not tarnish it by any act of hesitation at a critical moment. Nor will I tolerate any act of aggression against the British race from whom I am descended—for my fathers helped to build the India of today, and though only an East Indian denied the political rights that have already been granted to Muslim and Hindu, yet I and the 1,00,000 able bodied young East Indians, the majority of whom bear arms as volunteers, will never flinch when duty calls...." Shameless as he was, his letter carried no logical argument to defend his act, and he tried to justify it in the name of 'British Race'.

Virendranath Chattopadhyaya, in support of Savarkar, wrote to *The Times.* "Sir, I have read with much satisfaction Mr. V.D. Savarkar's letter in todays issue of *The Times.* Being detained by urgent business, I was unable to be present at the protest meeting held yesterday in the Caxton Hall. But it was my intention to proceed there, and in the event of M.L. Dhingra's criminality being assumed by the supporters of the resolution, to enter an emphatic protest. I am glad this was done by Savarkar. Had I been present I would have supported him at the risk of being ejected, and there would have been two voices raised against the resolution. In saying this I do not express any sympathy with the assassinator. In my opinion the programme of the terrorists is an absolutely suicidal one. But I think we all have the right to express our opinions honestly, and if we take objection to the words of the resolution, I see no reason why force should be used to expel us."[31]

Chattopadhyaya was well aware of the consequences and effect of the political assassination upon the progress of national movement. He wrote, "But, anxious as I am to see 'anarchism' obliterated from my country. I cannot consciously help the British Government to suppress it, as I am firmly convinced, as every nationalist is that their whole policy is wrong and is calculated to produce no other result than it has already done. You, Sir, have always advocated repression and coercion, and the vast majority of your countrymen accept this as the only method of continuing to rule India. But coercion will drive India headlong into destruction, and, if you still believe you are there in the interest of humanity, you will be disillusioned earlier than you think." He protested and warned the British administration of the coming consequences if they do not adhere to protests and petitions of the Indians. He warned the British administration, "The catalogue of coming assassinations will probably be a long one, and the responsibility for its length will have to be laid at the door of those who, instead of espousing the cause of Indian freedom, wish to hold India in the interest of Britain."[32]

An anonymous writer wrote to *The Times*, in reply to Savarkar's letter, the author highlighted certain facts about Savarkar and his comrades. He pointed to the address mentioned by Savarkar, in his letter to the editor. He wrote, "There lie before me the three last copies of *Swaraj*, the *Indian Nationalist*, and described as edited by 'Shriju' Bipin Chandra Pal, who at Saturday's meeting so strongly condemned political assassination, and the office of which 'Fortnightly organ of Indian Nationalism' is stated to be 140, Sinclair Road West Kensington, from where Mr. Savarkar addressed his letter to *the Times*."[33]

He also pointed out that these nationalist leaders were trying to launch another movement from foreign land as the British Indian Government had undermined their efforts in India. He disclosed to the press that Savarkar, Khaparde and Bipin Chandra Pal were planning to form a limited liability company called the Hind Nationalist Agency (Ltd.).[34] The list of objects of the agency was proceeded by a statement signed by Mr. G.S. Khaparde and Mr. Bipin Chandra Pal it was as followed—"During the present year there have been many significant occurrences in our country, and it is becoming increasingly manifest that the Indian Nationalist Party though it had suffered heavily by the exile or incarceration of its leaders, has been steadily gaining ground, and has already become a very powerful factor in shaping and determining the destinies of India. But the attitude of the British Government has made it almost impossible to conduct even an honest nationalist journal in India, while the suppression of our leading organs such as *Bande Matram*, has left a great gap which must be filled. It has, therefore, become eminently necessary that a journal should be published from Europe or America in the interest of the Indian nationalism and we think this an exceedingly opportune moment because we have among us here in England not only well-known nationalist, but one man in particular who has rendered conspicuous and meritorious service in the Nationalist Case."

The anonymous writer had questioned the credentials of the agency. "What were the significant occurrences to which Messers G.S. Khaparde[35] and Bipin Chandra Pal referred as strengthening the nationalist case other than the criminal acts and purpose of which the later now publicly declared his detestation?"

The correspondent challenged the attitude of the British Government resulting in a "great gap" in India, other than the exercise of its powers to repress and punish political crime and incitements thereto? He questioned: "Why was *Bande*

Matram of which Mr. Bipin Chandra Pal was one of the founders and first editor—suppressed after repeated prosecution of its printers and managers?"[36]

Unquestionably, the answer was to be found in the warning originally given to the conductors of the papers by Sir Andrew Frazer's Government more than two years ago. Under the sedition sections of the Indian Penal Code, unless the paper seized to use language instigating violence and lawlessness, legal proceedings would be taken against it.

He further wrote, "The conspicuous and meritorious services that Bipin Pal has rendered to the Nationalist case, is on record in the files of *The Times*, and elsewhere and his present protestation of the entirely lawful character of the movement would be more convincing were he to make confession of past mistakes in writing and in oratory." The effect of the provocative language on the impressionable minds has the potential of instigating anarchism, thus creating a serious problem of law and order for the government.[37]

The anonymous correspondent had laid specific charges on the prominent Indian leaders present at that time in England. For a moment, it seemed that the ingenuity of leaders had been exposed and soon they will come to their knees, as the writer had desired and planned, but the reply forwarded by Bipin Chandra Pal, the main accused in his defence, doomed such dreadful intentions. The allegations were severe and Bipin Chandra Pal answered them in detail, exhibiting his profound understanding on the subject matter, as such this letter is being produced below:

'The Extremist Attitude'

To the editor of *The Times*,

Sir, my attention has been drawn to a letter from an anonymous correspondence that appeared in *The Times* yesterday under the above heading. I hope you will do injustice to me personally and to the school of thought to which I have the honour to belong, permit to say a few words on the insinuation of this correspondence. Mr. Savarkar has for sometime past been living with me, if it is a crime to have entertained him as a "Paying Guest" in my house I plead guilty to it. This is the first time that I hear that a person is responsible for the act or opinion of those whom he entertain as guest paying or otherwise. In the next phase a few lines are quoted from the appeal of the Hindu Nationalist Agency. This appeal is not signed by Khaparde or myself, but our names appear as the organizers of the agency. If there is anything criminal or murderous about the appeal I plead guilty to the charge and am prepared to stand my trial upon the indictment. If to condemn official repression, which has been the psychological and origin of the various acts of violence in Bengal, be a crime, I plead guilty to it, and challenge to be brought to trial for it.

If to find and edit *Bande Matram* is a crime I cannot help pleading guilty to it also. But it is significant that no such prosecution was started against this paper as long as I was in-charge of it. Though it openly declare absolute autonomy as the nationalist ideal in India, as elsewhere. All the prosecutions were started after I left the paper, and as even then, accept the last, which lead to its suppression. The last article, too, was a reproduction of what the *Pioneer* had written, but it offered a sufficient plea to the government, too eager to suppress all honest expressions of political opinion favouring the ideal of national freedom and to crush it by the exercise of special powers assumed through a new enactment.

The writer speaks of my past mistakes in writing and oratory. I do not admit that these are mistakes. I do not budge an inch from my old position. I have nothing to alter and amend in anything that I have written and said during the last five or six years. If these opinions are criminal I am prepared to face the consequences of preaching them. Why was I not prosecuted for them? Why I was not punished for them even by the

Government of India, where justice means in political cases, often times a good deal more than what it mean here? I had never been hauled up for sedition even in India where almost anything can be construed as such.

It is not for me to say whether the murder of Sir Wyllie is political or personal. Those who discuss these questions now weave theories concerning them out of their own inner consciousness, encroach upon the function of the judge and the jury who will soon inquire into this matter, and commit thereby the contempt of court.

But the fairness of your anonymous correspondent is seen, however, from the fact that while he so eagerly quotes from the appeal, which formed no part of the editorial matter of the *Swaraj*, he suppresses the most unequivocal declaration of opinion and policy to be found there. In the very first page it stated:

"The political ideal of Indian nationalism has always been to work out a peaceful change in the constitution of the state organization in India, with a view to help the people to realize there divinely appointed destiny as a free nation among the free nations of the world. It is an essentially spiritually and humanitarian ideal. It is the desire of the spirit of the composite Indian nation to come to its own. It implies no enmity to any other people or the country. The sporadic outburst of violence in Bengal that had attracted excessive attention during the past year do in no way represent either the true ideal or the actual methods of Indian nationalism. These never had the support of the leaders of the movement, but were due entirely to the repressive acts of the Indian executives. The national leaders in India have always recognized the futility of political assassination as an instrument for the attainment of popular freedom. It may bring about a change of despots, but has never in any part of the world achieved popular freedom. The avowed methods of Indian nationalism have therefore been the peaceful methods of passive resistance."

Again, in commenting upon the murder of Mr. Ashutosh Biswas, the popular prosecutor at Alipur, he said: "We sincerely regret this crude scene of political violence. They retard the progress of our cause. They are recklessly increasing the cost of national freedom in India. They tend to indefinitely prolong and infinitely increase the bitterness of the struggle for civic rights everywhere. They are calling up the fury of animal passions in a race that had long brought these under control."

"Political freedom is valuable, not for itself, but for those opportunities of self-realizations, in every sense of the term, which it offers. The spiritual life is the truest life: politics and economics, art and literature, commerce and industry—all these are only contributories to it; and there value and significance are not in them but in their capacity to help the development of this spiritual life."

"But if these outrageous imitations of European revolutionary propaganda are adopted by us, that national end will be seriously injured by the brutal instinct and passion which they will necessarily arouse. That is the danger of these outbursts of political violence in India. They have a fatal tendency towards denationalizing the national movement and divorcing it from the eternal spirit of the Indian nation. If we lose that spirit, what it avail, even if we achieve the sovereignty of the three worlds?"

But not only do we condemn these as the higher grounds of ethics and religion, but we consider them even as suicidal to the cause of real national freedom. And we brought this out most clearly in the very issue of the advertisement column of which your correspondent makes his quotations. In page nine we said:

"Those who are pursuing this method of counter-violence do not seem to realize the risks that their acts involve to the political future of their nation. Either they will succeed or they will fail. And, but, if they succeed, they may make the government impossible. But to make the administration impossible by peaceful passive resistance is one thing and to make it impossible by breaking it up is another. In the former case popular freedom is secured by strictly constitutional methods; in the latter case, the country must pass through a period of military ascendancy which in view of the disorganized condition of the general civic population of India at the present time, and only mean for us a military dictatorship. In other words, a national autocracy, either Hindu or Mohammedan and more like a Mohammedan than Hindu, will, if these attempts ultimately succeed, suppliant the British Bureaucracy and that would mean another India's fierce struggle that will be measurably keen and more bitter than we have yet ever known. This is the risk of success of this campaign of political violence. If it does not succeed, it will mean greater and deeper demoralization of the people and the total ruin of the little work that has already been done. In the way of quickening a new national life in them in either case, thus, risks of this propaganda are very great; and no statesmanship would lend its support to it."

My utterances on this assassination have been prompted by sense of public duty. My God ordered me to speak, and I have spoken. I do not care as to who accept my sincerity and who does not. I am not a politician. I was asked by the press representative the other day whether this assassination was not exceedingly deplorable as likely to alienate British sympathizers from the Indian reformers. My reply was: "I do not care a pin about British sympathies or antipathies. I would condemn it even if the whole British Nation approved of it. I condemn it because it is wrong. I condemn it with God and I do so against all the world."

Bipin Chandra Pal[38]

110, Sinclair Road, West Kensington, July 9.

In reply to the anonymous letter, The Extremist Attitude,

Virendra Chattopadhyaya wrote to the editor of *The Times* clearing the stand of the Indian nationalist leaders who had been blamed of political violence in the country. In reply to the allegations, Chattopadhyaya commented, "I cannot imagine anything so grotesquely ignorant as the suggestion that Bipin Chandra Pal, of all people, is to be connected even remotely with the recent outrages. It is notorious that he has no place whatsoever in the council of those who advocate violence, and though I do not share his old world optimism as regard a 'peaceful revolution'. I am constrained to say that on no occasions, whether at a public gathering or in the secret intimacy of his own circle, has he ever countenanced violence of any description."[39]

Chattopadhyaya admitted for having drawn the prospectus which appeared in the journal *Swaraj*. He wrote, "I am responsible for having drawn it up with the sanction of Messrs. Khaparde and Pal." It is not to be expected, when we speak of services rendered to the nationalist cause by any leading man, that the British Government will consider them as "services" also. But that is just where the conflict lies, "We do not accept as crime every act which our foreign rulers in their own interest chose to call a crime. It is no crime, for instance, to boycott British goods or the British services or the British ideas or British men (and women). It is no crime to produce a moral and mental attitude in the people of India which will deprive our ruler of their moral support. And so long as we allow ourselves to hurt or kill no one, and to create no breach of peace, we are justifying in carrying our work in bringing about such a cooperation among the people of India as shall render the further existence of the British Government unnecessary."

Bampfylde Fuller, the former Lieutenant Governor of Bengal, had earned the wrath of the Indians for promulgating an order restricting the chanting of *Bande Matram*, a song that had become famous during Swadeshi and Boycott Movements. It encouraged a widespread agitation under Banerjee, and others in Bengal, against the draconian order and virtually leading to his exit. That dismissal perhaps, he could never forget and when the name and fame of Banerjee echoed in England, he decided to settle his old score with him.

He utilized the tense atmosphere, created by the 'Act of Dhingra' and tried to malign Banerjee's character through his letter to the editor of *The Times.*[40] The phraseology of his letter undoubtedly proves the point. He wrote, Sir, "At the recent conference of the Empire's Press, a representative who has been treated with special distinction is Mr. Surendranath Banerjee. He is the editor of the *Bengali*, published in Calcutta, which has acquired a remarkable influence over the student community by means of the virulent ability of its leading articles and the pruriency of its advertisements." He lamented over the distinctive status being accorded to him in England. He held him responsible for misguiding the youth of Bengal with his malignant writings.

He accused him for promoting, if not originating, boycott of British goods in India, causing huge economic loss to the British industry. He projected him as a staunch enemy of the British Kingdom in India. He blamed him for creating gulf between Hindus and Muslims, resulting in communal clashes.[41] His list of allegations did not end here. He wrote, "He is one of those who initiated the school 'volunteer corps' (now suppressed by law), which developed into nurseries of anarchy and led many unfortunate youths in the dock and some to the scaffold. At least one of the Bengali gentlemen who is now imprisoned without trial owes his perversion to Mr. Surendranath influence. Eighteen months ago Mr. Banerjee's services were acknowledged by a ceremony in which he was crowned 'King of Bengal'. This is the gentleman whom we have been delighting to honour. What must his Mohammedan opponent what must his Bengali friend—be thinking of us?"[42]

He levelled every possible charge against Banerjee which his mind could reflect, and thought could guide. Thereby, Bampfylde launched a well-planned and calculated move to counter Banerjee, while in England. Anyone else might have fumbled at the allegations, but Banerjee was a man of strong conviction, determination and straightforwardness, not to be towed or mowed down by such accusations. He framed his answer and posted it to *The Times*, which was duly published on July 13.[43] It was a lengthy letter where Banerjee responded to all the contentions levelled against him, fully extenuating his stand, and finally apprehending Fuller in his self-concocted cocoon.

Banerjee sent his reply to *The Times*, which was duly published next day:

To the editor of *The Times*

Sir, on Saturday last I was the subject of an attack by an ex-Lieutenant Governor of Bengal. I find in your issue of today that I am the honoured recipient of a similar measure of attention from another ex-Lieutenant Governor. This time it is Sir Bampfylde Fuller, who, you will remember, was the first Lieutenant Governor of the new province and the author of that respective policy which in respect of many of its most important features Lord Morley found it necessary to discontinue. Sir Bampfylde Fuller, in a letter published in *The Times* said:

"If Mr. Banerjee did not originate the boycott of British goods, he was its principal sponsor, and is more than anyone else responsible for a movement which has thrown Hindus and Mohammedans into violent opposition.

It is a literary achievement of no small merit to be able to put so many misleading statements in so terse form and within so brief a compass. With regard to the part I have played in connection with the Swadeshi movement, I will repeat what I said in reply to the observations of your's Calcutta correspondence, which, unfortunately, you were not able to publish, viz. that I was indeed the leading spirit of the Swadeshi Boycott Movement, which is not anti-British at all, the object of the movement being, as expressed in the terms of the resolution creating it, "To call the attention of the British public to the contemptuous disregard of the Indian public opinion" in the matter of the partition of Bengal. An anti-British movement would not appeal to the British public for justice. Sir Bampfylde Fuller seems to think that this movement has thrown Hindus and Mohammedans into a violent opposition. Let me say in reply that in addition to the partition of Bengal his own policy as Lieutenant Governor of the new province was largely responsible for this result. Does he remember the historic occasion when he said that he had two wives—the one a Hindu and the other a Mohammedan, and that the Mohammedan was the favourite wife? It was said that half in jest, half in seriousness; but the Hindu population were at no loss to grasp the new situation and the new policy—the policy of preference of one class over another; that was the genesis of that class bias in the administration of the new province which still survives, and which has done so much to sow the seeds of bitterness and discontent among the Hindu population. Sir Bampfylde Fuller says that the Swadeshi movement has thrown Hindus and Mohammedans into violent opposition. This is a very ancient official view which has again and again been exploded, but which has as often been reaffirmed by its supporters with a magnificent disregard of facts. On the face of it one theory is absurd; for the Swadeshi movement is calculated to benefit Hindus and Mohammedans alike, and the Mohammedans even more so than the Hindus; for the bulk of the weavers of home-made cloth (the *Julahas*) are Mohammedans. The *Musselman*, an organ of Mohammedan opinion published in Calcutta, takes this view of the matter and gives facts and figures with which I will not trouble your readers, but I am prepared to submit them if necessary. The special correspondent of the *Statesman* newspaper, who was an Englishman, and went down to Jamalpur, in Eastern Bengal, in 1907, in connection with the riots that broke out there, says, "They (the Mohammedans) might not have been previously interested in the Swadeshi movement. They may not have liked or approved of the boycott, but they did not appear to think that there was any reason to take upon themselves the task of suppressing the Swadeshi ebullitions by physical force". He added: "Some mysterious influence seems to have been at work here and elsewhere" to create this violent opposition between Hindus and Mohammedans. Mr. Romesh Chandra Dutt, C.I.E., who was for three years magistrate of Mymensigh in East Bengal and possessed intimate knowledge of the situation thus observed in relations to the ill-feelings between Hindus and Mohammedans in some of the Districts of East Bengal: "The Swadeshi movement is not the cause; insofar as its interests the more ignorant Mohammedans that are rather in its favour, as it widens their industries and adds to their earnings."

I do not know what Sir Bampfylde Fuller means by saying that "I initiated the school volunteer corps", "which has now been suppressed by law", and which he says developed into "nurseries of anarchy". There is not, and there never was to my knowledge, such a thing as school volunteer's corps. I am connected with a great educational institution; there never was a school corps attached to this institution. On the occasions of great public function such as religious fair or a political or social demonstration, young men organized themselves as volunteers to help the pilgrims who come to the fairs, or the delegates who attend the conferences and the congresses, and they have always rendered splendid service. The government acknowledged the services of these volunteers on the occasion of Ardhodaya Joga in Calcutta in February 1908; this was a religious fair attended by poor 1,00,000 people. The volunteers protected the women, attended the sick, and cremated the dead. In April last a large body of volunteers helped the hundred thousand pilgrims who attended the Tarakeshwar Fair and elicited the warm recognition of the authorities. What Sir Bampfylde Fuller probably means is that some *samitis* or societies have been suppressed by the government such as the Anushilan Samiti and the Bandhub Samiti. I was not connected with either of them; and as far the Bandhub Samiti, I desire to say that it did splendid work in connection with the famine at Barisal, and that the Anushilan Samiti. It also rendered valuable help on the occasion of recent famine in parts of Bengal. The suppression of these *samitis* without formulating any charges against them, or giving them an opportunity of explanation in defence, is a proceeding which may commend itself to Sir Bampfylde Fuller, but will, I am sure, be strongly condemned by the majority of Englishmen.

As for the crowning incidence, the less said the better; for I believe even those who concocted this lie are ashamed of it. It is an ordinary incidence of Indian life accompanied by garlanding and other accessories which takes place everyday. At Manchester my countrymen garlanded me as a mark of honour at every marriage ceremony the bridegroom is garlanded and crowned. That Sir Bampfylde Fuller should rake up this incident and try to make capital out of it shows that he is profoundly ignorant of ordinary Indian life, although he lived in the country for over thirty years, or that he makes an attack upon me which he must know to be absolutely baseless. For myself, I am not surprised at this attack, for I lead agitation against his repressive policy which culminated in his resignation. He talks about my having "perverted" one of the deportees. Nobody has a right to say—

not even Sir Bampfylde Fuller—anyone of them was "perverted" either by me or anyone else, in the absence of any definite charges against them or of proof in support of such charges.

Surendranath Banerjee[44]

Flat 83, 3 and 4, Clement's Inn, London, W.C., July 12.

Banerjee's letter in *The Times* attracted the attention of C.A. Elliott. He immediately wrote back to the paper, and his letter was duly published under the title 'Indian Loyalty'.[45] Elliott challenged Banerjee's contentions and wrote, "He asserts that I was mistaken in my charge against him"—that he "Never raised his voice in Calcutta to assert his detestation of the policy of assassination." If he can show that he organized or assisted at any public meeting to protest against the attempts made on the life of Sir Andrew Frazer, the shooting of Mr. Allen, the murder of the two ladies at Muzzaffarpur and other similar crimes, I will admit my error. He challenged Banerjee, "I have been a careful reader of Indian news, and have seen nothing of the kind reported. That he joined in a meeting to protest against Ashutosh Biswas, a countryman of his own, only emphasizes the omission for which I condemn him." Elliott in his early letter to the editor of *The Times* had accused Banerjee that he never raised his voice in Calcutta.[46] Elliott in his letter wrote, "I do not understand his meaning when he says that this is not the only misstatement in my letter. I wrote that while the Indian 'Parliamentary Committee' passed a vote of condolence and sympathy with poor Lady Wyllie they did not signify their abhorrence of the crime. This he cannot deny. I said that it was not enough for Indian student to attend a meeting at which the resolutions of abhorrence were passed. His only reply is that such a meeting was held. We know that at Caxton Hall meeting there were at least two dissentients. We do not know how many more of those present shared in such views. What I have suggested is that all who wish publicly to disassociate themselves from the campaign of assassination should voluntarily sign a declaration to this effect."[47]

Banerjee replied, "It is absolutely untrue that I never raised my voice in Calcutta to assert my detestation of the policy of assassination there practised". At public meetings and in the column of the *Bengali*, of which I am the editor, I have throughout strongly and persistently denounced the anarchical crime, which I deplore, in common with my countrymen. The meetings, one of the students' of Calcutta and another of the general public held in the Town Hall, held after the assassination of the public prosecutor of the 24 Parganas, were largely organized by me. I presided at the students' meetings and I was the principle speaker at the Town Hall meeting. My speeches on both occasions were published in the newspapers. But Sir Charles Elliott writes with an ignorance of facts deeply to be regretted in one who was lately a Lieutenant Governor of Bengal; nor is this the only misstatement of facts in the short letter which he writes.[48]

Elliott further asserted, "Mr. Banerjee's speech at the New Reform Club was very significant of the real inwardness of his profession. He said that he and his community were willing to cooperate with the government, but that if there representations (e.g. on the partition of Bengal) were brushed aside (they were most carefully considered) they had no power to help the government. In other words, they would only cooperate if the government did nothing they disagreed with. By this we may gauge the loyalty of Mr. Banerjee."[49]

In reality, Banerjee's answer had left Fuller dumb founded. To make his face saving he wrote back to *The Times*, but his reply lacked the thrust, and support to substantiate his argument. He tried to save his skin by saying, "I cannot be expected to enter the lists against Mr. Surendranath Banerjee with a defence of my administration of the new province, or an elaboration of statements the literal truth of which is perfectly well-known to everyone in Bengal."[50] Banerjee had grounded him and his allegations.

Banerjee had emphasized that the partition of Bengal and

the policy of Sir Bampfylde Fuller had been largely responsible for encouraging disunity among Hindus and Muslims in Bengal. He had also reminded Fuller the historic occasion when he said that he had two wives—the one a Hindu and the other a Mohammedan, and that the Mohammedan was the favourite wife?[51] In reply to the accusations laid by Banerjee, Fuller wrote, "In the course of a private visit, a Bengali gentleman of some standing in the province expressed a desire to use his efforts to reconcile the Hindus with the government and with the Mohammedans. I accordingly explained the situation to him with frankness, and, falling into the parable form with which the East is so familiar, I likened myself to a man with two wives one Hindu and other Mohammedan, with equal claims, but one of whom was doing her best by her behaviour to throw him into the arms of the others. The similitude had the merit of expressing exactly the facts of the position. The conversation was, as I have said, private. But my visitor went from my room to the *Telegraph* office and reported it, to a good deal embroidered, to the Bengali newspapers."[52] Once again he seemed to reach for words to answer Banerjee's counter charges.

Banerjee's letter attracted the attention of another critic who wrote an anonymous letter to the *Times* stating that the charges levelled by Fuller that Banerjee is the editor of the *Bengalee*, published in Calcutta, which has acquired remarkable influence over the student community by the means of the virulent ability of its leading articles and the pruriency of its advertisements,[53] he further added, "May I direct his attention to the last five words of that sentence?" These five words were 'The pruriency of its advertisements'. The writer further wrote, "On September 13, 1906, you published a letter attacking Mr. Banerjee upon this very ground in the course of which writer spoke of Mr. Banerjee newspaper as follows—Bengali which, on remunerated terms for itself, supplies the precocious youth of Bengal with so much suggestive information as to the means of mitigating the evil consequences of sexual indulgence, is edited by Mr. Surendranath Banerjee, the headmaster of one of the largest native schools in Calcutta." He concluded, "A gentleman who conducts a large boy school in Calcutta, and at the same time edits a paper trading in filth of this kind, is a person to whose professions of civic virtue no respectable Englishman who knows the fact is likely to pay any attention."[54]

The letters to the editor in the newspapers were mostly related to the problem of unrest in India, the burning topic which had attracted the attention of many to its fold after the 'Act of Dhingra', and everyone was busy in finding causes for its genesis and growth. The letters to the editors reflected the mood of the public in general in England. The editor of *The India*, in reply to Mrs. Flora Annie Steel's assumption that "There is no line of demarcation in the minds of millions of India between the unrest which produces the crop of disloyal questions in Parliament or edits a paper like *The India*, and the anarchism which wantonly murders a friend simply because he is an Englishman."[55]

He further wrote that the members of Parliament who are attacked in this indiscriminate fashion are quite capable of taking care of themselves. But I must ask you to be so good as to allow me to reply at once to the insinuations made against the paper which I have the honour to edit. It would be interesting to know how many numbers of *The India* Mrs. Steel has read; but I unhesitatingly challenge her to quote a single editorial utterance from its columns in which the methods of strictly constitutional agitation have not been persistently and earnestly advocated. It is much to be deprecated that, at moment like this, attempts should be made to irritate the great body of moderate and the loyal opinion which India, strives to represent and which it is so important in Lord Morley's words to, "Rally" and strengthen in its adherence to British rule in India.[56] The British administration feared the rising tide of the public opinion against the Crown. They had gone to India to rule and loot, but under the garb of progress, growth, development and modernization. The handful educated Indian elite had discovered their hidden intentions and making it public. It was causing unrest and resentment among the masses, for whom the *mai baap* had turned out to be the real culprit. It was the effort of the administration to curb any such medium which propagate and spread 'Truth' in the people and as newspapers were the medium, were severely curbed, banned and its associates were arrested or exiled, the only way left for the administration to curtail the 'rising voices' against the Crown.

Those who questioned the utility and impact of Dhingra's act should know that his action had forced the British Government to pay considerable attention to the grievances of the Indians. It had forced the government to look into their flaws and plug the loopholes. The British Government never wanted to aggravate the situation. After the final verdict of the court on Dhingra, the following questions were raised in the Parliament of England, which were directly related to the Indian's grievances and certain extracts of such queries are being produced below.[57]

The Master of Elibank, M.P., Under Secretary of State for India, admitted at a Liberal Social Council, meeting held at Woodford-Green on Saturday evening, that the people of India were peace and justice loving.[58] When he came to look at the figures he was surprised to find that only one in 15,000 had made himself amenable to the criminal law; and he was certain that if the statistics of the other European countries were taken it would be found that percentage was considerably higher. Out of the 232 millions of people in British India and the vast number in the native states, only a small section were in any way imbued with disloyal sentiments to this country and his hearers might be perfectly certain that Lord Morley would do his duty undeterred by any criticism, and that he would deal drastically with those who, while keeping themselves in the background, maliciously, incited to disloyalty and disaffection towards this country. It was necessary that these rebellious agitations and waves of disloyal feelings should not be permitted to attain maturity, or the result would be most calamitous, not only to the agitators themselves but to the great Empire that was making such great progress in internal prosperity and civilization. He felt confident that the strong policy he was pursuing Lord Morley would have behind him the full backing of the country. Lord Morley was himself in favour of Indian reforms, as had been clearly shown by his India Council Bill, and by other legislation.

Mr. Kennedy (Cavan, W, Nat.) asked the Under Secretary of States for India, if he would state the number of deaths recorded in India as attributable to a famine for the last hundred years; what was the annual amount of revenue collected in India, giving the amounts of the same allocated for local and Imperial purposes, respectively; and would he say how many persons have been imprisoned or deported from India under the ordinary law and otherwise for the last five years?[59] Such queries could become possible, and Indian grievances got highlighted, only after Dhingra's act.

The Master of Elibank (Peebles and Selkirk, Min.)—The number of deaths in India in the last hundred years from starvation and famine is not ascertainable, as death registration is of comparatively recent origin in British India and is only very imperfectly established in native states. The gross revenue received in India in 1908-09, according to the revised estimates, was £ 69,035,100, of which about 45 millions was allocated to Imperial and about 24 millions to provincial purposes. These figures include considerable receipts of which arc not taxation. The total number of persons sentenced to imprisonment in British India in the five years ending 1907 (the last for which figures are available) was 785,857. The number of persons dealt with for the five years ending 1908 under Bengal Regulation

III of 1818 and the two other similar modes of procedure is 22:11 of these cases were connected with seditious movements against the British Government of which some cases were in May 1906, and nine in December 1908.

Mr. Rees asked the Under Secretary for India, whether seeing that prior to British Rule no mortality statistics were kept in India, that deaths attributable to famine and diseases resulting from famine had progressively declined during periodic failures of crops in the period for which statistics were available under British Rule, that the Mughal Emperors collected from the territories under their sway a larger land revenue than the British Government obtains from immensely larger Empire, the government could give any information regarding the mortality from famine in ante-British days for purposes of comparisons.[60]

The Master of Elibank—Such information as exists is necessarily of general kind, but it points to the conclusion that the mortality from famine in former times was much in access of anything that is now conceivable under British administration. The answer did not carry any substantiate proof.

Captain Faber (Hands Andover Opp.), asked the Under Secretary of States for India if he would state whether the Government of India had drawn the attention of the India Office to the danger caused by India House, and to the fact that leaders of sedition were posting to India large numbers of postcards and pamphlets.[61]

The Master of Elibank (Peebles and Selkirk, Min.)—The answer is in the affirmative. This Majesty's government is well aware of the character of these operations and the Home Office is taking such measures as or available for frustrating them.

Dr. Rutherford asked the Under Secretary of State for India, how many famines were there in India during the 25 years ending in 1887 and in 1907, respectively, with the official estimate of the loss of life involved during each period; and the names of the provinces which suffered more severely.[62]

The Master of Elibank (Peebles and Selkirk, Min.)—Omitting draughts of limited extent there were four great famines during the first period, the Orissa famine of 1865, the Northern India and Rajputana famine of 1868-70, the Bihar famine of 1873, and the Southern India famine of 1876-78. The Famine Commission of 1880 estimated the mortality in British India in these four famines at about 8,000,000 in excess of the normal. Much of the excess mortality was due to epidemic diseases obscurely connected with seasons of draught and privation. In the second period, there have been four great famines, the Upper India and the Central Province famine of 1893, which extended to Madras and Bombay and to Bengal and Punjab, the Rajputana and Central India famine of 1899, which also affected Bombay and Central Provinces, the Gujarat famine of 1899-1902, the United Provinces famines of 1907 which extended to parts of the Central Provinces and Punjab. The excess mortality in British India in 1895 has been estimated at 750,000 and in 1907 at 1,000,000. I am not aware that estimates have been made for the later famines. In the 1907 famine in the United Provinces, the provincial death rate was 36.47 per 1,000 against a normal 34.89, but there were only 11 deaths which after full enquiry could be attributed to want of food.

Mr. Rees and Mr. Gooch asked in the House of Commons to the Master of Elibank—Whether the cases of the nine deported Bengalis came up this month for reconsideration by the Government of India, or were merely reported in the manner prescribed by the regulation as a matter of administrative routine.[63]

Colonel Seeley (Liverpool Abererombie, Min.) replied that the regulation requires the officer in whose custody a state prisoner is to submit twice a year a report to the Government of India on the 'Conduct, health and comfort' of such state prisoners, in order that the Government of India may determine whether the orders for his detention shall continue in force or be modified.[64]

Indian leaders observed that the electors of the United Kingdom were the real rulers of India, but unfortunately the great bulk of the British people took little or no interest in Indian affairs. Governors and administrators were appointed, and the British public thereupon imagined its responsibilities were over and the task of administering India was left in the hands of the appointed few. Indian leaders held British administration and its repressive policies in India responsible for the rise of anarchism and terrorism in the country. The British administrators, on the other hand, blamed the Indian nationalist leaders for the deteriorating situation in the country. Banerjee reminded the government that formerly a parliamentary committee was appointed every 30 years to inquire into Indian administration. But this practice had been stopped. There was no reason why this practice should not be revived.[65] Public in England was justly agitated at the assassination of Sir Wyllie.[66] The circumstances were painful, but as case was still in the court, they did not wish to discuss it in the papers on which further light will presumably be thrown at trial, and therefore preferred to remain silent for the present.

There were many in the Parliament like Henry Cotton, who well understood the reasons for India's unrest, and people spoke openly against the repression of their own government. In Eng'and, the efforts of the leaders, like Gokhale, Banerjee, Bipin Chandra and Lajpat Rai seemed to have left a deep impact on some of the liberal Parliamentarians in England. They all were against the oppressive measure of the government and were in favour of responsive form of administration. Henry Cotton detested against the assumption that the murder afforded any evidence of the existence of any general or widespread anarchist conspiracy in India.[67] He said, "It is a question whether any such conspiracy exists. The judicial findings of the District and Sessions Judge of Alipur and of the High Court of Calcutta in Alipore and Midnapore conspiracy cases afford very strong reason for holding that it does not, and that there never was any Grave menace to very foundation of public peace and security." He further insisted, "When conspiracy charges after elaborate public trial extending over many months are found to breakdown completely and to rest, in fact, on false evidence concocted and manipulated by a corrupt police, there is at all events room for doubting whether high reputation and character have been imprisoned and deported without charge or trial is not also tainted and untrustworthy. It is true that there have been deplorable outrage in India, most of which have been appropriately punished. No one would wish to minimize the gravity of these offences, but no calm or judicial person would jump to the conclusion that they establish the existence of a general or widespread conspiracy. If these outrages constitute a system of terrorism on the one hand, it is indisputable that spies and informers and false and tutored witnesses constitute an equal system of terrorism on the others. I do not know what motive could have influenced the wretched murder of Colonel Wyllie—that will no doubt come at the trial; but I protest against the unwarranted assumption which without any proof in support of it connects this crime with a conspiracy in India."[68]

The Indian Nationalist Party, though it had suffered heavily by the exile or incarceration of its leaders, yet was steadily gaining ground, and had become a powerful factor in Indian political scene. But the attitude of the British Government had made it almost impossible to conduct even an honest nationalist journal in India. The majority of the moderate Indian leaders believed that revolution was no solution to India's ill. They knew well that radicalism could retard the progress of national freedom and constitutional progress in India. The letter of Bipin Chandra clearly indicated that Indian leadership was against adopting violent means for political gains.[69] The interesting point to be noted was that Chattopadhyaya, otherwise critical about Bipin Chandra Pal's policy and die-hard admirer of Dhingra, objects to an anonymous writer's accusation that Bipin Chandra Pal advocated violence. In fact, he defended Pal by stating, "I am constraint to state that on no occasions, he ever approved of violence of any description."[70]

The definition of violence and crime seemed to have taken a new shape in the context of Indian leaders and foreign rulers. What our leaders considered to be their basic right, British administration considered it an outrage against the Crown. For instance, boycott of British goods was adopted by the Indian National Congress Party as a peaceful means to force the British Government to accept their demands, but the government took it as affront to its economic and administrative policies, and tried to crush it with heavy hand. The Congress Party was trying to woo the Indian people to the cause of freedom struggle against the British Empire, the latter looked upon it as an aggression. Similarly, the freedom of the press was considered as a fundamental right by the Indians while the British administration considered it a headache, and tried to suppress it. Indian leaders were enjoying the liberal practice in England where the freedom of speech and expression was granted to all. This right had been denied to the people in India.

Commenting on the role of terrorism after the incidence W.S. Blunt wrote in his diary, "People talked about the political assassination as defeating its own end, but that is nonsense. It is just the shock needed to convince selfish rulers that selfishness has its limits of prudence. It is like the other fiction that England has her face slapped, she apologizes, not before."[71] As far the question of repression on the Indians was concerned, Henry Cotton emphasized, "I protest also against the insinuation which has been generally made, and from which yours columns are not exempt, that this crime is in any way attributable to or connected with the parliamentary agitation against the policy which is favoured by the government of repression by means of *letters de cachet* against individuals who are now lying in prisons without having been charged, and much less tried, for any offence. I and those with whom I am associated will continue through good and evil repute in our campaign against this un-English and intolerable procedure in respect of British subjects."[72]

The Indian leaders made it quite clear that for the unrest the government was largely responsible. The government had provided them education, the liberty of press, the local self-government and expanded councils, containing the germs of representative institutions but slowly and steadily the government was putting restrictions, on one pretext or the other. The leaders did point out that isolated cases of assassination should not divert Great Britain attentions from measures of reforms.[73]

Lord Morley's scheme of reforms had somewhat eased the situation, but could not fully satisfy the aspirations of the educated Indians. They were not fully satisfied but they took the scheme as a beginning of great possibilities. In fact, the reforms, which crystallized into the Act of 1909 were little more than an attempt to broaden the representation authorized by the Council Act of 1892. At the Centre, the maximum number of members for the Governor-General's Council was raised from sixteen to sixty, while in the provinces of Bengal, Madras and Bombay, the strength was increased from twenty to fifty. The number in the United Provinces was raised from fifteen to fifty. It is true that the principle of election was introduced for the first time, but the concession became a serious liability to the country since it was based on sectional and religious representation. The Act entitled members to move resolutions on the budget and on other subjects, but the basic character of the legislature as a mere deliberative body remained unchanged. The reforms gave no responsibility whatsoever to Indians to administer the affairs of their country.

The Morley's reforms had failed to revoke the partition of 1905, the major point of contention and resentment among the Bengalis.[74] Morley had denounced the partition of Bengal in the House of Commons as "a measure which was against the wishes of the majority of the people concerned", but government was not prepared to provide remedial measure for the same.[75] It was this settled fact that Bengal and the rest of India decided to unsettle. In Bengal, young and old, educated and unlettered, the landless labourer and the rich *zamindars*, all joined in one mighty effort to undo the partition. Indian leadership considered it as the root-cause of the present discontent.

The British administration had taken the plea that the population of Bengal had multiplied and it was difficult to maintain the finances and progress of such vast area. But the truth was that if "Finance was the test of efficiency, at that time the partitioned province was in a state of bankruptcy." The 'Swadeshi' movement gained a great impetus during the agitation, thus giving hope and encouragement to the India entrepreneur to start new enterprises for replacing British imports.[76]

The Indian leaders appealed to the British administrators to end the policy of coercion, repression and deportation without trial, the major cause of resentment among the Indian youths. Racial discrimination towards the Indian subjects was one of the major concerns and causes of discontent among the Indians including the tallest among them. Henry Cotton records in his book, *New India or India in Transition*, how Mr. Justice Mahmood, son of the famous Sir Syed Ahmed Khan, was not allowed to visit the Madras Club even though he had accompanied Sir Charles Turner, the Chief Justice on the ground that he was a 'native'.[77]

The fair-minded Englishmen like Sir William Wedderburn and Henry Cotton were distinguished officers of the Indian Government. They won the gratitude of the Indian people by their vigorous championship of the Indian cause and in grateful recognition of their services; they were elevated to the

Presidentship of the Congress. The number of British friends of India was indeed large and included such stalwarts as John Bright and Charles Bradlaugh.

The Times correspondence established the fact that Dhingra's act was his own plan and it was not a planned conspiracy as believed by many. The confusion was mainly created by the statement made by the British Prime Minister Asquith, just after the assassination of Curzon Wyllie, "The crime afforded emphatic evidence of a seditious conspiracy on the part of a section of Indian people."[78]

Morley and his colleagues saw in Wyllie's assassination not only a tragic episode which had cost a precious life, but a symptom of things fraught with dangerous consequences on a wider scale. Morley had sent a telegram on 2 July, to Viceroy, Minto in India: "A most important thing to ascertain is whether the crime was the result of individual action or criminal conspiracy."[79] Morley was convinced that the crime was politically motivated.[80] Dhingra's own evidence in the course of proceedings entirely bore out this view; and in today's press there is published a statement drawn up by him, though not read at the trial, which opens as follows: "I admit the other day I attempted to shed English blood as a humble revenge for the inhuman hangings and deportations of patriotic Indian youths. In this attempt I have consulted none but my own conscience. I have conspired with none but with my own duty."

The majority of people abhorred the assassination and condemned Dhingra and his act except, a few revolutionary comrades, like Shyamji Krishna Varma, Madame Cama, Hardayal, Savarkar, Chattopadhyaya, etc. His family was the first to abhor his act. It went to the extent of disowning him. The family felt disgraced and they bitterly repeated it their letters to the government that their son had completely ruined the family prestige by his mad act. Family believed that he was used as a puppet in the hands of the revolutionaries. They considered him innocent, who had fallen into the trap of shrewd anarchists, and was misused by them. The family abhorred Madan Lal Dhingra's act publicly and openly declared that his act had nothing to do with the family. The family had fully realized that Madan Lal Dhingra had gone astray and would not listen to their advice. That is why his brother had written to Wyllie to look into the matter and help him, to come out from the influence of India House. The family refused to accept Madan Lal Dhingra as martyr, as the extremist would desire. We look upon him as a lunatic (who could not be influenced by the traditions and instincts of the family) and his act as a detestable role. May God punish the real culprits, and throw light so that everybody may be judged correctly.

Among Dhingra's critics, M.K. Gandhi was the severest of all; he was more elaborate and ruthless in his denunciation, and there was no trace of emotion in his attack. He had gone to England with H.O. Ali in a delegation sent to protest the notorious 'Black Ordinance' requiring the registration of Asiatics and during his short stay there, Dhingra's case came up in old Bailey. He posted his views to Natal for publication in the *Indian Opinion* his views on Wyllie's murder.[81]

One should not forget that Gandhi had his own ideology of 'Non-violence', and he struck to it till the end of his life. Similarly, there were others, who believed that through violent means the British administration and its repressive and coercive policies on Indians could be checked and freedom could be won. Both considered their ideology, and methodology to be the best. As such Gandhi had his own line of thinking where anarchism had no place and for radicals the policy of pleading and appeasement was shameful and disgraceful. From this context, the criticism of Dhingra by Gandhi does not surprise.

Syed Amir Ali, a leading member of the London branch of the All India Muslim League,[82] Sheikh Umar Baksh, the Chairman of All India Congress Committee, Lahore, Pandit Madan Mohan Malviya, Harkishan Lal and Mohd. Shafi from Punjab, and even Malik Umar Hyat Khan, who at one time had been associated with Savarkar and the India House, went to the extent of describing Savarkar and his other associates as "low-caste men". There is no doubt that the dominant Indian political elite deprecated Dhingra's act, but does that undermine the 'Act of Dhingra'? Perhaps, it does not. It might have helped the British administration to nip the rising tide against the Crown in a systematical way and their staunch 'loyalists', might have earned the goodwill of their 'My Lords', for condemning the 'act', but these accusations and tactics could not withhold the valour of Dhingra forever.

Many members of the India House deliberately joined the London Indian Society and East India Association, with a purpose to get hold of the associations. Their growing influence on Indian students in Britain and their activities caused the British authorities a considerable worry, and police began to shadow Indian students in general. King had written to Minto, "They (Indian students in U.K.) only learn sedition, and treason which they infuse into the minds of their countrymen both in England and India."[83] The members of the India House were always looking for some opportunity to be in the limelight. To do something spectacular and to each popular imagination, Kunjlal Bhattacharya and Vasudeb Bhattacharya slapped Lee Warner in the India Office during interview. During their trial, they made full use of the opportunity to defame British Rule in India. Those who got themselves involved in such act were well aware of the consequences of such daring acts.

There were certain leaders who supported the 'Act of Dhingra' like Savarkar and Chattopadhyaya. Chattopadhyaya earned the British government wrath for his one statement.

"The catalogue of coming assassination will be a long one, the responsibility for which must rest at the British". Mr. Asaf Ali writes that sentence of his earned him his expulsion from Inn, and I hold to this day that but for that expulsion he would have come back to India as a barrister and would have been in the front rank of the country's lawyers and public men.

That disbarring sealed his career as a wandering revolutionary who wasted his genius on fruitless pursuits.[84] Such was the attitude of the revolutionaries. They were least bothered about the loss of a career and perks and this made them stand different in the crowd. Chattopadhyaya's words, "Instead of espousing the cause of Indian freedom, wish to hold India, in the interest of the British" clearly exposed the economic exploitation of India by British Government. He had written, which was already well-known and well-established fact, but it required nerves to condemn publicly. Many like Banerjee, Pal and others, held it a futile exercise as there was nothing new in it. Such utterances could invite trouble to one's career, and it did affect many, but here lies the difference between a revolutionary and a politician. Such men were intoxicated with their own ideas and ideology and had their own line of action and they lived to die to fulfil their desired dreams, without caring for petty material gains. The condemnation of such men and their actions cannot undermine their sacrifice and valour exhibited by them. It is easy to call Dhingra's act as 'coward' but difficult, even to think and tread a that path.

Shaheed-i-Azam Sardar Bhagat Singh had aptly stated: "Such singularly exceptional rebels, who challenge the powers that be, and jump into flames of their wrath, forget all about their own well-being, while beautifying the world at large; and the human society moves forward by virtue of their mortification. Such heroes descend from time to time. India too had them, has them and shall continue to have them. Within India, Punjab had a plentiful share of such gems. In the twentieth century, the trail was blazed by Madan Lal Dhingra."

NOTES

1. A.C. Bose, *Indian Revolutionaries Abroad, 1905-22*, p. 27.
2. *The Times*, London, July 6, 1909.
3. The Indian problem could never be solved by the mischievous activities of a few fanatics, but only by the well-considered movement of the great body of the people, who realized the inestimable blessings

which the paramountcy of Britain had conferred upon his native land: *The Times*, London, July 6, 1909.

4. Indulal Yajnik, *Shyamji Krishna Varma*, p. 272.
5. From the chief of Jamkhandi, the Indian student at Cambridge, Edinburgh Parses Union and Indian Society of Edinburgh, and the Manchester Parses and Indian Society: *The Times*, London, July 6, 1909.
6. Government of India, Home Department, Political B, August 17, 1909, No. 10.
7. His geniality and modesty of demeanour, and above all the unostentatious manner in which he served his sovereign on the one hand and on the other carried on the necessary official intercourse with princes and also private visitors from India and safeguarded the interest of the numerous students who sought his help and advice made him an ideal occupant of a difficult office. Hence, his death was great public loss to India and England. He had a rare gift for building up personal friendship with many of the prominent men of India and endearing himself to them in a way that had made most of them feel this terrible loss to a degree that words could not describe. This happy trait of character further served the high imperial purpose of increasing the devoted affection Indians even felt for the Crown he represented to them: *The Times*, London, July 6, 1909.
8. They had to render to his memory also their tribute of sorrow and esteemed. He had no doubt that meeting would perform that pious duty in both cases in a way which in some degree should efface the foul stain which had been caste upon the fair name and fame of their beloved country.
9. The File: Government of India, Foreign Department, *Proceedings, Political Intl.*, Part B, August 1909, No. 96, carries the messages of the native chiefs expressed at the death of Sir Curzon Wyllie and Dr. Lalcaca. The people in India too had expressed their feeling on the assassination and sympathized with the family of the deceased.
10. He had the pleasure of personal intercourse with Dr. Lalcaca since his arrival in this country a few weeks ago after an absence of twenty years, and he could say that a more courageous citizen and more loyal subject India had never known. By the manner of his death he had retrieved to some extent the stain upon India. It was a foul Indian hand that fired those fatal shots but they were proud to think that it was a noble Indian hand that tried to interpose. *The Times*, London, July 6, 1909.
11. Amid a silence which could almost be felt air. Theodore Morison, a member of the India Council, led to the dias young Indian youth.

Mr. Morrison said that the youth was the brother of Madan Lal Dhingra. With his hand resting on his shoulder he said that the youngman had that morning came to him and asked what he should do to show his repugnance of his brother's crime. Mr. Morison told him that it was his duty to come there to show that he dissociated himself from the crime. The dramatic suddenness of this incident created a sensation in the hall, and many of those present were openly moved to tears: *The Punjabee*, Lahore. Dhingra in London: Brother's Story; July 7, 1909.

12. This was Mr. Savarkar, whose name has come into prominence in recent months in connection with India House whose call to the Bar had been suspended by the Bencher's of the Grey's Inn pending inquiry into his conduct: *The Times*, London, July 6, 1909. For the refusal of the Benches of the Grey's Inn to admit Savarkar to the Bar see File: Government of India, Home Department, Political 885-887, August 1909, Nos. 135-137.
13. At the meeting Sir Mancherjee Bhownagari, Sir Aga Khan, Sir Surendranath Banerjee, B.C. Pal and Khaparde were loud in their denunciation. The meeting was attended by Maharaj Kumar of Cooch Behar, Sir Dinshaw Petit, Fazalbhoy Curimbhoy and others. The resolution was put to vote and was unanimously accepted except for one, "I say, No. Not Unanimous": Dhananjay Keer, *Veer Savarkar*, p. 53.
14. *The Times*, London, July 6, 1909.
15. In India, letter of His Highness, the Maharaja of Benaras condemning Madan Lal Dhingra, suggesting measures to meet the present situation in India can be seen in Government of India, Home Department, Political Deposit, August, No. 14.
16. Contribution from public funds of a sum not exceeding of ₹ 1500 to the memorial to Dr. Lalcaca, who was assassinated by an Indian in London: Government of India, Home Department, Political B, August 1909, Nos. 179-186.
17. Submission of copies of resolution, etc., expressing condemnation of the murder of Sir Curzon Wyllie and Dr. Lalcaca: see Government of India, Home Department, Political Deposit, August 1909, No. 35. Also see Curzon Wyllie, KCIE, CVO message of condolence from native Chiefs and Dr. Lalcaca, Government of India, Foreign Department, *Proceedings, Political Intl.*, August 1909, Part B, No. 96.
18. Submission of copies of resolution, etc., expressing condemnation of the murder of Sir Wyllie Curzon and Dr. Lalcaca—The speech of the Lt. Governor of Bengal in the Council of Bengal; Government of India, Home Department, Political Deposit, August 1909, No. 35.

19. From the report in yesterday's *Daily Chronicle* of the Indian meeting of indignation held at Caxton Hall on July 5, 1909.
20. *The Panjabee, Lahore*, Dhingra in London: Brother's Story; July 7, 1909
21. *Ibid.*
22. On one occasion he went to Ventnor, on the Isle of Wight, and stayed there with a family. The daughter of the landlady, as was customary in such families, took the guests out for a walk: Yogesh Chadha, *Rediscovering Gandhi,* Arrow, London, 1998, pp. 24, 27, 29.
23. It is a natural question: and even those who believe, as I do, that probably 90 per cent, of these youths are free from the seditious taint would welcome any evidence on the part of these 90 that is the case: *The Times*, London, Indian Students in London, July 3, 1909.
24. *The Times*, London, Indian Students in London, July 3, 1909.
25. *The Times*, Opinion of the Members of Parliament, London, July 3, 1909.
26. Government of India, Home Department, Political B, July-August 1909, Nos. 151-153. Also see *The Times*, Opinion of the Members of Parliament, London, July 3, 1909.
27. *The Times*, Indian Indignation, London, July 3, 1909.
28. *Ibid.*
29. *The Times*, Savarkar Statement, London, July 6, 1909.
30. The letter was written by Palmer on July 6: *The Times,* Caxton Hall Meeting, London, July 8, 1909.
31. He had written the letter on July 6, *The Times,* To the Editor of *The Times*, London, July 9, 1909.
32. *The Times*, To the Editor of *The Times*, London, July 9, 1909.
33. *The Times*, The Extremist Attitude; by a correspondent, London, July 8, 1909.
34. Khaparde notes on doing in England; Government of India, Home Department, Political Deposit, April 1909, No. 21.
35. Khaparde G.S., Note on doings in England, Government of India, Home Department, Political Deposit, April 1909, No. 21.
36. *The Times*, The Extremist Attitude; by a correspondent, London, July 8, 1909.
37. "Those who have followed the extremist agitation and know the effect which the willed language employed by the agitators is calculated to produce on impressionable youngmen will not easily credit the theory which now seems to be adopted by the police that the murder of Sir Curzon Wyllie was not a political crime but the outcome of some imagining personal grievances. *The Times*, The Extremist Attitude; by a correspondent, London, July 8, 1909.

38. *The Times*, The Extremist Attitude, A letter to the Editor by Bipin Chandra Pal, London, July 12, 1909.
39. *The Times*, The Extremist Attitude, A letter to the Editor by Virendra Chattopadhyaya, London, July 12, 1909.
40. *The Times*, To the Editor of *The Times*, by Bampfylde Fuller, London, July 12, 1909.
41. If Mr. Banerjee did not originate the boycott of British goods, he was its principal sponsor, and is more than anyone else responsible for a moment which has thrown Hindus and Mohammedans into a violent opposition: *The Times*, the Editor of *The Times*, by Bampfylde Fuller, London, July 12, 1909.
42. *The Times*, To the Editor of *The Times*, by Bampfylde Fuller, London, July 12, 1909.
43. *The Times*, Surendranath Banerjee on Bampfylde Fuller's letter to the Editor of the Times, July 13, 1909.
44. *The Times*, Surendranath Banerjee on Bampfylde Fuller's letter to the Editor of *The Times*, July 13, 1909. The speech of the Lt. Governor of Bengal in the Council of Bengal; Government of India, Home Department, Political B, July, Nos. 140-142.
45. *The Times*, Indian Loyalty by C.A. Elliott, London, July 13, 1909.
46. *The Times*, Letter to the Editor by Surendranath Banerjee, July 10, 1909.
47. *The Times*, Indian Loyalty by C.A. Elliott, London, July 13, 1909.
48. The Times, To the Editor of *The Times*, by Surendranath Banerjee, July 10, 1909.
49. *The Times*, Indian Loyalty by C.A. Elliott, London, July 13 1909. Also see the speech delivered by Lt. Governor of Bengal in connection with the assassination of Sir Curzon and Lalcaca; Government of India, Home Department, Political B, August 1909, Nos. 99-102.
50. *The Times*, Indian Loyalty by Bampfylde Fuller, London, July 15, 1909.
51. *The Times*, to the Editor of *The Times*, by Surendranath Banerjee, July 10, 1909.
52. *The Times*, Indian Loyalty by Bampfylde Fuller, London, July 15, 1909.
53. *The Times*, to the Editor of *The Times*, by A.B.C., London, July 13, 1909.
54. *The Times*, to the Editor of *The Times*, by A.B.C., London, July 13, 1909.
55. *The Times*, A Defence of India, to the Editor of *The Times*: From Editor of the *India*, London, July 6, 1909.
56. Challenging to the editor of the *India*, Steel wrote to *The Times*, "I cheerfully admit, that so far as I am aware no 'editorial' in that paper has advocated any but so-called constitutional methods

allowable today in England. That is why I made it typical of the so-called loyalty that does harm today in India. For it is frankly impossible to adjudicate on the same lines for the two countries." She further wrote, "The Editor of *India* will scarcely deny that the incidence of education, even in Bengal, when rightly divided between the higher and the lower castes, leaves but a bare six per cent for the latter. The plough man and his kind are not in touch, therefore, with high class editorial: but in village *bazaars* or at the *Dharmsala* they do hear of boycott and such so-called constitutional methods." She further insisted that "Above all they hear petty slanders against their rulers which even the best native newspapers seldom fail to reproduce from the miserable broad sheets which disgrace India. To play the part of Mrs. Candour is not enough for true loyalty; that is not confined to editorial; it needs every syllable that is printed. I repeat, therefore, with more emphasis, that everyone who seeks to sow unrest amongst the millions of India cares little if the crop be anarchism": *The Times*, A Defence of India, to the Editor of *The Times*: From Editor of the *India*, London, July 6.

57. For parliamentary questions and answers regarding the assassination of Sir Curzon and Dr. Lalcaca see Government of India, Home Department, *Proceedings*, Political B, July-August 1909, Nos. 151-153. This section appeared in *The Times* after July 24, 1909.
58. Government of India, Home Department, Political B, July-August, Nos. 151-153. Also see *The Times*, The Master of Elibank on India, London, 26 July 1909 and for parliamentary questions and answers; see Government of India, Home Department, Political B, July 1909, No. 18, 146.
59. *The Times*, "India", London, 22 July 1909.
60. Government of India, Home Department, Political B, July-August, Nos. 151-153. Also see *The Times*, "British Rule in India", London, July 22, 1909.
61. Regarding the danger caused by India House and the dissemination from London of a large number of postcards and pamphlets by the leaders of the sedition see File: The Government of India, Home Department, Political B, August 1909, 87. Also see *The Times*, "India House", London, July 23, 1909.
62. *The Times*, "Famines in India", London, July 23, 1909.
63. Government of India, Home Department, Political B, July-August, Nos. 151-153. Also see *The Times*, "The Deported Bengalis", London, July 27, 1909.
64. The verbal conflict in *The Times*, continued till the verdict on Dhingra was reached. In it, the editors of the newspapers like *The Times*,

Chronicle, *The Statesman*, the *Punjabee*, *The India*, the *Bengalee*, etc., also contributed one way or the other, besides prominent Indian leaders Bipin Chandra Pal, Surendranath Banerjee, Virender Chattopadhyaya, Savarkar, and British administrators, Members of Parliament, and others like, Henry Cotton, F.A. Steel, Bampfylde Fuller, G.R. Hadaway, B.H. Rutherford, Ramsay Macdonald, C.A. Elliott, Tantum, Frederick Mackarness, etc.

65. The official objections that the machinery of the government would be dislocated, he answered by remarking that he had more faith in the stability in that machinery than apparently those who worked it. That faith was justified by the lessons of experience for recently a Decentralization Commission had been holding a most minute inquiry, yet the government of India survived the disaster. He claimed that if the old committees had been kept up and there recommendations had been given effect to in the spirit of statesman like sympathies the government would not have found itself face-to-face with the unrest and excitement and all that it implied. For the unrest the government was largely responsible: *The Times*, "The Situation in India", by Surendranath Banerjee, July 14, 1909, London.
66. He was one of the best of men, whose long and distinguished service was devoted to the interest of the Indian people.
67. *The Times,* To the Editor of *The Times*, by Henry Cotton, London. July, 10.
68. *Ibid.*
69. See the letter published in the same chapter.
70. *The Times*, The Extremist Attitude, already discussed on p. 195. Savarkar also let the Eurasian go! And the meeting ended. All the revolutionaries in London got angry with B.C. Pal. M.T.P. Acharya wrote a letter to the *Indian Sociologist*, saying they were grateful to Pal for his past service; but they should boycott him because he called Dhingra a cowardly assassin: Dhanajay Keer, *Veer Savarkar*, p. 54.
71. Man Behari Majumdar, *Militant Nationalism in India*, Calcutta, 1966, p. 179.
72. He had asserted, "It is a constitutional campaign on which we are embarked, and there can be only one result to it. Profoundly shocked as we are, and as everyone is at the dreadful crime that was lately perpetrated at the Imperial Institute we know quite well, as of course everyone must know whose judgment is not warped by prejudice, that our efforts are disinterested and our souls aim the reputation and vindication of the British justice. To associate our actions in the smallest degree with this atrocious crime, or to suppose that anyone

in India, however ignorant, could connect our action in anyway with poor Wyllie's murder implies a sense of moral insufficiency and obliquity to; which I am sorry that some should have sunk": *The Times*, To the Editor of *The Times*, by Henry Cotton, London, July, 10, 1909.

73. He had strong opinion which he thought it a public duty to express that isolated cases of assassination should not divert Great Britain by one hair's breadth from the policy of accompanying conservative reform by measures of appeasement such as would be the release of those who had been imprisoned under the deportation ordinance. *The Times*, "The Situation in India", Surendranath Banerjee, July 14, 1909.
74. Lord Morley had said that he would be no party to reversal of the partition. He earnestly hoped that his Lordship was not precluded from considering proposals not for the reversals, but for the modification of the partition, if any one was to tell him there was no hope of modification he would tell them that there was no hope for the conciliation of the Bengal: *Ibid.*
75. V.B. Kulkarni, *British Dominion in India and After*, Bhartiya Vidya Bhawan, Bombay, 1964, p. 108.
76. *Ibid.*, p. 110.
77. Gokhale himself was grossly insulted on a railway train but refused to disclose the name of the British offender despite the earnest entreaties of Lord Curzon. It was customary for Lady Minto, the wife of the Viceroy, to call their guests, the Amir of Afghanistan, a barbarian. Pandit Motilal Nehru, father of the late Prime Minister of India, declined to accept the suggestion of Sir John Edge, Chief Justice of the Allahabad High Court, that he should apply for the membership of the European Club in the city. As his son wrote, "Any subaltern could blackmail him, and he would rather not offer himself for election under these circumstances". Jawaharlal Nehru, *A Biography*, Bodley Head, 1936, pp. 288-89.
78. *The Times*, to the editor of *The Times* by Frederick Mackarness, House of Commons, 18 August, 1909.
79. Government of India, Home Department, *Proceedings*, Political A, September 1909, Nos. 66-68.
80. He asked the Viceroy to keep close watch on all the telegrams from Europe, especially from London, and Paris. He believed that Dhingra was a tool in the hands of the conspirators. But the measures hardly yielded any result: V.N. Datta, *Madan Lal Dhingra and the Revolutionary Movement*, p. 60.

81. V.N. Datta had noted in detail the arguments that Gandhi had forwarded in case of Dhingra, because it supported his earlier assumption, the consumption of *bhang*. V.N. Datta, *Madan Lal Dhingra and the Revolutionary Movement*, p. 71.
82. He called Dhingra's act a "National disaster".
83. Indulal Yajnik, *op. cit.*, p. 263.
84. *The Times*, to the Editor of *The Times*, 9 July, 1909, London.

□

10

Who's Who

The Bande Mataram, Calcutta was a daily paper in English started in November 1906 by Auroindo Ghose. The paper was closely linked with *The Yugantar*, a paper published in Bengali. *The Bande Mataram* was intended to appeal to the selected elite class while *The Yugantar* catered the masses.

The Yugantar (New Era) was the first and most pernicious of the revolutionary papers of Calcutta. It was started in 1906 by Barindra Kumar Ghose and Abhinash Chandra Bhattacharjee (members of the Maniktola conspiracy) and Bhupindra Nath Dutt, the brother of Swami Vivekananda, founder of Ram Krishna Mission. The paper received warning from the government for its articles, had no effect on it and it continued to publish seditious literature. In 1907, Bhupendra Nath Dutt was prosecuted and was sentenced to one year imprisonment. *Yugantar* and *Bande Matram* were two influential papers of Bengal which supported the nationalist movement, vehemently criticized the partition of Bengal, and supported the agitation of Swadeshi and Boycott.

The Sandhya. closely connected with the *Yugantar* was *The Sandhya* (Twilight), published from the same press in Calcutta. It also received warning and in 1907 its manager

Saroda Charan Sen, Editor, Brahmo Bandhap Upadhyaya and the printer and publisher Hari Charan Das were arrested. While the case was pending the Editor Brahmo Bandhap Upadhyaya died.

The Karamyogin, weekly magazine started by Aurobindo Ghose in June 1909, but soon it came under surveillance of the government. Aurobindo ran away to Pondicherry and its printer Manmohan Nath Ghose was sentenced six months rigorous imprisonment. Aurobindo did not come back to Calcutta and the magazine stopped.

The Suprabhat, a magazine in Bengali was started by Miss Kumudini Mitter, daughter of K.K. Mitter, Editor of *Sanjibani* newspaper, in 1907 from Calcutta. It contained articles related to freedom of the country. In July 1908, it published the photograph of the dead body of Prafullla Chaki, taken at Mokamesh station after he had committed suicide. A poem, containing the dialogues between Profula and the "Mother", was also published in the magazine. Similarly, the magazine honoured Khudiram Bose and other assassins in its 1908 issue, after their executions.

The Kesari, a weekly in Marathi was started by Bal Gangadhar Tilak from Poona in 1880. Another similar weekly, but by different editors in English the *Maharatta* was also started by Tilak. *The Kesari* became very popular among the masses and by 1907 about 20,000 copies were printed weekly. Among the extremists organs *The Kesari* occupied the foremost place. On 12 May 1908, an article of *The Kesari* 'The Country's Misfortune' on the subject of recent bomb outrage at Muzaffarpore, led to Tilak's arrest in June. Another article 'These remedies are not lasting' again led to his prosecution. Tilak was sentenced three years imprisonment and a fine of rupees one thousand. On other case six years transportation, but later commuted to simple imprisonment.

The Free Hindustan was first published from Vancouver in April 1908 by Taraknath Das as its manager. *The Free*

Hindustan magazine was an imitation of *The Sociologist* in general get up and in style but with much less ability. In September 1908, Taraknath Das had sought admission in Northwich University to receive military training. The manager of the institution had warned him earlier to not to indulge in political activities against England which he could not resist and had to leave the institution. Even after that he continued to publish the magazine from New York but without much success.

The Times, London was founded by publisher John Walter on 1 January 1785 as *The Daily Universal Register*, with Walter in the role of Editor. Walter changed the title on 1 January 1788 to *The Times.* The paper contributed articles in the fields of politics, science, literature, and the arts to build its reputation. It faced financial extinction in 1890 under Arthur Fraser Walter, but it was rescued by an energetic Editor, Charles Frederic Moberly Bell. The paper covered national and international news and was considered reliable for providing liberal opinion.

The Panjabee newspaper known to be Lala Lajpat Rai paper, was conducted under his guidance and launched in October 1904 as bi-weekly. According to Feroz Chand, the policy of the paper would be generally guided and controlled by Lala Lajpat Rai. He appointed K.K. Athawale as its first Editor at the suggestion of Bal Gangadhar Tilak, and himself wrote signed articles quite frequently, besides almost regularly writing unsigned editorials. The very first issue contained the criticism of the doings of the several officials. It was not in much demand among the European community. Mr. Mant delivered his judgment in *The Panjabee* case inflicting two years rigorous imprisonment on the proprietor and the Editor respectively. *The Panjabee* worked most effectively week after week local grievances, police high-handedness and race arrogance were dealt with. Then there were India wide issues like the University Bill of Lord Curzon and foreign and internal events which could be used to further the same end. From the very beginning *The*

Panjabee devoted great attention to the lessons of the Japanese victories against Czarist Russia.

The Times of India was founded on 3 November 1838 as *The Bombay Times and Journal of Commerce* in Bombay during the British Raj. Published every Saturday and Wednesday, *The Bombay Times and Journal* of *Commerce* was launched as a semi-weekly edition by Raobahadur Narayan Dinanath Velkar, a Maharashtrian Reformist. It contained news front Britain and the world, as well as the Indian subcontinent. The daily editions of the paper were started from 1850 and in 1861, the *Bombay Times* was renamed as *The Times of India* after amalgamation of three more newspapers.

The Talvar*: *Madan's Talwar, later known as ***The Talvar***, was an early-20th century Indian Nationalist periodical published from Berlin. Originally named after Madan Lal Dhingra, one of the heroes of the Indian independence movement who had been executed for the political assassination of William Hutt Curzon Wyllie, the publication was established in 1909 in Paris by Bhikaji Cama. Editorial responsibilities lay with Virendranath Chattopadhyaya in Berlin. The weekly aimed to incite nationalist unrest and sought to sway the loyalty of the British Indian Army Sepoys. Similar to the *Bande Mataram* that was published from Paris by the Paris Indian Society, it continued the message of *The Indian Sociologist* that had earlier been published from London.

The Pioneer was founded in Allahabad in 1865 by George. Alien, an Englishman who had had great success in the tea business in north-east India in the previous decade. It was brought out three times a week from 1865 to 1869 and daily thereafter. In 1866, a supplement, the *Pioneer Mail*, consisting of "48 quarto-size pages", mostly of advertisements, was added to the publication. In 1872, Alfred Sinnett became the Editor of the newspaper. Although he was later to be known for his interest in theosophy, he oversaw the transformation of the newspaper to one of exercising great influence in British India. In 1874, the weekly *Pioneer Mail* became the *Pioneer Mail and India Weekly News* and began to also feature short stories and travel writings. Author Rudyard Kipling (1865-1936), in his early 20s, worked at the newspaper office in Allahabad as an assistant editor from November 1887 to March 1889. In July 1933, *The Pioneer* was sold to a syndicate and moved from Allahabad to Lucknow, Uttar Pradesh, at which time the *Pioneer Mail and India Weekly News* ceased publication.

The Statesman was incorporated and directly descended from two newspapers, *The Englishman* and *The Friend of India*, both published in Calcutta (now Kolkata). *The Englishman* was started in 1811 by a Mr. Robert Knight, who was previously the principal founder and editor of *The Times of India*. Mr. Knight then founded a new newspaper called *The Statesman and New Friend of India* on 15 January 1875. The name was soon shortened to the present one—*The Statesman.* During the British occupation of India, the British ran and managed *The Statesman,* but it was not until after India's independence was realized that *The Statesman* finally passed into the hands of the people of India.

The Civil and Military Gazette in 1876 in Lahore (English daily), was distinctly an organ of British conservative opinion. *The Times of India, the Pioneer, the Statesman and the Civil and Military Gazette* organs mostly supported and defended the views and actions of the British Government in India.

The Amrit Bazar Patrika, an Anglo-Bengali weekly, was founded by Ghose brothers, Hemendra Kumar, Shishir Kumar and Motilal in 1868. In 1878, it was converted into English weekly. In 1891, it was launched as an English Daily. It propagated strong nationalist views and was a nationalist paper.

The Tribune, English daily, was started in Lahore by Sir Dayal Singh Majithia in 1877. It soon became an important paper of the Punjab with liberal nationalist outlook.

The Hindu, English weekly from Madras in 1878, later

converted into English daily in 1889. It had liberal outlook, supported though critically the policies of the Indian National Congress.

The Bengali, in English was started by Surendranath Banerjee in 1879. It propagated the views of the moderates of the liberal school of Indian political thought.

M.P. Tirumala Chari Alias Tirumal Acharya (of Madras): Born about 1887. Vaishnava Brahmin by caste. Cousin of S. Srinivasa Chari, and associate of G. Subramania Bharati in Pondicherry and one of the promoters of the seditious Tamil paper India. He was known in London and Paris as Acharya. In London, Acharya lived at the India House from January 1909 until the house was closed just before the Curzon-Wyllie murder (1 July 1909) . It was reported at this time that Savarkar and others were urging him to become a 'martyr'. He attended the Egyptian National Congress at Brussels (September 1910) . He is said to have copied out for the press most of the English version of Savarkar's book on the Mutiny.

Ram Bhaj Dutt Chaudhari (of Lahore): Born about 1867. Son of Radha Kishen, Brahmin of the Gurdaspur District. Educated at the Forman Christian College, Lahore; B.A. of Panjab University; Pleader of the Chief Court, Lahore. Ram Bhaj Dutt was a leader of the local Arya Samaj and worked as its Secretary. In October 1905, he got married to Sarala Devi who was already prominent in Nationalist circles in Calcutta. He was proprietor of the Hindustan newspaper, of which Amba Parsad was a sub-editor. The press and the paper were purchased by him from Dina Nath and Ishri Parshad. In July 1908, it was privately reported that both Ajit Singh and Amba Prasad were receiving pecuniary assistance from Ram Bhaj Dutt.

Lala Lajpat Rai: Born about 1862 to Radha Kishen, Jain (Khatri) by caste of Jagraon in Ludhiana District. His father was employed by the Education Department as a Persian teacher. Lajpatrai passed the Entrance Examination of the Punjab University and started practice in Hissar in 1891, moving next year to Lahore. In 1897, he gave up most of his legal work and devoted himself to the Arya Samaj, by which he was employed as a preacher.

In 1905, Lajpatrai was selected by the Indian Association, Lahore, to represent the Punjab on the Congress deputation then sent to England. From England he proceeded to America and returned to India in November 1905. During 1906, he toured and lectured in the Punjab, nominally on the Swadeshi movement. In December 1906, there was a demonstration in Sialkot against the enhancement of certain octroi rates. In March 1907, he addressed at Lyallpur two meetings of protest against the Canal Colonisation Bill held by members of the Chenab Colony. He said foreigners could not rule unless the people were divided and disunited. Lajpatrai was one of the proprietors of *The Panjabee*, and when the Editor was prosecuted (and convicted) he defended him free of charge. He was arrested on the morning of the 9 May 1907 and deported to Mandalay. He was released in November 1907. In December 1907, he attended the Surat Congress.

Kirtikar: He was planted an informer in India House by the government. Savarkar found out who Kirtikar really was. When exposed and threatened with life, Kirtikar gave all the information he had about the police operations to Savarkar. After this incident, Kirtikar's reports were likely screened by Savarkar before they were passed on to Scotland Yard.

Mahatma Gandhi: Popularly known as Father of Nation played a stellar role in India's freedom struggle. He was born on October 2, 1869 in a Bania family at Kathiawar, in Gujarat. His real name was Mohandas Karamchand Gandhi (M.K. Gandhi). The title Mahatma was given to him by Swami Shradhanand of Gurukul Kangri. Mahatma Gandhi's main contribution lay in the fact that lie bridged the gulf between the intelligentsia and the masses and widened the concept of Swaraj to include almost every aspect of social and moral regeneration.

Shaheed Bhagat Singh was born on September 27, 1907

to a Sikh family in village Banga in Layalpur district of Punjab. He was the third son of Sardar Kishan Singh and Vidyavati. Bhagat Singh's family was actively involved in freedom struggle. His father Kishan Singh and uncle Ajit Singh were members of Ghadr Party founded in the U.S to oust British rule from India. Family atmosphere had a great impact on the mind of young Bhagat Singh and patriotism flowed in his veins since childhood. He established 'Naujavan Bharat Sabha' to spread the message of revolution in Punjab. He also formed 'Hindustan Samajvadi Prajatantra Sangha' along with Chandrasekhar Azad to establish a republic in India. He assassinated a police official Saunders to avenge the death of Lala Lajpat Rai, and dropped bomb in Central Legislative Assembly, Delhi along with Batukeshwar Dutt. He believed that the overthrow of British rule should be accompanied by the socialist reconstruction of Indian society and for this political power must be seized by the workers. He was against individual terrorism but favoured mass mobilization.

Gopal Krishna Gokhale: Born in 1866 was one of the socio-political leaders of Indian's National Movement. He was a senior leader of Indian National Congress and founder of servants of India Society. He favoured British Education System and wanted this to be applied to India. He was considered the leader of the moderates and had confrontation with Tilak on ideological basis who was the leader of the extremists. Gandhi considered him as his political mentor.

Jayaswal, Kashi Prasad: Born in 1883, son of Mahadev Prasad Kalwar, a carpet merchant Mirzapore. Kashi Prasad went to England to study law in 1906 and there he came into contact with V.D. Savarkar and V.V.S. Aiyar and other revolutionaries. He left England in 1910. On his return to India he started his practice in law.

Jaswant Rai: Born in1875 in Hisar. He started *Punjabee* newspaper in 1904 in Lahore. He was prosecuted for his article in which he had suggested that a native policeman died due to his superior European officer. He was sentenced to two years imprisonment and a fine of rupees 1,000. Later on his sentence was reduced to six months. His paper did not improve much after that. In 1910, it was taken over by a syndicate.

Joshi, Dattaraya Pandurang of Aurangabad was a friend of A.L. Kanhere and was involved in Nasik conspiracy.

Joshi, Waman Gopal son of Gopal Rao Joshi, was born in 1878 at Amroati, Central Provinces. In 1904, he set-up a club at Amroati where Shivaji's and Ganpati celebrations were held. He was member of Abhinav Bharat Society and a protégé of G.S. Kharparde.

Kandikar, Raghunath Pandurang: Born in about 1857, at Pandharpur in Sholapur District. He was a close friend of B.G. Tilak. When Tilak was arrested in 1908, Karandhikar was the first to go to meet him in jail and later he left for England to appeal to the Privy Council.

He did attend the meetings arranged by the revolutionaries there but never known to have addressed any public gathering and his presence in the India House was never reported.

Saraladevi Chaudhurani: She was born in the old Tagore house at Jorasanko on 9 September 1872 and spent there some of the most impressionable years of her childhood, when her father was in England. Her mother was the well-known writer and editor Swarnakumari Devi, daughter of Maharshi Debendranath Tagore and granddaughter of the famous Prince Dwarkanath Tagore. Her father was Janakinath Ghosal, said to be one of the founders of the Indian National Congress. Rabindranath was her mother's younger brother. Unlike other girls of the day, she was not married off to a suitable bridegroom until much later. She continued her musical training with zeal and soon became well-known as a fine and original singer. She sang Bankimchandra's song, Bande Mataram, from the platform of the Indian National Congress. She composed many patriotic songs, later included in her book *Satagan*, literally 'A hundred songs'. Among these songs 'Hindusthan' and 'Namo Bharata Janani' are unique in their beauty and passion. In 1904, she opened a Swadeshi shop called Lakshmir Bhandar. She collected and sent Swadeshi goods to the Bombay Congress and was awarded a gold medal for her endeavours. She married Rambhaj Datta Chaudhuri, a Punjabi Brahmin, living at Lahore. This was probably in 1905. Rambhaj was interested in the Arya Samaj movement and was lawyer by profession. He was an ardent patriot and editor of an Urdu paper called *Hindusthan*. This drew down the displeasure of the British Government and Rambhaj had to suffer harassment and was later arrested. Saraladevi then took over the editorship and even published English versions of the paper. Her excellent management drew the praise of Englishmen like Ramsay Macdonald. She worked for women's education in the villages around Lahore and had larger plans for the education of purdah women, which she revealed during the Congress session at Allahabad in 1910. This led to the foundation of the Bharat Stri Mahamandal, with branches in many Indian cities and villages. In 1930, she opened the Bharat Stri Shiksha Sadan, a school for girls, in Calcutta.

The Indian Sociologist, a monthly magazine was started in London by Shyamji Krishna Varma in January 1905 and appeared regularly every month till July1914. Its import to India was prohibited under the Sea Custom Act September 19, 1907, but copies continued to be smuggled to India from time to time. The August 1909 issue was printed and published for the proprietor by Guy A. Aldred of the Bakunin Press, at 35, Stanlake Road, London. It contained eight pages instead of four. Two articles in the magazine attracted attention, "Passing Reflections" and "Sedition". A warrant was issued against Aldred and he was arrested and was sentenced to onc year imprisonment. The September 1909 issue of *the Indian Sociologist* was printed from Paris. Its main attraction was "How to manufacture bombs and handgrenades, etc."

Balmokand, C. Srikishen was son of Rai Balmok and

judge in Hyderabad State. He was educated in Nizam College and went to England in 1908 to study law. In London, he came in contact with Savarkar and Aiyar and became a regular visitor of India House. There he came close to Chattopadhyaya. He went back to India in June1910.

Pal, Bipin Chandra: Born in 1860, he belonged to Sylhet District. He started *New India* paper. He joined as a member of Aurobindo Ghose's *Bande Mataram.* He became active during the Bengal partition agitation in 1905. He propagated the worship of Shakti (the Goddess of power) to encourage people to join revolutionary movement against the British.

In 1908, he went to England and joined Savarkar, Chattopadhyaya and other revolutionaries active in London at that time. But soon he became to withdraw himself from the front rank and started opposing revolutionary methods.

Rama Rao, Chanjeri: Born in 1878, went to England in 1909 to study sanitary science. He came under the influence of Savarkar and started working for him. In January 1910, he left for Paris and went back to India. On his arrival at Bombay, a pistol along with eighty cartridges and material of banned book of *The Indian War of Independence 1857* was found in his possession for which he was sentenced to two years of rigorous imprisonment.

Niranjan Pal was the son of the moderate Indian nationalist Bepin Chandra Pal. He came to Britain in the early twentieth century to study in London, and lived in a boarding house with Sukhsagar Datta, Ashutosh Mitter and his father. It was to this boarding house at 140 Sinclair Road in London that David Garnett was invited to by Datta and where he was introduced to Pal, who was also known as Nanu. In *The Golden Echo*, Garnett described Pal's politics as not clearly defined, but more sympathetic to Indian revolutionaries in contrast to his father's moderate views.

Niranjan Pal tried to revive the interest in Indian affairs by celebrating *Dussera.* A dinner was arranged at Holborn Restaurant and scenes from *Ramayana* were played. Many Indians along with British dignitaries like Mr. Henry Cotton, Dr. and Mrs. Rutherford, Mr. W.T. Stead and Mr. Navison were present. The speakers were B.C.Pal and Mr. Stead. The scene of Sita abduction was played signifying the abduction of India by the foreign ruler. All the characters except the slave girls were performed by the Indians, Sukh Sagar Dutt (brother of Ulhaskar Dutt who along with Hemchandra Das made bomb used by the Maniktola) and Sita role was played by Niranjan Pal.

G.D. Savarkar was son of Damodar Savarkar and elder brother of Vinayak Damodar Savarkar. Both the brothers started taking active part in the agitations launched against the partition of Bengal in 1905. They both were the leader of the *Mitra Mela*, an association started in 1899 in connection with Ganpati celebrations. Ganesh used to supervise the drill and physical training of its members. Ganesh had written two books and had prepared a song for the *Mitra Mela.* Ganesh was arrested in sedition case in February 28 in Bombay. His house was searched and a copy of manuscript of making bomb was found in his possession for which he was sentenced to transportation for life on June 09, 1909. On the Sunday meeting at India House, Savarkar was very violent and advocated wholesale murder of the English in India.

The Bande Mataram of Geneva, a monthly organ of Indian Independence was started in September in 1909, by Paris Indian Society. Founded by Madam Bhikaji Cama, the paper along with the later publication of *Talvar* was aimed at inciting nationalist unrest in India and sought to sway the loyalty of the Sepoy of the British Indian Army. It was founded in response to the British ban on Bankim Chatterjee's nationalist poem of Bande Mataram, and continued the message of *The Indian Sociologist* that had earlier been published from London. In an article "Dhingra, the Immortal", he was portrayed as a hero whose words and deeds should be cherished by the whole world for the centuries to come. It wrote, "In time to come when the British Empire in India shall have been reduced to dust and ashes, Dhingra's monument will adorn squares of chief towns, recalling to the memory of our children the noble life and the nobler death of him who laid down his life in a far-off land for the cause he loved so well."

Maniktola Bomb Conspiracy was brought to light by a bomb outrage which took place at Muzaffarpore on April 30, 1908. The bomb was thrown at the carriage, at about 8.30 p.m., in which Mrs. and Miss Kennedy, the wife and daughter of a local barrister were coming back from the club, opposite the gate of Distrct Judge Mr. H.D. Kingsford, I.C.S. The bomb was meant for Kingsford. Both the ladies died. Kingsford was coming in another carriage. Why? Kingsford had tried the cases against the *Yugantar, Bande Mataram, Sandhya*, and *Navshakti* and had convicted persons connected with them. Khudiram Bose involved in the bomb case was arrested from Waini station. The other accomplice, Profulla Chandra Chaki committed suicide.

Ajit Singh (1881-1947), patriot and revolutionary, was born in February 1881 at Khatkar Kalari, in Jalandhar district of the Punjab. He was son of Arjan Singh, father and Jai Kaur, mother. He had his early education at Sain Dass Anglo Sanskrit High School, Jalandhar, and D.A.V. College, Lahore. He later joined the Bareilly College to study law, but left without completing the course owing to ill health. He became a teacher of Oriental languages, establishing himself at Lahore.

Ajit Singh came into the political arena during the passing of the Punjab Land Colonization Bill (1906) and enhancement in the rates of land revenue and irrigation tax.

Ajit Singh supported the agitators by setting up in 1907 of a revolutionary organization, Bharat Mata Society, with headquarters at Lahore. A large number of protest meetings and demonstrations against the Colonization Bill were held.

Besides referring to the immediate problems the peasantry faced, he encouraged the people to strive for the freedom of the country and end foreign rule. The Government of India deported Ajit Singh to Mandalay on 2 June 1907. Upon his release in November 1907, Ajit Singh returned to the Punjab amid much popular acclaim. He did not wait long to resume his anti-British activities.

E.J. Beck: was Honorary Secretary of the National Indian Association from 1905. She was the younger sister of Theodore Beck, Principal of the Mahomedan Anglo-Oriental College in Aligarh, and lived in India with him when he was Principal. After his death, she returned to London and became involved in the National Indian Association. On the death of E.A. Manning in 1905, Miss Beck became Honorary Secretary. She did not however edit its organ, *The Indian Magazine and Review*, for long, and employed Miss A.A. Smith to take on editorial duties. Beck was present at the NIA event at the Imperial Institute at which Madan Lal Dhingra assassinated Sir Curzon Wyllie and was called as a witness to Dhingra's trial. She retired in 1932 and *The Indian Magazine and Review* stopped printing.

She died in Allahabad on 1 January 1936 while on a tour of India to visit friends. Cornelia Sorabji was in Allahabad at the time and recounted the last days of Miss Beck for the NIA.

Duleep Singh, Sophia was the fifth child of six children of the Maharaja Duleep Singh. Her father became the Maharaja of Punjab in 1843 when he was five years old. The Punjab was subsequently annexed to the British Empire in 1849. The Maharaja was converted to Christianity and eventually settled in England, becoming a naturalized British citizen and receiving a British pension. Sophia's mother, Bamba Müller, came from German and Ethiopian ancestry. The family settled in Elveden Hall in Norfolk where Sophia was born in 1876. In 1896, Queen Victoria gave Sophia 'Faraday House' in Hampton Court as a 'grace and favour'.

Sophia was highly involved in the patronage of Indians in Britain such as in the establishment of the Lascars' Club in the East End of London. Sophia was also involved in bringing attention to the contribution of Indian soldiers in the First World War. She visited wounded Indian soldiers in Brighton. She organized Flag Days to raise money for wounded soldiers—the first of which was on October 19, 1916 at Haymarket—where British and Indian women sold Indian flags decorated with elephants, stars or other objects. She also entertained Indian soldiers who were part of a peace contingent at her home in Hampton Court in September 1919. Sophia joined the Suffragette Fellowship after World War I and remained a fellow until her death. During the Second World War, Sophia left London and her home in Hampton Court to live in the village of Penn in Buckinghamshire, in a bungalow named 'Rathenrae'.

David Garnett (March 09, 1892-Feb. 17, 1981) was an English novelist, journalist, war reporter and editor, whose path crossed that of Savarkar in London in the year 1909. He was profoundly impressed by Savarkar's magnetic personality. He even made an unsuccessful attempt to rescue Savarkar from the Brixton Jail. This, from an Englishman, can only be called an act of treason against Britain, his homeland! In the first volume of his autobiography, *The Golden Echo* (Harcourt, Brace and Company, New York, 1954, 271 pp.), Garnett frankly and openly recounts the Savarkar chapter of his life. His abiding deep respect and admiration for Savarkar is evident, though he has made some efforts to whitewash his role in the scheme of things and writes condescendingly of Indians and India.

David Garnett writes that one morning at the Cearne, opening the paper, I read the news that Sir Curzon Wyllie had been assassinated at a soiree for Indian students at the Imperial Institute by a young Indian called Dhingra. A Parsee doctor, who had flung himself between the assassin and his victim, had also been killed. Dhingra had been overpowered before he could commit suicide. The name Dhingra meant nothing to me. But I thought it extremely probable that some of my acquaintances were implicated and I wandered down under the great beech tree at the end of the garden as I thought the matter over. Curzon Wyllie! Was it possible that the Indian student thought it was Lord Curzon? Or was that too idiotic?

Edward suddenly approached me, the newspaper in his hand, looking pale and shaken. He asked me if I knew Dhingra; was he one of my friends? Did I know anything out him or about this assassination? It was obvious that Edward drew a very sharp distinction between Indian and Russian terrorists. Not that he was ever an advocate of violent measures.

I was able to reply quite truthfully that I had never heard Dhingra's name before and knew nothing whatever about him. But I went up to London that afternoon to find out.

Naturally enough my friends were in a fine frenzy, and as soon as I had got hold of Dutt and Mitter I heard all the details. Dhingra, it turned out, was the Byronic young man I had met at India House, who had stopped the Harry Lauder record at my request. Mitter was furious at the frivolity of the assassination. Bepin Chandra Pal was scared and angry because Nanu had been to India House. Dutt was calm. None of the three had known Dhingra intimately: Savarkar and some of the others were his friends.

One result of this assassination was that India House was closed and its inhabitants dispersed. When Dhingra came before the magistrate he asked to be allowed to read aloud a statement. This was refused. I met Savarkar shortly afterwards, and he gave me a copy of Dhingra's statement and asked me if I could get it published. That was easy. I took my first and only journalistic scoop to Robert Lynd, then on the staff of the *Daily News*, and it appeared in that paper next morning. Savarkar was extremely pleased. Curiously enough, after being deprived of his statement, Dhingra had been unable to express himself nearly so well or quite to the same effect. It occurred to me that someone might have written it for him and that he had not bothered to learn it by heart. If so, I guessed who the author of it was and realized that he was an accessory. In due course Dhingra was tried for murder and hanged. During the trial seditious pamphlets with photographs of the martyr who had struck down one of the oppressors of his country, and the patriotic statement which had been suppressed, began to circulate among the Indian students in London. I strongly suspected that Dhingra had been briefed to assassinate Lord Curzon, or at all events someone more important than Sir Curzon Wyllie. But I never obtained, nor tried to obtain, evidence bearing out any of my suspicions. My friends were from that time forward kept under close watch by Scotland Yard, and there was usually a detective hanging about, watching their lodgings or following them in the street. It was an easy matter to shake these detectives off in the tube railways.

Curzon Wyllie, a very high ranking officer, who entered the British Army in 1866 and the Indian Political Department in 1879. He earned distinction in the Afghan War of 1879-80, in Oudh, in Nepal, in Central India and above all in Rajputana where he rose to the highest rank in the Service. In 1901, he was chosen to be Political *Aide-de-Camp* to the Secretary of State for India. David Garnett informs that Curzon Wyllie was also the head of the Secret Police, a fact not mentioned in contemporary British newspapers. He had compiled an extensive file on Savarkar.

Khaparde, Ganesh Srikrishna (August 27, 1854 - July 1, 1938) was a renowned Indian lawyer, scholar, political activist.

Born at Ingroli in Berar, Khaparde studied Sanskrit and English Literature before beginning law. He graduated with an LLB in 1884, which led him to government service. He served as a Munsiff and an assistant commissioner at Berar between 1885 to 1890. Closely associated with Bal Gangadhar

Tilak, he took a keen interest in politics and in 1890 resigned from service to begin his own law practice at Amrawati. He attended, along with Tilak, the Shivaji Festival of the Congress at Calcutta in 1906. He was associated with the "extremist" camp within the Congress, led by Lal-Bal-Pal trio of Lala Lajpat Rai, Bal Gangadhar Tilak and Bipin Chandra Pal. A close ally and one of the most trusted lieutenants of Tilak, Khaparde's strong and singular personal influence in the Central Provinces earned him the epitaph of "The Nawab of Berar". Between 1908 and 1910, Khaparde travelled to England to conduct Tilak's appeal to the Privy Council. Intelligence reports indicate that along with Bipin Chandra Pal, he was associated with the India House.

Shyamji Krishna Varma: Born at Mandvi, in Kathiawar in 1857, the son of a poor *bania* (merchant) he got in touch with the nationalist Swami Dayananda Saraswati, a radical reformer and an exponent of Vedas, who had founded Arya Samaj. He became disciple of Swami Dayanand Saraswati and was soon conducting lectures on Vedic philosophy and religion. He came to the attention of Monier Williams, an Oxford Professor of Sanskrit who offered Shyamaji a job as his assistant. Colonel Curzon Wyllie was appointed Resident at Udaipur, where Shyamji had been member of the State Council from 1893 to January 1895. Shyamji got employed with Maharana, and when in 1896 Lord Elgin visited Udaipur, Curzon Wyllie did not let Shyamji be present in Viceregal Durbar. Shyamji went to England never to come back. He made his debut in Indian politics by publishing the first issue of his English monthly, *The Indian Sociologist*, an organ of freedom and of political, social and religious reform in London. On February 18, 1905, Shyamji inaugurated a new organisation called The Indian Home Rule Society and became its President. As many Indian students faced racist attitudes when seeking accommodations, he founded India House as a hostel for Indian students, based at 65, Cromwell Avenue, Highgate. This living accommodation for 25 students was formally inaugurated on 1 July by Henry Hyndman, of the Social Democratic Federation, in the presence of Dadabhai Naoroji, Lala Lajpat Rai, Madam Cama, Mr. Swinney (of the London Positivist Society), Mr. Harry Quelch (the Editor of the Social Democratic Federation's *Justice*) and Charlotte Despard, the Irish Republican and Suffragette. Most of the British press were anti-Shyamji and carried outrageous allegations against him and his newspaper. He defended them boldly. *The Times* referred to him as the "Notorious Krishnavarma". His movements were closely watched by British Secret Services, so he decided to shift his headquarters to Paris, leaving India House in-charge of Savarkar, in early 1907.

In 1914, his presence became an embarrassment as French politicians had invited King George V to Paris to set a final seal on the Entente Cordiale. Shyamji foresaw this and shifted his headquarters to Geneva. Here the Swiss government imposed political restrictions during the entire period of World War I. He kept in touch with his contacts, but he could not support them directly. He spent time with Dr. Briess, President of the Pro India Committee in Geneva, whom he later discovered was a paid secret agent of the British Government.

He published two more issues of *Indian Sociologist* in August and September 1922, before ill health prevented him continuing. He died in hospital at 11:30 p.m. on March 30, 1930 leaving his wife, Shrimati Bhanumati Krishnavarma. Shyamaji Krishnavarma did not live to witness the independence of Bharat, but his confidence in India gaining its freedom from British rule in future was so strong that he made prepaid arrangements with the local government of Geneva and St Georges cemetery to preserve his and his wife's ashes (*Asthis*) at the cemetery for 100 years and to send their urns to India whenever it became independent during that period.

Vinayak Damodar Savarkar, a Konkanasth Brahman by caste, born in 1883 in a landowner family in the Nasik district of Bombay. He graduated from Fergusson College, Poona. His elder brother Ganesh Das was involved in freedom movement of the country. Savarkar was a poet, writer and playwright. Savarkar founded student societies Abhinav Bharat Society and the Free India Society. He wrote *The Indian War of Independence.* He analyzed the circumstances of 1857 uprising and assailed British rule in India as unjust and oppressive. It was through this book that Savarkar became one of the first writers to allude the uprising as India's First War for Independence. He translated the life of Mazzini in Marathi but was unable to get it published. Vinayak Damodar Savarkar won the scholarship started by Shyamji Krishna Varma and left for England in 1906 and stayed at India House. He encouraged India House to celebrate May 10, 1908 as fifty years of the first war of independence 1857. On every Sunday a meeting was held in the India House to discuss some important topic. The policy of assassination was many a time advocated in the meetings. In June 1908, Dr. Desai who was studying in London delivered a talk on methodology of making bombs. In November 1908, Savarkar delivered a talk on the subject "Are we really disarmed". He pointed out that in spite of the Arms Act there was plenty of war-like material available in India. He suggested that the native troops will be sufficient to turn out the British. He commented, the advent of the bomb had terrified the British public. We must teach our people to hate the foreign oppressor and success is sure."

Savarkar published an article in which he endorsed the act of Dhingra and worked to organize support, both political and for Dhingra's legal defence. At a meeting of Indians called for a condemnation of Dhingra's deed, Savarkar protested the intention of condemnation and was drawn into a hot debate and angry scuffle with other attendants. A secretive and restricted trial and a sentence awarding the death penalty to Dhingra provoked an outcry and protest across the Indian student and political community. Savarkar was arrested in 1910 for his connections with the revolutionary group India House. Following a failed attempt to escape while being transported from Marseilles, Savarkar was sentenced to two life-terms amounting to 50 years' imprisonment and was moved to the Cellular Jail in the Andaman and Nicobar Islands.

Hemchandra Das: He was a cattle pound inspector in Midnapore District but was dismissed for his anti-government activities in 1906. He left for Paris and stayed there for a year. He had great respect for Lala Lajpat Rai and Sardar Ajit Singh, as he expressed his feelings to his wife in a letter. From there he went to London and stayed at India House. He was a guest of Shyamji Krishna Varma in 1908. Hemchandra returned to India in 1908. He had become expert in making of bombs.

Chaturbhuj Amin was employed as a cook in India House. In February 1909, he came back to India. Savarkar took advantage of his return journey and concealed twenty Browning pistols in his box. He was to handover the consignment to V.M. Bhat, an old friend of Savarkar and founder member of *Mitra Mela.* He delivered the goods to Bhat who further handed it to G.K. Patankar. In the meantime Ganesh Savarkar was arrested (February 28, 1909). The arrest upset the plan of Nasik conspirators and Patankar sent the consignment to a place named as Pen, in the Colaba District. From there Karve took away five pistols and later two more. After Madan Lal Dhingra had committed the act, in December 21, 1909 Mr. Jackson, District Magistrate of Nasik was shot dead at Vajyanand theatre by a Brahmin youth named Anant Lakshman Kanhere. The weapon used in the murder was Browning pistol.

Varacaneri Venkatesa Subramaniam Aiyar was born on April 2, 1881 in a middle-class Brahmin family in the suburb of Varahaneri in Tiruchi. After his early education he studied in St. Joseph's College and took his B.A in History, Politics, and Latin; he studied for the Law profession and passed the Pleader (junior lawyer) examination from the Madras University in 1902. He practiced as pleader in the District Courts of Tiruchi.

Aiyar then moved to Rangoon in 1906. In 1907, he moved to London and joined Lincoln's Inn to study law. While in London, V.V.S. Aiyar came into contact with Vinayak Damodar Savarkar, an Indian revolutionary, at the India House. Under Savarkar's influence Aiyar began to take an active role in the militant struggle for Indian independence.

Aiyar's militant attitude prompted the British Government in 1910 to issue a warrant for his arrest for his alleged involvement in an anarchist conspiracy in London and Paris. Aiyar resigned from the Lincoln's Inn and escaped to Paris. Although he wished to remain in Paris as a political exile, he had to return to India. Aiyar landed in Pondicherry on December 4, 1910 disguised as a muslim to escape arrest. While in Pondicherry, Aiyar met with fellow revolutionaries Subramanya Bharathi and Aurobindo.

On 22 September 1914, the German cruiser SMS *Emden* entered the Madras harbour and bombed the city. The British Government blamed this on the activities of the exiles in Pondicherry, and urged the French Governor to deport V.V.S. Aiyar and his companions to Africa. The French police brought several charges against the revolutionaries, but failed to convict them. Aiyar returned to Madras after World War I and worked as the Editor of the newspaper *Desabhaktan* (*Patriot*). He was arrested in 1921 on sedition charges and spent nine months in prison. While in prison Aiyar wrote the book *A Study of Kamba Ramayana*. He died on 3 June 1925.

Rana, Sardar Singhji Rewa Bhai: Singh Rewabhai Rana was born to a high-caste Rajput family in the Kathiawar district, and was a claimant to the throne of the princely state of Limbdi hence also Rana's title of 'Sardar'. Rana was educated at Elphinstone College, graduating with a baccalaureate from Bombay University in 1898.

In 1899, Rana left for Paris, where he began a jewellery business trading in pearls. He is known to have lived with a German woman who—although she was not married to him—

came to be known as Mrs. Rana. It was at this time that Rana came to associate with Indian nationalist politicians, including Lala Lajpat Rai who is known to have visited Paris and stayed with the Ranas. In 1905, Rana became one of the founding members of the Indian Home Rule Society, of which he was the vice-president. Together with Munchershah Burjorji Godrej and Bhikaji Cama, he founded the Paris Indian Society that same year as an extension of the Indian Home Rule Society on the European continent. Rana announced three scholarships in memory of Rana Pratap Singh for Indian students, each worth ₹ 2,000.

Together with Cama he came to develop close links with the French and Russian Socialist movements and with her attended the second Socialist Congress at Stuttgart in 1907. From then on, he was a regular contributor to *Bande Mataram* (published by Cama from Paris) and *The Talvar* (from Berlin).

The years immediately prior to World War I were however the turning point for Rana's personal and political life. Along with his dying son Ranjit and his German wife, he was expelled by the French Government to Martinique in 1911. The activities of the Paris Indian Society were curtailed.

Surindranath Banerjee: Born in 1848, educated in Calcutta passed B.A. in 1868 went to England, qualified Indian Civil Services, came back to India in 1871, posted at Sylhet District. His was declared unfit to act as magistrate and fourteen charges were framed against him by the commission, removed from the services and was given rupees fifty as monthly allowance. He took active part in the Partition of Bengal agitation 1905 and headed the boycott and Swadeshi movement. He was Editor of the *Bengalee* newspaper. He was in England in 1909 when Dhingra episode took place.

Bapat, Pandurang Mahadev: Born in 1880, son of Mahadev Bapat of Parner in Ahmednagar District, went to England for higher studies, wrote an essay on "British Rule in India" which resulted in loss of his scholarship as it was considered disloyal to the government. In May 1907, he went to Paris and stayed with H.D. Varma. There he met Hemchandra Das, Subodh Bose Mirza Abbas and S.R. Rana. From a Russian anarchist Nicholls Safranski he learnt the art of making bomb. The same bomb Manuel copy was found from Maniktola members. In March 1908, Bapat left for India and went to Calcutta, joined Maniktola members.

Cama, Bhikhaiji Rustom: The first National Flag of Hindustan was unfurled on 21 August 1907. This is an attempt to commemorate the occasion and remember the lady who then led from the front: "Daughter of India" Madam Cama. She: born on 24 September 1861 in Bombay to Sorabji Framji Patel a lawyer by training and a merchant by profession. She had her early education at Alexandra Native Girl's English Institution.

On 3 August 1885, she married Rustom Cama, a wealthy, pro-British lawyer. It was not a happy marriage. In 1896, the Bombay Presidency was hit by famine, and shortly thereafter by bubonic plague. Bhikhaiji joined Grant Medical College to provide care for the afflicted and subsequently contracted the plague herself, but survived. Severely weakened, she was sent to Britain for medical care in 1901. There she came in contact with Shyamji Krishna Varma, Dadabhai Naoroji, Singh Rewabhai Rana, and others. Cama supported the founding of Varma's Indian Home Rule Society in February 1905. Later she shifted to Paris where she was joined by Singh Rewabhai Rana and Munchershah Burjorji Godrej. There she founded the Paris Indian Society. Cama published *Bande Mataram* (founded in response to the Crown ban on the poem *Bande Mataram*) and later *Madan's Talwar* (in response to the execution of Madan Lal Dhingra). These magazines were smuggled into India.

On 22 August 1907, Cama attended the International Socialist Conference in Stuttgart, Germany, where she unfurled the "Flag of Indian Independence". That flag, a modification of the *Calcutta Flag*, was co-designed by Cama, Vinayak Damodar Savarkar and Syamji Krishna Varma from which the current national flag of India was created.

In 1910, Savarkar's attempt to escape from Marseille harbour failed but it was linked to Cama. The British Government requested Cama's extradition, but the French Government refused to cooperate. In return, the British Government seized Cama's inheritance.

With the outbreak of World War I in 1914, France and Britain became allies, and all the members of Paris India Society except Cama and Singh Rewabhai Rana left the country. Cama and Rana were briefly arrested in October 1914. In January 1915, the French Government deported Rana and his whole family to the Caribbean island of Martinique, and Cama was sent to Vichy, where she was interned. In bad health, she was released in November 1917 and permitted to return to Bordeaux provided that she report weekly to the local police. Following the war, Cama returned to her home at 25, Rue de Ponthieu in Paris.

Cama remained in exile in Europe until 1935, when, gravely ill and paralysed by a stroke that she had suffered earlier that year, she petitioned the British Government through Sir Cowasji Jehangir to be allowed to return home. Writing from Paris on 24 June 1935, she acceded to the requirement that she renounce seditionist activities. Accompanied by Jehangir, she arrived in Bombay in November 1935 and died nine months later, aged 74, at Parsi General Hospital on August 13, 1936.

Chakravati, Chandra Kanta: Born in 1882, in Bakarganj District, his father was a priest. He studied at Brojo Mohan Institution. He was found involved associated with the Maniktola members. It was later found that he knew the formula of making bomb. In 1908, a reward of five hundred was offered by the government for his arrest. He was the first one to print leaflet for *Yugantar* which contained the detailed information of making bombs. After the warrants he went into hiding. Later on the news was received that a man named Chakarvati or Chatterjee was planning a conspiracy in connivance with Ajit Singh. He was thought to be the same Chandra Kanta. In February 1909, he was in Paris and from there he reached England and appeared in India House. After staying there for a few days he disappeared. Later on he was found in New York. There he joined Vedanta Society. In 1917 he was arrested.

Chatterjee, Janendra Nath was born in 1894, son of Rai Bahadur Brojendra Nath Chatterjee, a retired Superintendent of Calcutta Police. He came under the influence of the revolutionaries and left his home. He went to California in 1908 and joined Berkley University. He changed his name to J.N. Sharma. He was in communication with Shyamji Krishanvarma in Paris.

Chattopadhyaya, Virendranath alias Chatto was born in 1880. He was the eldest son of Dr. Aghorenath Chattopadhyaya (Chatterjee), who was an ex-principal Nizam College, in Hyderabad. Aghorenath's other children Sarojini Naidu and Harindranath Chattopadhyaya were famous poets. Viren was a polyglot and was fluent in the Indian languages Telugu, Tamil, Bengali, Urdu, Persian, Hindi, as well as English; later he was to learn French, Italian, German, Dutch, Russian and the Scandinavian languages as well. He graduated from the University of Calcutta.

In 1902, Viren went to England and joined Middle Temple to study law. He met Shyamji Krishna Varma and joined India House. In 1906, he met V.D. Savarkar and befriended him. In 1907, Viren was on the editorial board of Shyamji's *Indian Sociologist* and in August, along with Madame Cama and S.R. Rana, he attended the Stuttgart Conference.

In 1908, at India House he came in contact with a number of important "agitators" from India: G.S. Khaparde, Lajpat Rai, Har Dayal, Rambhuj Dutt and Bipin Chandra Pal. In June 1909, at an India House meeting, V.D. Savarkar violently advocated assassinations of the Englishmen in India. On 1 July, at the Imperial Institute in London, Sir William Curzon Wyllie, political *aide-de-camp* at the India Office, was assassinated by Madan Lal Dhingra, who was deeply influenced by Savarkar. Viren published a letter in *The Times* on 6 July in support of Savarkar, and was promptly expelled by the Benchers of the Middle Temple. In November 1909, he edited the short-lived but virulent nationalist periodical *Talvar* ('The Sword').

In May 1910, a warrant issued for his arrest and he went to France. In 1912, Viren married Miss Reynolds. In April 1914, he went to Berlin for furthering the revolutionary activities. In Germany, he formed a "German Friends of India Association". Its other prominent members were Har Dayal, Taraknath Das, Mohammad Barakatullah, Bhupendranath Datta, M.P. Tirumal Acharya, Herambalal Gupta, Jodh Singh Mahajan, Jiten Lahiri, Satyen Sen, and Vishnu Ganesh Pingley.

On November 20, 1914, Viren sent Satyen Sen, V.G. Pingley and Kartar Singh to Kolkata with a report for Jatindranath Mukherjee or Bagha Jatin. Bagha Jatin conveyed a note through Pingley and Kartar Singh to Rash Behari Bose asking him to expedite preparations for the proposed armed uprising. In 1915, when Viren went to meet Raja Mahendra Pratap in Switzerland and convey him the Kaiser's personal invitation, there was an attempt to murder Viren, while he was dogged by British agent, Donald Gullick.

In January-February 1934, he had a correspondence with Krupskaya (Lenin's widow) and on March 18, 1934 he gave a talk about his reminiscences of Vladimir Lenin. Viren was arrested on July 15, 1937. Death sentence was pronounced by Military Collegium of the Supreme Court of the USSR on September 2, 1937 and the same day he was shot.

Dube Vishnu Prasad, son of Prasad Dube, a loyal pleader of Hoshangabad. He went to England in 1908 to study law and got associated with V.D. Savarkar and other members of India House. He was a close friend of Chattopadhyaya and was arrested and interned in England.

Sisir Kumar Ghose, Born in 1889, son of Tarni Charan Ghose of Keshabpur, Bengal. He was the member of Maniktola Conspiracy and sentenced to five years imprisonment.

Haidar Raza or Riza: Born in 1883 in Muzzafarnagar in United Province. His father Ahmed Raza was a teacher who died in 1889 and Raza was brought up by his uncle, a petty government officer Naib Tehsildar in Rewari, Gurgaon District. Raza passed his BA from St. Stephens College, Delhi and became a teacher. In 1905, he got attracted to Swadeshi Movement and joined in its bandwagon of agitation. He started a newspaper *Aftab* from Delhi. He took part in the agitation launched in 1907 in the Punjab after the deportation of Lala Lajpat Rai. Due to his political activities his paper was stopped. Finding it difficult to stay in India he communicated with Shyamji Krishna Varma in England who awarded him scholarship and sent him rupees five hundred to visit England. He, along with Asif Ali and Rauf Ali, left for England from Bombay on January 16, 1909. The three (Raza, Asaf and Rauf) first went to Paris and from there they went to England. In London, they stayed at India House. Raza stayed in India House till July 1, 1901. After the assassination of Curzon Wyllie he moved out. On October 9, 1909, he wrote a letter to the *Tribune* in which he denied having any relation with India House.

Lala Hardayal was born in October 14, 1884, in Delhi. His father Gauri Dayal Mathur was a reader in the district court. He received his early education at Delhi and then went to Lahore for further studies. He stood first in MA in English literature. He also scored distinction in MA History and went to England for further studies. He came in close contact with revolutionaries men like C.F. Andrews, Bhai Parmanand, Shyamji Krishna Varma and Savarkar who encouraged him to join them in their struggle for independence. He started contributing to Indian Socialist. He raised his voice against the arrest and deportation of Lala Lajpat Rai and Sardar Ajit Singh in 1907. In 1908, he came back to India and met Tilak and Gokhale. He contributed his articles in newspapers especially in the *Punjabee*. When after the murder of Curzon Wyllie, the revolutionaries in India House moved out to Paris, Lala Hardayal too shifted to Paris. He worked for the monthly journal *Bande Mataram*. From there he went to U.S.A. and later on joined *Ghadar movement* and became its General Secretary in 1913.

Tilak, Keshav Bal Gangadhar was born on July 23, 1856 in Maharashtra to a Chitpavan Brahmin family. He graduated from Deccan College, Pune in 1877 and started teaching mathematics in a private school in Pune. Later he became a journalist. Tilak joined the Indian National Congress in 1890. He opposed its moderate attitude, especially towards the fight for self-government. He was one of the most eminent radicals at the time.

A plague epidemic spread from Mumbai to Pune in late 1896, and by January 1897, it reached epidemic proportions. In order to suppress the epidemic and prevent its spread, it was decided to take drastic action. A Special Plague Committee, under the Chairmanship of W.C. Rand, was formed to look into the matter. On June 22, 1897, Rand and another British officer, Lt. Ayerst were shot and killed by the Chapekar brothers and their other associates. Tilak was charged with incitement to murder and sentenced to 18 months imprisonment.

Following the partition of Bengal in 1905, Tilak encouraged the Swadeshi and the Boycott movement. Tilak opposed the moderate views of Gopal Krishna Gokhale, and was supported by fellow Indian nationalists Bipin Chandra Pal in Bengal and Lala Lajpat Rai in Punjab. They were referred to as the Lal-Bal-Pal triumvirate. In 1907, the Congress Party split into two factions moderates and extremists, Tilak following the latter.

On April 30, 1908, two Bengali youths, Prafulla Chaki and Khudiram Bose, threw a bomb on a carriage at Muzzafarpur, in order to kill the Chief Presidency Magistrate Douglas Kingsford of Calcutta fame, but erroneously killed some women travelling in it. While Chaki committed suicide when caught, Bose was hanged. Tilak, in his paper *Kesari*, defended the revolutionaries and called for immediate *Swaraj* or self-rule.

The government swiftly arrested him for sedition and was sent to Burma from 1908 to 1914. Tilak had mellowed after his release in June 1914, more because of the diabetes and hardship in Mandalay prison.

Later, Tilak re-united with his fellow nationalists and re-joined the Indian National Congress in 1916. He also helped found the All India Home Rule League in 1916-18, with G.S. Khaparde and Muhammad Ali Jinnah and Annie Besant. After years of trying to reunite the moderate and radical factions, he gave up and focused on the Home Rule League, which sought self-rule.

□

Bibliography

(I) Primary Sources

(a) Records of the Government of India (Home Political Department Reports)

Government of India, Home Department, Political B, 7 August 1909, No. 10.
———, Political 97, February 1909, No.13-3A.
———, Political Deposit, April 1909, No. 21.
———, Political Branch B, November 1909, No. 32-41.
———, Political Deposit, August 1909, No. 35.
———, Political B, October 1909, No. 51.
———, Political A, September 1909, Nos. 66-68.
———, Political B, August 1909, 87.
———, Political Intl., August 1909, Part B, No. 96.
———, Political B, August 1909, 99-102.
———, Political 885-887, August 1909, 135-137.
———, Political B, July, 1909, Nos. 140-142.
———, Political B, July 1909, Nos. 18, 146.
———, Political B, July/August 1909, Nos. 151-153.
———, Political 967-976, October 1909, Nos. 145-153.

Gandhi, M.K., ***The Collected Works of Mahatma Gandhi,*** Vols. VIII and IX, Ahemdabad, 1963;

*Jawaharlal Nehru, **A Biography***, Bodley Head, 1936.

Lala Lajpat Rai, ***Young India,*** New York, 1916.

Shyamji Krishna Varma. Director Criminal Intelligence, Departments Report to the Government, File Home Department Political B, August 1907, No. 3.

Speeches of Gopal Krishna Gokhale (2nd Edition) G.A. Natesan & Co. Madras, 1916.

(b) Newspapers

The Times, London, July 2, 1909
"Curzon Wyllie Shot by an Indian"
The Times, July 3, 1909:
"Murder of Sir Curzon Wyllie"
"Their Majesties Sympathies"
"Tribute to Sir Curzon Wyllie"
"Indian Students in London"
"Opinion of the Members of Parliament"
"Indian Indignation"
The Times, July 4, 1909
"A Political Crime"
"Assassination of Curzon Wyllie"
The Times, July 6, 1909
"Savarkar Statement"
"The Indian Murder"
"The Inquest on Dr. Lalcaca"
"Dhingra's Statement"
"Funeral Arrangements"
"Tributes to Dr. Lalcaca—to the Editor of *The Times* by Henry Morris"
"The Scene at the Imperial Institute"
"Speech by Aga Khan"
"A Dissident Expelled"
"Dhingra's Brother"
"Condolences"
The Times, July 8, 1909
"Caxton Hall Meeting"
"A Letter from Dhingra's Father"

"Gokhale on Political Aspirations—A report from Bombay, from *The Times* correspondent"

"The Council of India"

"The Extremist Attitude by a Correspondent"

"A Defence of India"—to the Editor of *The Times*: From the Editor of ***India***, the letter was written by Palmer on 6 July 1909

The Times, July 9, 1909

"To the Editor of *The Times,* a letter by Virendra Chattopadhyaya"

"Funeral of Dr. Lalcaca"

The Times, July 10, 1909

"To the Editor of *The Times*, by Surendranath Banerjee"

"To the Editor of *The Times*, by Henry Cotton"

The Times, July 12, 1909

"Sir Lesley Probyn's Evidence"

"Other Evidence"

"Prisoner Revolver Practice"

"Prisoner's Statement"

"To the Editor of *The Times,* by Bampfylde Fuller, Surendranath Banerjee

"Henry Cotton, in House of Commons"

"Indian Loyalty to the editor of *The Times* by F.A. Steel"

"Viendra Chattopadhyaya on Extremist attitude, letter to the Editor"

'The Murder of Sir Curzon Wyllie'

"On the Extremist Attitude", a letter to the editor by Bipin Chandra Pal.

The Times, July 13, 1909

To the Editor of *The Times*, by A.B.C.

"Indian Loyalty" by C.A. Elliott.

Surendranath Banerjee on Bampfylde Fuller's letter to the Editor of *The Times*

House of Commons—Sedition in India, Unrest in India—A report from Simla

The Times, July 15, 1909

"The Situation in India", anonymous letter to the Editor on S. Banerjee's response

"Indian Loyalty" by Bampfylde Fuller

"Gray's Inn and Savarkar"

The Times, July 18, 1909

"Indian Sedition"

The Times, July 19, 1909

"Indian Unrest"

"Measures adopted in Bengal"

"Indian Sociologist—Charges of seditious libel"

"Police Evidence"

"Indian students in England"

"House of Commons—On partition of Bengal"

The Times, July 20, 1909

"Indian States and Seditious Propaganda"

The Times, July 22, 1909

"In House of Commons"—Kennedy on number of deaths caused due to starvation and famines

"In House of Commons"—Mr. Rees on availability of statistics

"In House of Commons"—Captain Faber on danger caused by India House

"In House of Commons"—Dr. Rutherford on details of fami :es in India

"British Rule in India"

The Times, July 24, 1909

"Central Criminal Court" July 23, 1909

"The Indian Socialist"

"The Attorney General's Statement"

"Lord Chief Justice's Address"

"The Assassination of Curzon Wyllie"

"Revolver Practice"

"Prisoner's Statement"

The Times, July 25, 1909

"Central Criminal Court"

The Times, July 26, 1909

"Indian Sedition Report From Allahabad"

"The Master of Elibank on India at Liberal Social Council Meeting"

The Times, July 28, 1909

"The Deported Bengalis"

The Times, August 05, 1909

"Agitation in Bengal"

The Times, August 07, 1909

"Mr. Elibank's speech—by correspondent from Simla"

The Times, August 13, 1909

"House of Commons—Sedition in India"

The Times, August 18, 1909

"Indian Sedition"

The Times, August 19, 1909

"Sedition in India"

"The Execution of Dhingra"—by Frederic Mackarness, House of Commons, to the Editor of *The Times*

The Times, August 20, 1909

"Execution of Dhingra"—G.C. Withworth

Dhingra's Alleged Statement

"Callous to the End"

The Tribune, Lahore, November 9, 1905

The Tribune, November 25, 1905

"*Swadeshi Vastu Prachar*" : Swadeshi has brought to the fore the exposure of talent which under normal conditions would have remained dormant.

The Tribune, July 03, 1909

"Trial Court Proceedings"

The Tribune, July 04, 1909

The letter was written to the newspaper with a request to publish it by Sahib Ditta Mal, from Dhingra Buildings, Amritsar

Sir Curzon was the Political *Aide-de-camp* to the Secretary of State for India, Lord Morey. His father General William Wyllie

G.C.B. had served with distinction in the first Afghan War, 1838-40. Born in 1848, Curzon Wyllie had joined the Indian Staff Corpse (later called the Indian Army) in 1869, was selected for service in the Oudh Commission in 1870, and joined the Political Department of the Government of India in 1879. During the Afghan War (1879-80) he served in Kandhar. He was Military Secretary to the Governor of Madras, 1880; Resident in Nepal, 1893-98; Viceroy Agent in Central India, 1898-1900; Agent in Rajputana, 1900-01; Political A.D.C. to the Secretary of State for India, 1901-09; Knighted, 1902.

Assassination of Sir William Curzon Wyllie and Dr. Lalcaca at the Imperial Institute, London.

The Tribune, July 06, 1909

"Punjabi Members on the Tragedy"

The Tribune, July 09, 1909

"Sir, I am sending herewith for your information copies of two of the letters addressed by the lamented Sir Curzon Wyllie to the address of my eldest son, Mr. K.L. Dhingra, who went to England two years ago for business. The original letters have been sent to Colonel Dunlop Smith. ***You will observe how deeply we have been indebted to Sir Curzon, whom my cursed son killed in a fit of madness.*** I shall feel grateful to you if you will kindly express in the *Pioneer* the abhorrence of the family at this dastardly crime of my son, who has thus deprived us of one of our kindest friends in London."

"Thanking you in anticipation, I am yours faithfully,

"S. Ditta Dhingra, Rai Sahib, retired Civil Surgeon".

The Tribune, July 21, 1909

The Tribune, Chandigarh, December 13, 1976

"The body of Madan Lal Dhingra was repatriated to India".

The Tribune, December 20, 1976

"The last remains of the Madan Lal Dhingra"

The Tribune, December 24, 1976

"How *the Tribune* Covered Dhingra's Episode".

The Tribune, 17 December, 1976

"A Rebel From Aristocracy"

The Tribune, September 07, 1990

"The Memorial to Martyr, Madan Lal Dhingra"

The Tribune, September 15, 2010.

"Mistakes: Our Life Long Companion"

The Panjabee, Lahore, April 24, 1905

People had gathered outside the Town Hall protesting against Lord Curzon's aspersions on Indian character in his address at the Calcutta Convocation

The Panjabee, September 18, 1905

"Boycott is the order of the day in every creek and corner of the land"

The Panjabee, October 16, 1905

"Swadeshi meetings"

The Panjabee, July 6, 1909

"Indians, at Caxton Hall, in London, and His Highness the Aga Khan"

Morrison told, "When he came to me to ask what he should do, how he should express his own horror at the crime, I said to him, 'Your proper course is to purge yourself before your own countrymen and to tell them that, though the man who committed the crime is your brother, you wish to join with your countrymen in repudiating it'. Therefore this man desires to add his words of support to the resolution".

The Panjabee, July 7, 1909

"Dhingra in London: Brother's Story"

The Amrita Bazar Patrika, Calcutta, 1906

The Panjabee, *August 23, 1909.*

"Hindu View on London Tragedy"

The Indian Mirror, February 28, 1906

The Dacca Gazette, Dacca, March 5, 1906

The Statesman, Calcuttta, July 04, 1909

Indian Sociologist, July 21, 1909

"Heathen Dog"

The Pioneer, Allahabad, July 07, 1909

"London Assassination"

"Statements in House of Commons"

"Indian Telegrams"

"The murder of Sir Curzon Wyllie"

The Pioneer, July 08, 1909

"Aga Khan"

"Caxton Hall Meeting Report"

The Pioneer, July 09, 1909

"Letter from Dr. Sahib Ditta Dhingra"

"Letters written by Sir Curzon Wyllie to Dr. Sahib Ditta Dhingra"

The Pioneer, July 25, 1909

"At Home and Abroad"

"Madan Lal Dhingra Sentenced"

The New Mail's News, July 9, 1909

"London Assassination"

Virendra Chattopadhyaya concluded, "The catalogue of coming assassinations will probably be long one."

The Amrita Bazar Patrika, Calcutta, February 28, 1906

The Daily Milap, (Urdu), Jalandhar, November 25, 1975

"Freedom Fighters Association"

The Daily Milap, November 26, 1975

"Shaheed Madan Lal Dhingra Asthiyan Bharat Layeen Jayen: Amritsar Mein Shaheed Ka Makan Tahbil Mein Le Liya"

Indian Daily News, July 10, 1909

"Was Dhingra Mad?—father's story of Dhingra's eccentricities"

The Civil and Military Gazette, Lahore, July 20, 1909

"Narratives of Eye-witnesses"

The English Mail, London, July 10, 1909

"Mr. Banerjee's Defence"

"Sir Henry Cotton's View"

The English Mail, July 20, 1909

"Execution of Dhingra"

The English Mail, July 23, 1909

"Trial of Dhingra"

The English Mail, August 20, 1909

"Execution of Dhingra: Callous to the End"

The Daily Chronicle, August 18, 1909

"Execution of Dhingra: Assassin of Sir Curzon Wyllie dies Unrepentant"

(c) Interviews

The nephews of Madan Lal Dhingra: Shamsher Dhingra and Vikram Dhingra were interviewed at his residence and factory respectively in February and June 2009.

Police Commissioner, Varinder Kumar Sharma was interviewed on 22 July 2010, at 4.15 p.m. at his office in District Court Amritsar.

(d) Micro Films

Madan Lal Dhingra, Micro Film, No. 1853. At National Archives New Delhi.

(II) Secondary Works

Bandyopadhyay, Shekhar, *From Plassey to Partition : A History of Modern India*, Orient Black Swan, New Delhi, 2008.

Banerjee Surendranath, *A Nation in the Making:Being The Reminiscences of Fifty Years of Public Life*, Humphrey Milford Oxford University Press, Bombay,1925.

Bhatia, B.M., *Famines in India: A Study in Some Aspects of the Economic History of India (1860-1965)* (2nd Ed), Asia Publishing House, Bombay, 1967.

Blunt, W.S., *My Diaries: Being a Personal Narrative of Events, 1900-1914*, Vol. II, London,1919.

Bose, A.C., *Indian Revolutionaries Abroad 1905-1922*, Bharati Bhawan, Patna, 1971.

Brown, Emily, *Har Dayal: Hindu Revolutionary and Rationalist*, Manohar, Delhi, 1975.

Chadha, Yogesh, *Rediscovering Gandhi*, Arrow, London, 1998.

Chandra, Bipan, *India's Struggle For Independence*, Penguin, Books, Delhi,1989.

—*Nationalism and Colonialism in Modern India*, Orient Longman, New Delhi, 2003.

—*The Rise and Growth of Economic Nationalism in India*, New Delhi, 1966.

Chaturvedi, Avdhesh Kumar, *Madan Lal Dhingra*, Bhartiya Granth Niketan, New Delhi, 1999.

Chatterji, Joya, *Bengal Divided : Hindu Communalism and Partition (1932-47)*, Cambridge University, New Delhi, 1996.

Chatterjee, Saral Kumar, *Builders of Modern India : Bipin Chandra Pal*, Publications Division, Ministary of Information and Broadcasting, Government of India, Bengal Printing Press, New Delhi, 1984.

Chaudhry, Sukhbir, *Encyclopedia of Indian Nationalism*, Volume I: Political Nationalism (1800-1918), Anmol Publications, New Delhi, 1994.

Chopra, P.N. (Ed.), *A Comprehensive History of Modern India*, Sterling Publishers, New Delhi.

Cotton, Henry, *India and Home Memories*, T. Fisher Unwin, London, 1911.

Datta, V.N. , *Madan Lal Dhingra and the Revolutionary Movement*, Kay Kay Printers, New Delhi, 1978.

Deol, G.S., *The Role of the Ghadar Party in the National Movement*, Sterling Publishers Jalandhar, 1969.

Desai, A.R., *Social Background of the Indian Nationalism*, Popular Parkashan, Bombay, 2003.

Dhananjay Keer, *Veer Savarkar*, Popular Prakashan Bombay, 1966.

Dharamavira, *Lala Har Dyal and Revolutionary Movements of His Times*, Indian Book Company, Delhi, 1970.

Dutt, Rajni Palme, *India Today and Tomorrow*, People's Publishing House, New Delhi, 1955.

Frazer, Lovat, *India Under Curzon and After*, Willian Heineman, London,1911.

Fuller, Bampfylde, *Studies of Indian Life and Sentiments*, John Murray, London, 1910.

Gilbert, Martin, *Servant of India: A Study of Imperial Rule From 1905-1910* as told *Through the Correspondence and Diaries of Sir James Dunlop-Smith*, Longmans, London, 1966.

Gupta, Subhadra Sen, *Saffron White and Green*, Puffin Books, New Delhi, 2008.

Hardas, Balshastri, *Armed Struggle for Freedom*, Kal Prakashan, Poona, 1958.

Hector Bolitho, *Jinnah: The Creator of Pakistan*, John Murray, London, 1954.

Jim, Masselos, *Indian Nationalism: A History*, Sterling Publication, New Delhi, 1985.

Josh, Sohan Singh, *Bhagat Singh and on Other Early Revolutionaries*, Communist Party Publication, New Delhi, 1976.

Joshi, V.R. (Marathi), *Martyrs Madan Lal Dhingra, Udham Singh and Vishnu Ganesh Pingale*, Manorma Prakashan, Bombay, 1991.

Ker, James Campbell, *Political Trouble in India*, Oriental Publishers, Delhi, 1973.

Khullar, K.K., *Madan Lal Dhingra*, Ministry of I.&B. Government of India, 1983.

Kulkarni, V. B., *British Dominion in India and After*, Bhartiya Vidya Bhawan, Bombay, 1964.

Leonard, Mosley, *Curzon: The End of an Epoch*, Longmans, London, 1960.

Maighowalia, B.S., *First Indian Martyr: Executed in Pentonville Prison London on the 17th August 1909*, V.V.R.I. Sadhu Ashram Hoshiarpur, 1974.

Majumdar, Man Behari, *Militant Nationalism in India*, Calcutta, 1966.

Martin Gilbert, *The Servant of India*, Longman, London, 1966.

Mathur, D.B., *Gokhale: A Political Biography:A Study of Services and Political Ideas*, Manaktala, Bombay, 1966.

Mazumdar, Amvika Charau, *Indian National Evolution:A Brief Survey of the Origin and Progress of the Indian National Congress and Growth of Indian Nationalism*, G.A. Nalesan, Madras, 1917.

Minto, Mary Coroline, *Countless of India Minto and Merley,1905-1910:* Comp. from the Correspondence between the Viceroy and the Secretary of State, Macmillan, London, 1934.

Mukherjee, Hardas and Mukherjee, Uma, *Bande Matram and Indian Nationalism 1906-1908*, Firma K.L. Mukhopadhaya, Calcutta, 1957.

Nanda, B.R., *Gokhale: The Indian Moderate and the British Raj*, Oxford University Press, London, 1977.

Pandey, B.N., *The Break-up of British India*, Macmillan, St. Martin Press New York, 1969.

—, (Ed.), *The Indian Nationalist Movement, 1885-1947 Select Documents*, Macmillan Company of India, Delhi, 1979.

Pardhan, G.P. and Bhagwant A.K., *Lokmanaya Tilik: A Biography*, Jaico Publishing House, Bombay, 1959.

Prakash, Inder, *Life of Barrister Savarkar*, n.d., Lahore 1939.

Percival Spear, *The Oxford History of Modern India*, Oxford Press, New Delhi, 2002.

Pradhan, Ram Chandra, *Raj to Swaraj*, Macmillan, New Delhi, 2008.

Puri, Nina, *Political Elite and Society in the Punjab*, Vikas Publishing House, New Delhi, 1985.

Raghavan, G.N.S., *M. Asaf Ali: Memoirs: The Emergence of Modern India*, Ajanta Publication, N. Delhi, 1958.

Ralhan, O.P., *Indian National Movement: Punjabi Martyrs of Freedom*, Vol. V, Anmol Publications, New Delhi, 1994.

Rai , Satya M., *Punjab Heroic Tradition, 1900-1947*, Punjabi University Patiala, 1995.

Ram, Gopal, *Lokmanaya Tilak: A Biography*, Asia Publishing House, New Delhi,1956.

Robb, P.G., *The Evolution of British Policy Towards Indian Politics 1880-1920*, Manohar, New Delhi, 1992.

Sarkar, Sumit, *Swadeshi Movement in Bengal,* People's Publishing House, New Delhi, 1973.

—, *Modern India 1885-1947*, Macmillan India Limited, New Delhi, 1983.

Savarkar, V.D., *The Indian War of Independence 1857*, Rajdhani Ghantagar, New Delhi, 1970.

Sen, S.P. (Ed.), *Historical Writings on the Nationalist Movement in India*, K.C. Yadav, Paunjab, Basu Printing Works, Calcutta, 1977.

Singh, Fauja, *Eminent Freedom Fighters of Punjab*, Punjabi University Patiala, Department of Punjab Historical Studies, 1972.

Singh, Ganda, (Ed.), *The Freedom Movement of the Punjab: Deportation of Lala Lajpat Rai and Sardar Ajit Singh*, Vol. IV, Punjabi University Patiala, 1978.

—(Ed.), *The Freedom Movement of the Punjab: Seditious Literature in the Punjab*, Vol. V, Punjabi University, Patiala, 1988.

Srinivasmurthy, A.P., *History of India's Freedom Movement*, S. Chand and Company, New Delhi, 1987.

Valentine, Chirol, *Indian Unrest*, London, 1910.

Vasantha Madhava, K.G., *History of the Freedom Movement in India (1857-1947)*, Navrang, New Delhi, 1995.

Waraich, Malwinder Jit Singh, and Puri, Kuldip, *Tryst with Martyrdom: Trial of Madan Lal Dhingra*, Unistar Publication, Chandigarh, 2003.

Waraich, Malwinderjit, S., *The Hanging of Bhagat Singh: Complete Judgement and Other Documents*, Unistar Publication, Chandigarh, 2005.

Wasti, Syed Razi, *Lord Minto and the Indian National Movement, 1905 to 1910*, Clarendon Press, Oxford, 1964.

Yajnik, Indulal K., *Shyamji Krishanvarma:Life and Times of an Indian Revolutionary*, Bombay, Lakhani Publications, 1950.

(b) English Articles

Bruce, J.F., "Brief History of the University of the Panjab", *The Past and Present: Indian Science Congress Association*, January 1939.

Barrier, N.G., "The Punjab Government and Communal Politics, 1870-1908", *Journal of Asiatic Studies*, Vol. XXVII, No. 3, 1968.

Arora, A.C., "British Interference with Internal Administration of the Punjab State (1858-1905)", *Proceedings of Punjab History Conference*, Punjabi University Patiala, March 1976, pp. 115-31.

Rai, Satya, "Revolutionary Terrorist Movement in the Punjab", *Proceedings of Punjab History Conference*, Punjabi University Patiala, March 1976, pp. 298-315.

Kaur, Ravinder, "The Vernacular Press as the Representative

of the Public Opinion During 1885-1905", *Proceedings of Punjab History Conference*, Punjabi University Patiala, March 18-20, 2006, pp. 423-39.

Singh, Parminder, "Why Did Dhingra Shoot Wyllie?", *Proceedings of Punjab History Conference*, Punjabi University Patiala, March 14-16, 2008, pp. 292-303.

Bandhu, Vishav, "Madan Lal Dhingra in the Eyes of the Twentieth Century Historians", *Proceedings of Punjab History Conference*, Punjabi University Patiala, March 19-21, 2009, pp. 303-15.

Bandhu, Vishav, "Madan Lal Dhingra and the Press", *Proceedings of Punjab History Conference*, Punjabi University Patiala, March 12-14, 2010, pp. 342-51.

(c) Hindi

Brahma Nath Datta, *Amar Shaheed Madan Lal Dhingra*, Ludhiana, 1976.

Jagannath Sandhe, *Shaheed Madan Lal Dhingra*, Rakesh Prakashan, New Delhi, 1984.

Kesar Singh, *Amar Shaheed Madan Lal Dhingra*, Singh Brothers, Amritsar, 1977.

(d) Punjabi

Gill, M.S., *Hanerian Ratan Chamakde Tare,* Escort Press, Amritsar, 1997.

Pritam Saini (Ed.), *Shaheed Madan Lal Dhingra*, Punjabi University Patiala, 1991.

Sumit Sarkar, Bengal Mein Swadeshi Andolan (1903-1908) Granth Shilpi, New Delhi, 1997.

(d) Ph.D. Thesis

Barrier, N.G., *Punjab Politics and Disturbances of 1907* (Unpublished), Ph.D. Thesis, Duke University, USA, 1966.

Vishav Bandhu, *Arya Samaj and Education: A Case Study of DAV Institutions From 1947 to 2005* (Unpublished) Ph.D. Thesis, Guru Nanak Dev University, Amritsar, 2009.

□

Index

❑❑❑